Lecture Notes in Artificial Intelligence 5260

Edited by R. Goebel, J. Siekmann, and W. Wahlster

Subseries of Lecture Notes in Computer Science

T0238831

Carsten Ullrich

Pedagogically Founded Courseware Generation for Web-Based Learning

An HTN-Planning-Based Approach
Implemented in PAIGOS

 Springer

Series Editors

Randy Goebel, University of Alberta, Edmonton, Canada
Jörg Siekmann, University of Saarland, Saarbrücken, Germany
Wolfgang Wahlster, DFKI and University of Saarland, Saarbrücken, Germany

Author

Carsten Ullrich
DFKI, Deutsches Forschungszentrum für Künstliche Intelligenz
Stuhlsatzenhausweg 3, 66123 Saarbrücken, Germany
E-mail: ullrich.c@gmail.com

Library of Congress Control Number: 2008935889

CR Subject Classification (1998): I.2, H.3.5, H.5.3, K.3, H.5, I.7

LNCS Sublibrary: SL 7 – Artificial Intelligence

ISSN   0302-9743
ISBN-10   3-540-88213-8 Springer Berlin Heidelberg New York
ISBN-13   978-3-540-88213-8 Springer Berlin Heidelberg New York

Springer is a part of Springer Science+Business Media

springer.com

© Springer-Verlag Berlin Heidelberg 2008
Printed in Germany

Typesetting: Camera-ready by author, data conversion by Markus Richter, Heidelberg
Printed on acid-free paper   SPIN: 12539321   06/3180   5 4 3 2 1 0

This work is dedicated to Erica Melis and the ACTIVEMATH *research group.*

Foreword

Automatic course generation is a very important problem with numerous practical applications in e-learning. Therefore, it has been studied since the 1980ies in the areas of intelligent tutoring, AI and education, adaptive hypermedia and Web-based educational systems. Many approaches have been proposed, but hardly any have resulted in generic and practically applied systems. There are many problems that have remained unresolved, for example:

- Extracting from experts and representing pedagogical knowledge in a form suitable to guide instructional planning
- Deciding the level of granularity and appropriate pedagogical annotation of learning materials (objects) to allow for their reuse and retrieval; ensuring interoperability with different repositories of learning objects
- Balancing the pedagogical advantages of planning entire courses versus dynamically planning only the next step to ensure close adaptation to the individual student
- Allowing different degrees of involvement of the instructor and the learner in the planning process, rather than just "take it (the plan) or leave it"
- The limitation of having to focus on presenting single concepts imposed by the separation of content planning from presentation planning
- Ensuring smooth transitions between the individual learning materials in the course.

Carsten Ullrich's work addresses all these problems and brings about a new framework for course generation combining a variety of existing approaches, technologies, and techniques. This framework has been implemented and evaluated with good results in several domains, with users from different countries and universities in the context of an EU project. His work makes several significant contributions to the state of the art in the area of course planning.

First, it defines an extensive list of teaching tasks, methods and scenarios, which is a significant contribution. This knowledge has been extracted from pedagogic experts and literature and is represented in a form that can be processed computationally. Judging from my own experience, extracting, and representing in an explicit and unambiguous form such knowledge is very difficult, which explains the lack of repositories of pedagogical expertise.

Second, it defines a pedagogical ontology of instructional objects. The ontology is simple, general, and it is on a level of granularity that makes it easy for authors to add pedagogical annotation to their learning objects. In this way learning objects can be searched and retrieved by their pedagogical function. This is an important contribution not only for course planning, but for the entire area of e-learning, since the existing standards for learning object annotations (e.g., LOM) provide limited primitives for expressing pedagogical characteristics. An ontology-mapping language is proposed, that enables linking repositories using other ontologies.

Most instructional planners that separate content from presentation planning encounter a problem – the need to focus on the presentation of a single concept at a time. This problem is solved by the use of a hierarchical network planner. From the initial goal setting – selecting a learning goal and scenario – the proposed algorithm plans simultaneously the content and its presentation according to the instructional methods and tasks that are applicable.

The selection of a planning algorithm and the definition of dynamic tasks allow for an elegant solution to the old problem of whether to plan the entire course in advance (thus achieving a general roadmap for the learner which s/he can navigate in) or to plan dynamically only one step ahead (thus taking advantage of the most recent data in the learner model and being able to adapt the course closely to the needs of the learner). The dynamic tasks allow creation of a general course map comprising pedagogically meaningful stages (tasks) and then expanding each dynamic task further, when the time of execution approaches. This also allows for a degree of involvement for the instructor or the learner in the planning process, since the instructor or learner can manually create a plan for any dynamic task, while still enjoying the support of the system in selecting the general plan, creating sub-plan suggestions, selecting relevant learning objects etc. The effect is a pedagogical "neutrality" of the generated plan, allowing for self-directed learning.

A solution is proposed for ensuring smooth transitions between the individual learning materials in the course through generation of narrative text bridges. This is a novel and very useful contribution for the area of instructional planning. While the method of text generation using templates is not novel per se, the use of this technique to create "smooth" presentations in course planning has not been proposed before.

The planner is implemented as a Web service interacting with different learning objects repositories through a mediator that maps their ontologies to the one used by the planner. In this way interoperability with different repositories of learning objects is insured. This feature distinguishes this work from many others that are usable only in the context of one given system and domain.

Finally, the evaluation of the PAIGOS system both with respect to the technical performance and usability in four different studies (formative and summative evaluation) is a significant contribution by itself. The LEACTIVE-MATH project has provided an excellent domain for implementing the tutor and the possibility of evaluating the prototype with components developed by researchers and with students in several different countries and institutions. The fact that PAIGOS was evaluated on such a large-scale speaks for its viability. Such large scale (not so much in terms of number of users, but in terms of diversity of contexts) evaluation is not typical in the areas of ITS, AI and education, adaptive hypermedia, or even e-learning, and the results (both the problems encountered and the positive results) are very interesting and instructive for anyone building a course-generation tool.

July 2008   Julita Vassileva

Preface

This book presents the topic of course generation based on hierarchical task network planning (HTN planning). This course generation framework enables the formalization and application of complex and realistic pedagogical knowledge. Compared to previous course generation, this approach generates structured courses that are adapted to a variety of different learning goals and to the learners' competencies. The volume describes basic techniques for course generation, which are used to formalize seven different types of courses (for instance, introducing the learner to previously unknown concepts and supporting the learner during rehearsal) and several elementary learning goals (e.g., selecting an appropriate example or exercise).

The course generator presented in this volume is service-oriented, thus allowing the integration of learning supporting services into the generated course in a generic and pedagogically sensible way. Furthermore, learning environments can access the functionality of the course generator using a Web service interface. Repositories are treated as services that can register at the course generator and make their content available for course generation. The registration is based on an ontology of instructional objects. Its classes allow categorizing learning objects according to their pedagogical purpose in a more precise way than existing metadata specifications; hence it can be used for intelligent pedagogical functionalities other than course generation.

Course generation based on HTN planning is implemented in PAIGOS and was evaluated by technical, formative and summative evaluations. The technical evaluation primarily investigated the performance of PAIGOS; the formative and summative evaluations targeted the users' acceptance of PAIGOS and of the generated courses.

PAIGOS was developed over a period of three years in the ACTIVE-MATH group at the German Research Center for Artificial Intelligence (DFKI GmbH), Saarbrücken, Germany within the scope of the FP7 project LeActiveMath (contract number 507826).

I would like to thank my supervisor Erica Melis for her support during my years in the ACTIVEMATH group. Regardless of how much and what she had to do, Erica was always available for discussion and support, and a never dwindling source of ideas and suggestions. I am also deeply indebted for her careful proofreading of this book.

I also wish to thank Jörg Siekmann for letting me become a member of his research groups. His enthusiasm for artificial intelligence inspired my research from the very beginning.

My special thanks goes to Julita Vassileva for accepting to be the second referee of my thesis and to write the foreword of this book. I hope my research does honor to her pioneering work in course generation.

My gratitude goes to Prof. Ruimin Shen, who enabled me to explore the usage of course generation in a culturally different context in his e-learning lab at Shanghai Jiao Tong University.

Research always takes place within a context. In Saarbrücken, I had the privilege of being the member of two stimulating and encouraging research groups, first the Omega group and then the ACTIVEMATH group. A big thanks for proofreading parts of this book goes to Martin Homik, George Goguadze, Paul Libbrecht and Stefan Winterstein. A similar big thanks goes to Philip Kärger and Tianxiang Lu for implementing several of my ideas.

Large parts of this book were written during the month I was part of the Libbrecht family at "Chez Joséphine" in Saarbrücken. Merci à Paul, Corinne, Pénélope, Mercure, Eliott et Gaspard pour leurs encouragements.

Above all, I want to thank my wife Kerstin. Thank you for your support and patience. Without you, I wouldn't be standing here. Finally, I am deeply grateful to my parents whose support made my studies of computer science possible.

July 2008   Carsten Ullrich

Contents

Part III Conclusions

Part I

Preliminaries

1

Introduction

The concept of learning objects and their usage just-in-time, at the precise moment whenever necessary, adapted to the context, is as old as technology-enhanced learning itself:

> *The basic limitation of films in education is that the filmed material has not been programmed properly into the course of study. Only now, twenty years after the advent of the technique, are we beginning to think of eight millimeter, cartridge load, single concept films for education. Try to visualize two to ten minute segments of films, in self-load, self-thread cartridges, on the shelf in every classroom so that students or the teacher can display a demonstration of a scientific principle, explanation of a theorem, or an event in history, anytime during the class or course, simply by selecting the proper cartridge and pushing it into a rear screen projector. Such could be the potential of filmed material, properly programmed, in the future. [170]*

This quote, from the very first international conference on technology-enhanced learning in Germany in 1965 paints a future in which learning objects instantiated in video cartridges are "programmed" (the predominant jargon at that time of behavioristic learning theories) into the course, selected by students or teachers. This vision did not include the *automatic* selection of learning objects, albeit the necessary techniques were already under investigation for almost a decade.

About ten years earlier, in 1956, a conference in Dartmouth gave birth to the field "Artificial Intelligence". The aim of describing any feature of intelligence so precisely that machines can simulate it [98] today include the skill of teaching, resulting in applications that support the student in various ways while learning.

The work in this book describes teaching knowledge required for the automatic assembly of courseware in a previously unavailable level of detail. A large set of primitives, covering basic functionalities such as searching for learning objects, inquiring about the learner's competencies, inserting learning objects, and others, are formalized. From these basic building blocks, scenarios are assembled that support students in achieving complex learning goals. This set of pedagogical knowledge is then integrated into a Web-based, service-oriented architecture, in order to make this valuable expert knowledge available to others. At the same time, this work does not marginalize practical considerations. Thorough summative and formative evaluations assessed the acceptance of such unfamiliar paradigms by students, and technical evaluations made sure that the performance is suited for application in the real-world.

The idea of inserting learning objects just-in-time in a course is thus realized – albeit not based on film cartridges. In the following, we will start this chapter by putting the above example into the world of today, i. e., the world of digital resources.

1.1 Motivation

Today, the student interested in e-learning no longer faces the problem of finding *any* educational resources but he (throughout this work, I will randomly refer to the learner as "he" or "she") is confronted with a much greater challenge: finding the *appropriate* ones out of a very large set of possibilities. A compilation of the Center for International Education at the University of Wisconsin [11] lists about 50 publicly accessible learning object repositories, some of them cataloging more than 16 000 individual resources. This overwhelming amount makes it impossible for clients, be it learners, teachers, or educational systems to search manually through the repositories to find those resources that are appropriate for their current goals.

Say, the learner Anton wants to learn about the mathematical concept "derivative". This topic is new to him, but he has some rudimentary knowledge about more basic concepts, such as "functions". When searching for resources on the Web the first choice is usually Google. At the time of writing a search for "derivative" yields about 70 800 000 results. A refined search ("derivative mathematics") results in 1 260 000 links; a significantly smaller number but still too large to handle. Furthermore, the results are polluted by irrelevant links. Google (and other Web search tools) indexes all Web resources and does not allow restricting a search to educational resources. Therefore, explanations about the mathematical concept "derivative" are displayed alongside with advertisement about "financial derivatives".

Thus, in a second step, Anton searches learning object repositories. Browsing through all repositories one by one would cost too much time. Therefore, Anton accesses a Web-portal that offers *federated search*. Federated search allows uniform access to a multitude of repositories and enables a client (a human or a system) to pose queries that are answered by all repositories connected to the P2P network. Queries typically consist of keywords and additional information (called *metadata*) about the desired resources, such as learning context, typical learning time, etc.

Anton's search at the Web-portal MERLOT [181] returns 25 resources, which are of varying granularity and range from single applets to Web-sites that teach a variety of topics, including derivatives. Anton now faces the question which results are relevant for his goals and capabilities. In order to judge, he would need to inspect them one by one. This takes time and, in the first place, requires a very competent and self-organized learner who is able to assess and to structure the retrieved content. In particular low-achieving students do not always possess these skills and several empirical studies show that these learners benefit from content organized according to pedagogical principles [147, 137].

More abstractly speaking, posing queries to a multitude of repositories provides only one part of the functionality required for the task of finding and structuring appropriate educational resources. The task also requires pedagogical skills for finding and assembling the resources. That is where *course(ware) generation* comes into play. Course generation uses information about the resources, the learner and his learning goals to generate an adapted sequence of resources that supports the learner in achieving his goals.

However, previous course generators cannot handle *complex* learning goals. In most course generators the learning goal just consists of the target concepts the learner wants to learn about. But a user may have different objectives: when the content is unknown to him, Anton requires detailed, comprehensive information. Later, he might want to rehearse the content, which requires a different course. When preparing for an exam, Anton wants to use a workbook, which is yet another type of course.

While recent work on course generation often claims to use pedagogical knowledge, the quality and extent of most of the work cannot be judged due to insufficient descriptions. Schulmeister's [163] criticism on adaptive systems in general applies to course generation as well: a large percentage of existing work neither describes the characteristics of the learner used for adaptivity nor the methods and dimensions of adaptivity that are aimed at.

In addition, none of previous course generators has a service-oriented architecture. They cannot perform federated search, nor can they make their functionality available as a service to other systems.

1.2 Contributions

To overcome these and other problems, I developed the course generator PAI-GOS. I derived this term from the linguistic roof of "pedagogy", which is "paidagōgos". In ancient Greece, the paidagōgos was the slave who took the children to and from school [2]. Just like this slave, PAIGOS should provide guidance and support to the learner, when requested. PAIGOS advances the state of the art of course generation by using many of the possibilities offered by today's (Semantic) Web, Artificial Intelligence and technology-enhanced learning techniques. PAIGOS was developed in the context of the ACTIVE-MATH system [109]; however it is an independent module that can be used with other systems as well. The formalized course generation knowledge can be downloaded from http://www.activemath.org/pubs/cg.zip.

This work contributes to service-oriented course generation and modeling of pedagogical knowledge. Several empirical evaluations served to assess the practical value of PAIGOS.

1.2.1 Service-Oriented Course Generation

This work considers all software systems that are involved in course generation as *services*. This includes the course generator, repositories and additional tools that support the user during learning (called *learning-support services*).

A course generator service allows accessing course generation functionality by well-defined Web-service interfaces. This way, if a learning management system like Moodle [119] or any other system wants to offer course generation, it can re-use the functionalities made available by PAIGOS and is not required to implement the pedagogical knowledge itself.

Repositories are treated as services that can register at PAIGOS and make their content available for course generation. However, a difficulty is that the representation of resources often varies simply because different database schemas may be used in the repositories. In addition, despite standardization efforts such as LOM [180] almost every repository available uses its own description of learning objects (or at least a variant of LOM). PAIGOS uses a mediator architecture that is based on an ontology of instructional objects to overcome these problems.

Last but not least, PAIGOS views tools that support the learning process as services, too. PAIGOS integrates these services, not arbitrarily but in a pedagogically sensible way: during the learning process, at times the usage of a tool can be more beneficial than at some other time. For instance, reflecting upon the learned concepts may be most effective at the end of a lesson because attention is not split between cognitive and meta-cognitive (reflective) activity.

1.2.2 Modeling of Pedagogical Knowledge

PAIGOS implements realistic pedagogical knowledge developed jointly with pedagogical experts. This knowledge encodes how to generate courses that help the learner to achieve his learning goals. PAIGOS's domain knowledge realizes a large set of learning goals, ranging from selecting single resources such as examples and exercises to complete courses. This work contains a detailed description of the implemented knowledge, which addresses Schulmeister's criticism and thus allows judgment and comparison of the course generation knowledge.

The knowledge is generic, that is, independent of the actual content, which makes the knowledge reusable and applicable to other domains as well.

The basic pedagogical building blocks developed in this work are pedagogically neutral. In practice, researchers as well as practitioners disagree on the question which pedagogical principles to use for teaching. Hence, if a course generator aims at wide-spread applicability, it should not impose any specific learning theory. PAIGOS implements a novel competency-based pedagogical approach as well as a more traditional approach based on instructional design guidelines.

The courses that result from applying the formalized knowledge are structured according to pedagogical principles. This structure is made explicit by the nested sections of the table of contents and by bridging texts that are created during course generation. This structure and the bridging texts convey to the learner additional information about the learning process that he can later use to structure his own learning.

1.2.3 Adaptivity in Generated Courses

Course generation faces a dilemma: on the one hand it makes sense from a pedagogical point of view to generate a complete course immediately after receiving the learner's request, instead of selecting and presenting one resource after another: in one-shot generation, the learner sees how the content is structured and he can freely navigate. On the other hand, if a long time-span separates between the generation and viewing of a page, assumptions about the learner made during course generation may have become invalid, resulting in an inadequate course. Hence, if possible, the course generation should be dynamic in the sense that it uses the most up-to-date information about the learner that is available.

The solution presented in this work is based on dynamic subtask expansion: course generation may stop at a level that specifies what kind of educational resources should be selected but does not specify which ones. The specific resources are selected as late as possible, that is, only at the time when the learner actually wants to see them. An important aspect of dynamic subtask expansion is that this technique can be used by human "course generators" as well, i.e., authors that manually compose courses: an author can define a course where parts of the course are predefined and others dynamically computed, taking the learner model into account. In this way, an author can profit from the best of both worlds: she can compose parts of the course by hand and at the same time profit from the adaptive features of the course generator.

1.2.4 Evaluation

Evaluations are an integral part of this work. A technical evaluation investigated the performance of PAIGOS under various conditions. The results show that using the techniques described in this book the generation of courses with an approximated reading time of about 11 hours takes place in about half a second. The results also illustrate the drawbacks of service-oriented architectures: the above figures were obtained under optimal conditions, i.e., the latency of the services accessed during course generation was minimized. In real life, performance decreases, due to the large amount of queries send over the Web to the repositories and learner model.

Several formative and a summative evaluations investigated course generation from the learners' and teachers' point of view. In summary, users appreciate the tailoring of the content to their goals and they prefer dynamically generated over traditional, static books.

So, what would Anton's usage of PAIGOS look like?

Using the techniques described in this work, Anton is able to find what he is looking for. PAIGOS allows Anton to state his precise learning goal, in this case "discover derivatives", and to receive a structured sequence of educational resources that helps him to achieve his learning goal. Figure 1.1 contains the table of contents generated for Anton. At a later time, when Anton wants to rehearse the same content, he can use PAIGOS to generate a new course, which is again adapted to new his needs (Figure 1.2).

1.3 Overview

This book consists of three parts. Part I introduces the preliminaries of the work, Part II describes PAIGOS and Part III concludes the book with a description of related work, a summary and an outlook to possible extensions.

Part I Preliminaries

Chapter 2 describes the technologies relevant for this work. First, I introduce Semantic Web technologies, starting with the basic building block XML and then explaining how this general-purpose markup language is used to convey semantic information in RDF and OWL (Section 2.2). A second area relevant for this work is standards used for technology-enhanced learning. I describe these in Section 2.3. The basic concepts of course generation are the topic of Section 2.5. The AI framework I used to implement the pedagogical knowledge, i.e., Hierarchical Task Network Planning, is explained in Section 2.6. The first part concludes with a brief overview on non-technical information relevant for this work, namely descriptive and prescriptive learning theories (Chapter 3).

Part II PAIGOS

This part consists of four chapters. Chapter 4 introduces general principles for course generation. It starts with an ontology of instructional objects that allows describing educational resources such that pedagogically useful and

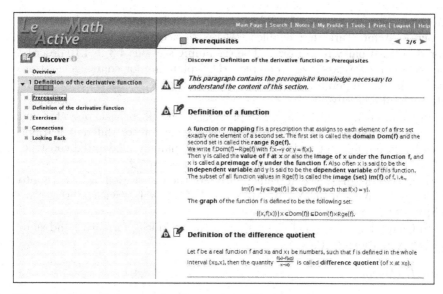

Fig. 1.1. A detailed course for Anton about "derivative"

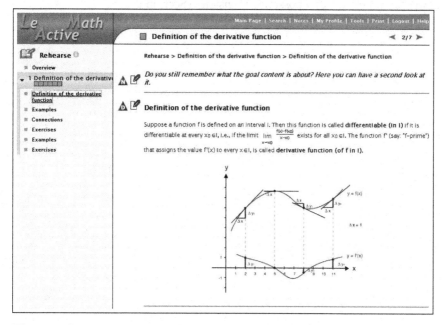

Fig. 1.2. A course supporting Anton to rehearse "derivative"

intelligent services become feasible (Section 4.1). In Section 4.2, I present a mediator architecture that enables PAIGOS to access educational resources stored in third-party repositories. The remaining sections 4.3 to 4.10 describe the techniques PAIGOS uses to employ HTN planning for course generation, such as the basic operators and methods and the conversion of generated plans into table of contents.

In Chapter 5, I explain how the previously described basic operator and methods are put into use to realize course generation for different learning goals based on different pedagogical paradigms, namely moderated constructivism (Section 5.1) and instructional design (Section 5.2).

Technical details of the implementation, of the integration of PAIGOS into the learning environment ACTIVEMATH, and of the Web-service interfaces are subject of Chapter 6.

In Chapter 7.2, I present the results of the technical, formative and summative evaluations of PAIGOS.

Part III Conclusion

This part concludes this book. I start with presenting related work (Section 8) followed by an outlook to possible extensions (Section 9).

2

Relevant Technologies

This chapter describes the technologies which are relevant for intelligent technology-supported instruction in the World Wide Web. The basic terminology, e.g., the concept of a learning object, is introduced in Section 2.1. Today's and tomorrow's World Wide Web, that is, the current basic standards and their extensions into the Semantic Web are topic of Section 2.2. Web-based technology-supported instruction heavily relies on standards describing learning materials and collections of learning material. These are presented in Section 2.3. The chapter concludes with a section on AI-planning (Section 2.6), which provides the basics needed to understand how PAIGOS implements pedagogical knowledge.

2.1 Basic Terminology

Learning Object

Wiley [209] defines a learning object as "any digital resource that can be reused to support learning". This definition points out three characteristics that are relevant for this volume:

- Digital: a learning object has to be available in some digital format, i.e., it is stored on a medium (say a hard disk, CD-ROM, Web page) and is visualized by a computer. This is in contrast to other definitions, e.g., [180], that include non-digital resources.
- Reuse: a learning object can be used in a way or context different from the one it was originally designed for (see Section 2.3 for more details on reuse of learning objects).
- Learning Support: a learning object is designed to serve the purpose of assisting a learner in this learning process. For instance, it can provide a definition of a concept in the domain, or an interactive opportunity used for exploration purposes.

According to Wiley [209], the concept of "learning object" is based on the object-oriented paradigm of software design. There, the goal is to create highly reusable software components that can be employed in a large number of contexts. Each object has a well-defined and specific functionality. Likewise, a learning object is a small piece of learning material that can be reused in different learning contexts.

However, the above definition is still too broad for automatic (re-)use of learning objects. It neither addresses the question of how to locate a learning object, nor its granularity. Thus in the scope of this volume, instead of learning object, I will use the term *educational resource*, with the following characteristics:

Educational Resource

An educational resource is an atomic, self-contained learning object that is uniquely identifiable and addressable by an URI, i.e., an Uniform Resource Identifier [12]:

- An educational resource must consist of the smallest possible (*atomic*) but still understandable and complete learning material (*self-contained*). If any content is removed from such an educational resource, then it can no longer be grasped without referring to additional resources. An example is a self-contained paragraph in a textbook. A complete course, although it might be self-contained, is not atomic, and hence does not classify as an educational resources as defined in this volume.
- Moreover, an educational resource is accessible through the Web (*addressable*), *identified* using an URI.

Course generation is a service that (re-)uses existing educational resources and arranges them adapted to a learner's individual context in order to create new learning opportunities. For a flexible and personalized reuse, these resources must consist of small entities, which can be presented in a Web-based learning environment (and thus must be identifiable and addressable).

I will distinguish between non-aggregated learning objects (*educational resources* and *learning-support services*) and learning objects that aggregate the basic learning objects (*pages*, *sections*, *courses*).

Learning-Support Service

A learning-support tool is any application that supports the learner during her learning process[1] in a targeted way and can be integrated into the learning process automatically. A related concept is "cognitive tool". According to Mayes [96], "[a] cognitive tool can be regarded as an instructional technique

---

[1] Here, learning process is used in the sense of the series of interactions or steps that take place during learning, and not in the sense of a cognitive activity taking place in the learner's mind.

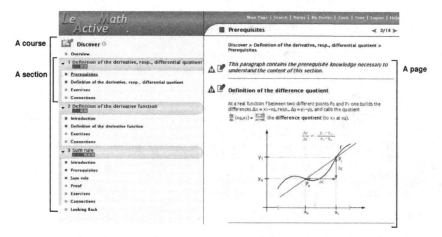

Fig. 2.1. An example of a course presented in ACTIVEMATH

in so far as it involves a task, the explicit purpose of which is to lead to active and durable learning of the information manipulated or organized in some way by the task". Work on cognitive tools often stresses that a specific cognitive process has to be supported [194]. In the scope of this volume, this requirement is too restrictive, as tools that support learning without targeting a specific cognitive process would then be excluded. Another difference to cognitive tools is the requirement that a learning-support tool needs to be available in a way that allows its automatic integration into a course. More specifically, it must be reachable by following a link, and, optionally, configurable via parameters. Later in this volume, I describe how the course generator itself can be used as a learning-support tool (Section 4.8) and how a template-based text generation can be used to extend courses with dynamically generated texts in order to support meta-cognitive learning (Section 4.9).

Page

A page is an ordered list of references to educational resources and learning-support services.

Section

A section consists of an ordered list of pages and/or sections.

Course

A course is a section that is an "instructionally complete" sequence of educational resources, i.e., it contains all resources required for a learner to reach a high-level learning goal, say "rehearse the difference quotient".

Figure 2.1 illustrates these concepts using a course presented in the learning environment ACTIVEMATH (for an overview on ACTIVEMATH, see Section 2.4.2).

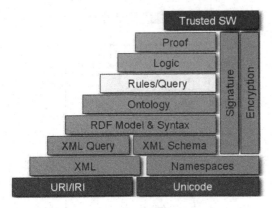

Fig. 2.2. The Semantic Web Layer Cake

2.2 Semantic Web Technologies

The vision of the Semantic Web as drawn by Berners-Lee et al. [13] describes
an extension of today's human-readable Web into a Web that represents information in a way that is meaningful for machines, too. Such a Web would
be crawled by agents the same way Google and Co. do today, yet working on
semantics, rather than on syntax. As a result, services that today still require
human intervention could cooperate automatically, thus resulting in a new
quality of services.

The Semantic Web is a major focus of the World Wide Web Consortium
(W3C), a consortium that designs and defines most of today's Web standards (called "recommendations" in W3C jargon), such as HTML, XHTML,
etc.[2] About half a decade after the initial paper by Berners-Lee et al., the
basic technologies of the Semantic Web have been developed and standardized. Some of these technologies are relevant for this volume and they will be
described below.

The "Semantic Web Layer Cake" illustrated in Figure 2.2 provides an
overview of the layered structure of the Semantic Web (diagram taken from
Wikipedia, [193]). I will use it in the following to guide the description of the
standards associated to the layers. Each layer builds on the lower layer. The
first three layers provide a common syntax (see the next section). The next
two layers add the semantics to the Web (see Section 2.2.2 and 2.2.3). The top
layers allow inferring new knowledge from the explicitly provided information
and to check the validity of the statements made in the Semantic Web. These
are not directly relevant for PAIGOS.

---

[2] http://www.w3.org [202].

2.2.1 Extensible Markup Language

The very basic layers of the Semantic Web provide a standard way to exchange symbols (UNICODE) and refer to resources (uniform resource identifier, URI, based on ASCII and internationalized resource identifier, IRI, based on UNICODE).

The "Extensible Markup Language" (XML) is a general-purpose markup language based on URI/IRI and UNICODE, which provides a syntax for structured documents [173]. Basically, it fixes a notation for describing labeled trees [176]. However, it imposes no semantic constraints on the meaning of these documents. Systems that use XML-based languages to exchange data have to agree on a common structure, provided either by Document Type Definitions (DTD) or XML-Schemas [203].

2.2.2 Resource Description Framework

The "Resource Description Framework" (RDF) is a first step towards semantics on the Web [93]. RDF allows making statements about resources using subject-predicate-object expressions called triples. The subject denotes the resource the statement is about and the predicate describes the relationship that holds between the subject and the object.

Example 2.1. The statement "`http://www.example.org/index.html`" was created on August, 16, 1999" could be represented by an RDF statement with the subject `http://www.example.org/index.html`,
the predicate `http://www.example.org/terms/creation-date`,
and the object "August 16, 1999" (example taken from [93]).

RDF can be expressed in a number of ways. The following is an example using the XML-syntax of RDF. The first line contains the XML declaration. It indicates that the content is provided in XML, version 1.0. The subsequent line begins an RDF element and introduces the namespaces `rdf` and `exterms` (line three). A namespace provides a context of the resources it contains and allows to distinguish between resources which share the same name. Lines four to six specify the relation described in Example 2.1: `http://www.example.org/index.html` was created on August, 16, 1999. The final line closes the RDF element.

Example 2.2. Expressing Example 2.1 using the XML-syntax of RDF:

```
1  <?xml version="1.0"?>
2  <rdf:RDF xmlns:rdf="http://www.w3.org/1999/02/22-rdf-syntax-ns#"
3      xmlns:exterms="http://www.example.org/terms/">
4    <rdf:Description rdf:about="http://www.example.org/index.html">
5      <exterms:creation-date>August 16, 1999</exterms:creation-date>
6    </rdf:Description>
7  </rdf:RDF>
```

RDF allows making statements about resources. However, it provides no means to define the vocabularies used in the statements. That is where RDF schema comes into play. RDF schema allows defining classes and properties, and how these are used together [93]. Basically, RDF schema provides a type system for RDF.

The following RDF schema statement defines the class `Instructional-Object`. `rdf:ID` (line six) is called fragment identifier and specifies that its value is to be interpreted relative to the base uri given in line five. Therefore, the `rdf:Description` element specifies that the resource located at `http://www.activemath.org/resources/#InstructionalObject` is of type `http://www.w3.org/2000/01/rdf-schema#Class`.

Example 2.3.

```
1  <?xml version="1.0"?>
2  <rdf:RDF
3    xmlns:rdf="http://www.w3.org/1999/02/22-rdf-syntax-ns#"
4    xmlns:rdfs="http://www.w3.org/2000/01/rdf-schema#"
5    xml:base="http://www.activemath.org/resources">
6  <rdf:Description rdf:ID="InstructionalObject">
7    <rdf:type rdf:resource="http://www.w3.org/2000/01/rdf-schema#Class"/>
8  </rdf:Description>
9  </rdf:RDF>
```

In addition to providing a vocabulary for defining classes, RDF schema allows describing properties of a class. The following RDF schema statement states that an instructional object has a learning context.

Example 2.4.

```
<rdf:Property rdf:ID="hasLearningContext">
  <rdfs:domain rdf:resource="#InstructionalObject"/>
  <rdfs:range rdf:resource="#LearningContext"/>
</rdf:Property>
```

While RDF schema provides some basic capabilities for describing RDF vocabularies, more advanced capabilities can also be useful. These are provided by ontology languages.

2.2.3 OWL Web Ontology Language

Ontology

Gruber [53] defines an ontology as "explicit formal specifications of the terms in the domain and relations among them". According to Noy and McGuinness [134], the principal advantages of making information explicit in ontologies include a shared common understanding of the domain among systems and to enable re-use of domain knowledge.

The "OWL Web Ontology Language" (OWL) provides a full-grown vocabulary for defining ontologies, i. e., describing classes, properties, relations between classes (e.g. disjointness), cardinality (e. g., "exactly one"), equality, richer typing of properties, characteristics of properties, and enumerated classes [193].

OWL provides the three sublanguages OWL Lite, OWL DL, and OWL Full, which offer on the one hand increasing expressiveness, yet on the other hand increasing computational complexity:

- OWL Lite provides the means to define classification hierarchies, together with simple cardinality constraints.
- OWL DL offers maximum expressiveness while retaining computational completeness and decidability. The "DL" illustrates the correspondence to the field of Description Logics.
- OWL Full provides the full, unconstrained expressiveness of the OWL vocabulary, yet without any computational guarantees.

We will encounter OWL again in Chapter 4.1, where it is used to describe an ontology of types of instructional objects.

2.3 E-learning Standards

The authoring of educational resources is one of the major cost factor of e-learning [162]. One approach to reduce the associated costs is to enable *reuse*, or, more specifically, *interoperability* of educational resources.

Reuse

Reuse can be defined as "[u]sing a digital learning resource in a way or in a context other than that for which it was originally designed" [154]. For instance, an author might be able to take an existing example for his course instead of having to develop his own. The definition does not impose any constraints on the effort required for reuse. The author might simply drag&drop the resource (a very efficient form of reuse) or he might be required to manually copy the content. The required effort is taken into account in the concept of *interoperability*.

Interoperability

Interoperability is "[t]he extent to which a digital learning resource will plug and play on different platforms" [154]. Interoperability implies a degree of automatization. Ideally, a resource developed in one context can be directly used in a different context. In reality, however, resources often require some adaptations.

Reuse and interoperability of resources require the involved parties to be able to interpret each others materials. While in principle, RDF, RDF schema, and OWL can be used for describing resources semantically, today, XML is still the most widely spread means to define the syntax and structure of resources. The vocabulary of what is being described is often described in *standards*:

Standard

A standard is "[a] specification that is recognized as the accepted way to achieve a technical goal either because it is widely adopted or because it has been accredited by a formal standards body" [154].

In field of e-learning, the IEEE Learning Technology Standards Committee (IEEE LTSC)[3] is the best known formal standard body. It is chartered by the IEEE Computer Society Standards Activity Board to develop accredited technical standards, recommended practices, and guides for learning technology [38].

In addition to the standardization bodies, several consortia carry out the technical work of designing the standards. Once a standard has been designed and agreed upon, they are submitted to the standard bodies. Consortia with a direct impact on educational technologies include the following.

- The "Advanced Distributed Learning Initiative" (ADL) was formed as a developer and implementer of learning technologies across the US Department of Defense.[4] ADL is best know for the Shareable Content Object Reference Model (SCORM, [36]), which aims to foster an overall specification for interoperability of learning objects among learning environments.
- The goal of the European ARIADNE Foundation is to create tools and methodologies for producing, managing and reusing educational resources.[5] In contrast to ADL's military motivated aims, ARIADNE emphasizes on societal objectives: "[f]oster cooperation between educational bodies ... . Keep social and citizenship aspects domination Education ... . Uphold and protect multilinguality .... Define by international consensus what aspects of ICT [information and communication technology]-based formation should be standardized and what should be left local" [7].
- The IMS Global Learning Consortium (IMS/GLC) encompasses vendors of learning management systems, authoring tools, and related products.[6] IMS/GLC's specification activities cover a wide spectrum of e-learning relevant aspects and are generally adhered to by all major commercial players. The subsequent sections will describe the IMS/GLC specifications relevant for this volume in more detail.

For a detailed description on standardization bodies and consortia, please refer to [38].

---

[3] http://ieeetlsc.org [61].
[4] http://www.adlnet.gov [99].
[5] http://www.ariadne-eu.org [7].
[6] http://www.imsglobal.org [64].

2.3.1 Learning Object Metadata

Metadata

IEEE LTSC [2002] defines metadata as "information about an object, be it physical or digital". Metadata thus provides descriptive information about an object in an explicit manner.

The IEEE LTSC Learning Object Metadata standard (LOM) provides a defined "structure for interoperable descriptions of learning objects" [180]. LOM is based on early work by ARIADNE and IMS/GLC and has been approved as a standard by IEEE LTSC.

LOM provides a vocabulary to describe educational resources, which is divided in nine categories (list taken from [180]):

1. The "General" category groups the general information that describes the learning object as a whole.
2. The "Lifecycle" category groups the features related to the history and current state of this learning object and those who have affected this learning object during its evolution.
3. The "Meta-Metadata" category groups information about the metadata instance itself (rather than the learning object that the metadata instance describes).
4. The "Technical" category groups the technical requirements and technical characteristics of the learning object.
5. The "Educational" category groups the educational and pedagogic characteristics of the learning object.
6. The "Rights" category groups the intellectual property rights and conditions of use for the learning object.
7. The "Relation" category groups features that define the relationship between the learning object and other related learning objects.
8. The "Annotation" category provides comments on the educational use of the learning object and provides information on when and by whom the comments were created.
9. The "Classification" category describes this learning object in relation to a particular classification system.

Although the standard only specifies an XML-binding, a RDF specification of LOM was proposed by [130].

LOM strives for general applicability, and hence it is the least common denominator for a large number of interested parties. As a result, some of its vocabulary can be criticized as being insufficiently precise for specific purposes. In Section 4.1, I will describe an instructionally motivated replacement of the learning resource type as defined in LOM's educational category.

2.3.2 IMS Content Packaging

LOM describes single resources, but it does not provide means for exchanging structured sets of educational resources. That is where IMS Content Packaging (IMS CP) comes into play [47]. It provides a standardized way of collecting and packaging educational resources to enable efficient aggregation, distribution, and deployment.

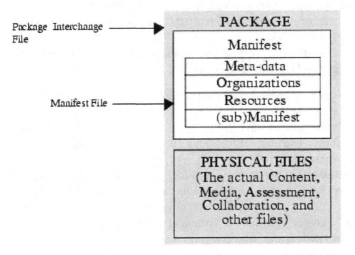

Fig. 2.3. An overview on the structure of an IMS Content Package (illustration from [47])

Figure 2.3 illustrates the structure of an IMS Content Package. The complete content package is exchanged as a *Package Interchange File*, a zip-compressed package. The package contains the educational resources (physical files) as well as structuring information, provided in the *manifest*. A manifest can contain sub-manifests. Each manifest contains a *metadata* section that provides information about the manifest, an *organization* section that describes the static organization of the content, a *resource* section the contains references to all of the resources and media elements needed for a manifest (including those from external packages), and optionally one or more logically nested manifests.

In theory, two systems that implement the IMS CP standard are able to exchange sets of resources by loading each others content packages. In practice, however, the formats of the resources play an important role: a Web-based system will have problems when integrating resources encoded in say Power Point format.

2.3.3 IMS Simple Sequencing

An IMS CP specifies the structure of a collection of educational resources. IMS simple sequencing (IMS SS) takes this approach one step further by allowing an author to specify sequences how a learner can traverse the resources [49]. Basically, an IMS SS structure consists of an IMS CP together with navigation paths.

Central to IMS SS is the notion of an *activity*. Each resource contained in an IMS CP can be associated with an activity. Each activity can be associated with *sequencing information*, *sequencing rules* and *learning objectives*.

Sequencing information covers the *control mode* of the interaction, e. g., whether the student can navigate freely or is guided through the content. Sequencing rules specify how to react depending on the learner's action, for instance, which activity to present next, or whether to display the current activity.

Learning objectives are specified very abstractly. They are objects, with a unique identifier, a satisfaction status (e. g., passed, failed) and an satisfaction measure (the degree to which the objective was achieved). The satisfaction status changes depending on the results of the student interactions. For instance, it is possible to specify that an objective is fulfilled if the student has a higher achievement in the current activity than 0.8.

As its name indicates, IMS SS provides a rather limited and simple approach to sequencing. It restricts itself to a single user in the role of a learner and does not address several simultaneous users and different roles. Furthermore, the ways of controlling the sequencing and navigation are limited.

Although the specification claims to be "pedagogical neutral", the very strict control of the learner navigation, based only on the performance, bears similarities to the restricted mode of interactions inherent in behavioral learning theories (see Section 3.1).

2.3.4 IMS Learning Design

IMS Learning Design (IMS LD) provides a pedagogical meta-model [48]. It allows describing how people perform activities using educational resources and how the activities are coordinated in a learning process.

IMS LD was originally developed at the Open University of the Netherlands, and is still widely known under its previous name "Educational Modelling Language" [86].

Key concepts in IMS LD including roles and activities of people. The overall design (the *play*) specifies how collections of activities performed by the involved people interact.

Due to its generality, IMS LD is a quite complex standard. It is hard to implement and is not yet completely supported by existing systems [67].

IMS CP, IMS SS and IMS LD are relevant for this work because they define potential output formats of the course generated by PAIGOS. Using a standardized format increases the range of potential clients of the course generator service. In Chapter 6, I will discuss the three different standards and their applicability with respect to course generation, and motivate why I chose IMS CP as output format.

2.4 Mathematics in the Web

This section describes ACTIVEMATH, the learning environment in which PAIGOS is embedded and OMDOC, the knowledge representation used in ACTIVEMATH.

2.4.1 OMDoc (Open Mathematical Documents)

OMDOC (Open Mathematical Documents) is a semantic markup language for mathematical documents [84, 85, 107]. It has evolved as an extension of OPENMATH [23] which is a standard for mathematical formulas. The main difference between OPENMATH and other representation formats for mathematical formulas, such as Presentation MATHML and LATEX, is that OPENMATH deals with the semantics of mathematical expressions rather than with their presentation. OPENMATH defines so-called Content Dictionaries in which mathematical symbols are declared and their semantics is defined. The semantic representation of formulas allows for automatic translation of these formulas to (and from) the languages of different mathematical systems (via so-called phrasebooks). This provides the basis for interoperability in different computer algebra and other reasoning systems.

OMDOC defines learning objects such as exercises, definitions, and relations between them. Such learning objects can consist of text mixed with formulas in OPENMATH format. The semantic information includes types, relations, and other mathematical and educational metadata. The type indicates a characterization of the items as collection, theory, concept or satellite items: an OPENMATH symbol defines a mathematical concept abstractly; a theory assembles concepts and it can import other theories; concepts (definitions, algorithms, and assertions/theorems) are the main items of mathematical contents, whereas satellites (exercises, examples, explanations, introductions) are additional items of the content which are related to one or several concepts. All items are accessible via a unique identifier.

2.4.2 The Learning Environment ActiveMath

ACTIVEMATH [106, 109] is a Web-based intelligent learning environment for mathematics that has been developed since the year 2000 at the Saarland University and at the German Research Center of Artificial Intelligence (DFKI).[7]

---

[7] www.activemath.org,[1].

ACTIVEMATH uses an extension of OMDOC to encode its educational resources. In addition to presenting pre-defined interactive materials, it uses PAIGOS for course generation.

A presentation component transforms the OMDoc documents represented in XML to the desired output format, e.g., HTML, XHTML +MATHML, and PDF. A learner model stores the learning history, the user's profile and preferences, and a set of beliefs that the systems holds about the cognitive and meta-cognitive competencies and the motivational state of the learner. The domain model that underlies the structure of the learner model is inferred from the content for that domain and its metadata.

A complex subsystem in its own right is ACTIVEMATH's exercise subsystem [51] that plays interactive exercises, computes diagnoses and provides feedback to the learner in a highly personalized way. It reports events to inform the other components about the users' actions.

In 2007, at the time of this writing, a significant amount of educational resources exists in ACTIVEMATH's repositories for Fractions (German), Differential Calculus (German, English, Spanish) at high school and first year university level, operations research (Russian, English), Methods of Optimization (Russian), Statistics and Probability Calculus (German), Matheführerschein (German), and a Calculus course from University of Westminster in London.

To realize a smooth and efficient cooperation of all components and in order to integrate further internal and external services, ACTIVEMATH has a modular service-oriented architecture. It includes the XML-RPC Web communication protocol for simplicity and remote support. In addition, an event framework enables asynchronous messaging between system components.

2.5 Course Generation

This section introduces the basics of course generation and the standard components a course generator typically consists of. Based on Brusilovsky and Vassileva [19], I will distinguish between *course(ware) generation* and *course(ware) sequencing*.

Course Generation

Course generation uses pedagogical knowledge to generate a structured sequence of learning objects that is adapted to the learners' competencies, individual variables, and learning goals. This generation happens upon request of a client (a learner or a software system). Ideally, the sequence is not a flat list of learning objects but is structured in sections and subsections. This structure can convey additional information relevant to the learning process. In course generation, the course is generated completely before it is presented to the learner. This early generation has the advantage that the course can be visualized to the learner, thereby informing her about the structure. In addition, the student can navigate freely through the course.

Course Sequencing

Course sequencing uses pedagogical knowledge to dynamically select the most appropriate resource at any moment, based on the current needs and goals of the learner. Thus, the course is not generated beforehand but step-by-step. The benefit of this approach is that it can react to the current context and thereby circumvent problems that arise in course generation if assumptions about the learner change. However, this local approach, with its transitions from resource to resource makes it hard to convey information about the structure of a course and the sequence from start to end can not be presented to the learner.

Course generation has long been a research topic and is also called "curriculum sequencing" and "trail generation". It has been reinvented several times, which leads to a vast amount of terminology used in the literature for the same technical concept. To avoid this confusion, I use the following sections to define the relevant basic concepts and describe them in relation to a *reference architecture*.

Reference Model

A reference model is an abstract representation of the entities and relationships of some environment. It is used as an abstract template for the development of more specific models of that environment. A reference model simplifies the comparison between different systems implementing the model [135].

A reference model for course generation systems has not yet been developed. However, reference models exist for *adaptive hypermedia system*, which Brusilovsky [18] defines as follows:

Adaptive Hypermedia System

"By adaptive hypermedia systems we mean all hypertext and hypermedia systems which reflect some features of the user in the user model and apply this model to adapt various visible aspects of the system to the user. In other words, the system should satisfy three criteria: it should be a hypertext or hypermedia system, it should have a user model, and it should be able to adapt the hypermedia using this model."

According to this definition, a course generation system can be classified as an adaptive hypermedia system. The visible aspects that are adapted are the sequences through the educational resources.

Several reference architectures for adaptive hypermedia systems do exist. The first, the Adaptive Hypermedia Application Model (AHAM), was proposed by De Bra et al. [32]. It is based on the Dexter hypertext reference model [54], and extends it to encompass adaptive hypermedia techniques. Koch and Wirsing [83] describes an object-oriented reference model formalized the Unified Modeling Language (UML) [136]. A logical characterization of adaptive hypermedia systems is given by Henze and Nejdl [59]. Their model allows formalizing parts of the adaptive features using first-order logic. In the following,

I mostly use the terms as defined by the AHAM reference model, which is the most wide-spread architecture. The basic ingredients of an adaptive hypermedia system are *concepts* and the three-tier architecture, consisting of a *domain model*, a *user model*, and a *teaching model*.

Concept

A concept is an abstract representation of an information item from the application domain.

Domain Model

The domain model contains the educational resources, and, depending on the specific system, the domain concepts. Additional information associated to the domain model includes metadata and the domain structure (often represented by a graph) that models the relationships between resources. In case the domain model contains resources as well as concepts, the connections between them are called anchors [32] or indices [19].

User Model

The user model (also called learner model) manages information about users. Based on observations of the user's interactions, it stores, infers and updates information about an individual user. Examples of user models are overlay models and stereotype user modeling. In the former approach, first proposed by Carr and Goldstein [24], the user model contains the knowledge of a domain expert. The individual user's knowledge is represented as a subset of that knowledge. In stereotype user modeling, proposed by Rich [155], each learner belongs to a specific class whose characteristics he inherits.

Teaching Model

The teaching model (or adaptation model) contains the knowledge how to adapt the behavior of the system, e. g., how to present content from the domain model taking into consideration the information provided by the user model. Often, this knowledge is provided as a set of rules.

Vassileva [199] distinguishes between two different functionalities provided by the rules of the teaching model, *content planning* and *presentation planning*.

Content Planning

Content planning reasons about the domain model and determines the domain concepts the generated course will cover. Usually, this process makes use of the domain structure.

Presentation Planning

For each concept selected during content planning, presentation planning determines the educational resources used to convey the information about the concept to the learner.

This distinction was originally coined by Wasson [205] (then called content planning and *delivery planning*), yet at that time in the scope of one-to-one tutoring. Other authors [e. g., 71] use the terms *concept selection* and *content selection* for these processes. The distinction between content and delivery planning is also made in other domains, e. g., natural language generation [153].

Course Planning

The process of producing a course is called course planning. The result of the planning is a *course plan* (plan in the AI-sense, see Section 2.6). From this plan, a course can be constructed.

Instructional Tasks

Following Van Marcke [197], I define a task as an abstract activity that can be accomplished during the learning process at various levels of granularity. In principle, tasks are generic, i. e., they can be applied across domains, or at least within a domain. The tasks developed in this volume are applicable for well-structured domains. They were mostly applied for learning mathematics, although one application target workflow-embedded e-learning in enterprise and office environments (see the section about evaluations for further details).

Instructional Methods

An *instructional method* specifies means to accomplish a task. It encodes domain expert knowledge how to proceed in order to perform the activity represented in a task. Typically, a method decomposes a task into subtasks, i. e., it breaks down an activity into smaller activities. Like tasks, most methods are generic, and can be applied in a large number of circumstances. Methods normally carry application conditions that specify the conditions under which a method can be applied. As an example, a method could decompose the task "rehearse content" into the subtasks "show content", "illustrate content", and "train content".

The distinction between *task* and *methods*, i. e., between *what* to achieve and *how* to achieve it clearly separates different kinds of knowledge [174].

2.6 Hierarchical Task Network Planning

In the following, I describe the planning algorithm used in PAIGOS and start with a general overview of Artificial Intelligence (AI) Planning that introduces the basic planning vocabulary. Sections 2.6.2 to 2.6.4 provide the details of the Hierarchical Task Network Planner SHOP2 and its Java version JSHOP2 employed in PAIGOS. These three sections owe a lot to [214] and [62].

2.6.1 Introduction to AI-Planning

AI-Planning/AI-Planning Problem

AI-planning provides an intelligent agent with the means of generating a sequence of actions that will achieve his goals [157]. Generally speaking, a planning problem consists of:

- the *initial state* that represents the state of the world at the time the agent begins to act;
- the *goal* the agent wants to achieve; and
- the possible operations that the agent can perform, formalized as *operators*.

Planner/Actions

The algorithm that is applied to a planning problem in order to solve it is called a *planner*. The result of the planning process, the plan, is a sequence of instantiated operators, which are called *actions*. The execution of the actions starting in any world that satisfies that initial state will achieve the goal.

Planning Language

The language that is used to describe the planning problem influences the kind of problems that can be solved by the planner. A language should be expressive enough to represent a variety of problems, while at the same time restrictive enough to allow efficient planning.

A classic planning language is STRIPS [41]. In STRIPS, a state is represented by a conjunction of positive ground literals. The goal state is partially specified. A goal g is fulfilled in a state s if s contains all literals of g. Operators consist of a *precondition* and an *effect*. A precondition is a conjunction of positive literals; an effect is a conjunction of literals. An action is an instantiated operator. It can be applied if the precondition is true in the state before the action is executed. The state changes that occur due to the application are represented in the effect: positive literals are asserted to be true, negative literals are asserted to be false.

It has been shown that STRIPS is insufficiently expressive for many real-world problems [157] and many language variants have been developed to overcome its limitations. The "Planning Domain Definition Language" (PDDL) provides a syntax that attempts to standardize planning languages [101, 42]. It is mainly used to benchmark and compare different planning approaches, e. g., at the AI Planning Systems Competition [100].

Planning Algorithm

Different planning algorithms exist. The standard approaches are forward state-space search and backward state-space search. Forward state-based planning (or *progression* planning) starts in the initial state and applies actions until the goal state is reached. Because naive forward planning does consider all actions applicable in each state, the search space quickly becomes too large to handle. In contrast, backward state-based planning (also called *regression* planning) only considers those actions that contribute to achieving unsatisfied literals, i. e., conditions that need be true in the goal state, but are not yet. One of those available operators is selected that has a literal on the effect list that matches an unsatisfied literal. The variables of the operator are instantiated, and the new goal state is calculated by deleting all positive effects of the operator and adding all preconditions of the operator (unless they already appear in the goal state).

These basic algorithms are insufficient for real-world problems. As a consequence, a number of different algorithms have been developed (see [157] for an introduction to planning). In the following, I will describe an approach that makes use of the hierarchical problem solving knowledge often available in a domain to guide the search through to search space.

2.6.2 Introduction to Hierarchical Task Network Planning

In Hierarchical Task Network planning (HTN planning), the goal of the planner is to achieve a partially or fully ordered list of activities. In HTN terminology, these activities are called *tasks*. For now, these tasks share only the name with instructional tasks as defined in Section 2.5; conceptually they are different. Only later in this volume, in Section 4.4, I will show how instructional tasks can be mapped onto HTN tasks. In the following sections, whenever I use the term "task", it means "HTN task".

An HTN planner solves a list of tasks (*task network*) by decomposing these top tasks into smaller and smaller subtasks until *primitive* tasks are reached that can be carried out directly. Sacerdoti [158] and Tate [177] developed the basic idea in the mid-70s. The development of the formal underpinnings came much later, in the mid-90s by Erol et al. [40]. HTN planning research has been much more application-oriented than most other AI-planning research, and most HTN planning systems have been used in one or more application domains [210, 29, 126].

HTN planning is a very efficient planning technique, as illustrated by the HTN planner SHOP2 that received one of the top four awards in the 2002 International Planning Competition. HTN planning is efficient because the task decomposition encodes domain-specific control knowledge that prunes the search space effectively. The goal is represented by a task network, and instead of considering all operators applicable in the current state, the planner only considers those that occur in the decomposed goal task [122].

2.6.3 SHOP2 and JSHOP2

The planners SHOP (Simple Hierarchical Ordered Planner [123]), SHOP2 [124], and JSHOP2 [63] were developed at the Automated Planning Group, University of Maryland. Unlike most other HTN planners, they decompose tasks into subtasks in the order in which the tasks will be achieved in the resulting plan. This search-control strategy is called *ordered task decomposition*. As a result of this strategy, the current state is known in each step of the planning process. This allows incorporating sophisticated reasoning capabilities into the planning algorithm, such as calling external functions, which can access predefined code in order to perform complex calculations or access external information sources. Nau et al. [124] show that the planning procedure of SHOP2 (and JSHOP2) is Turing-complete, and sound and complete over a large class of planning problems.

JSHOP2 is the Java version of SHOP2. It is a compiler that takes an HTN domain description as input and compiles it into a set of domain-specific Java classes that can later be used to solve planning problems in that domain. These classes implement a domain-specific instance of a domain-independent planner. The fact that JSHOP2 is a compiler rather than an interpreter helps optimizing the domain-dependent code it produces. Ilghami and Nau [63] provide evaluation results that show that the compilation technique can increase planning efficiency significantly.

2.6.4 JSHOP2 Formalism

In this section, I provide a detailed description of JSHOP2, where I will restrict myself to the features actually used by PAIGOS. The JSHOP2 manual [62] describes the complete set of features; and this section owes a lot to that manual.

The inputs to JSHOP2 are a *planning domain* and a *planning problem*. Planning domains are composed of *operators*, *methods*, *axioms*, and *external functions*:

- *planning operators* describe various kinds of actions that the plan executor can perform directly. These are similar to classical planning operators such as the ones in PDDL, with preconditions, add and delete lists. Each operator instance can carry out a primitive task associated with it. These operator instances change the world state upon their execution according to their add and delete lists.
- *Methods* describe various possible ways of decomposing compound tasks into eventually primitive subtasks. These are the "standard operating procedures" that one would normally use to perform tasks in the domain. Each method may have a set of preconditions that must be satisfied in order to be applicable.
- *Axioms* are Horn-clause-like statements for inferring conditions that are not mentioned explicitly in world states.

- External functions are code calls to external agents that the planner can make while evaluating a condition or calculating a binding during planning. As we will see in Chapter 4, they are used extensively in PAIGOS.

Planning problems are composed of an initial state that consists of *logical atoms*, and *tasks lists* (high-level actions to perform). The components of a planning domain (operators, methods, and axioms) all involve *logical expressions*, which are logical atoms connected through operators described below. Logical atoms involve a *predicate symbol* plus a list of *terms*. Task lists in planning problems are composed of *task atoms*. The elements of domains and problems are defined by various *symbols*.

Planning happens by applying methods to compound tasks that decompose them into subtasks until a level of primitive tasks is reached, and by applying operators to primitive tasks to produce actions. If this is done in such a way that all of the constraints are satisfied, then the planner has found a solution plan; otherwise the planner will need to backtrack and try other methods and actions.

This section describes each of the above structures. Following [62], the description is organized in a bottom-up manner because the specification of higher-level structures is dependent on the specification of lower-level structures. For example, methods are defined after logical expressions because methods contain logical expressions.

2.6.4.1 Symbol

The vocabulary of the language for the JSHOP2 planner is a tuple $\langle V, C, P, F, T, N, M \rangle$, where V is an infinite set of variable symbols, C is an finite set of constant symbols, P is a finite set of predicate symbols, F is a finite set of function symbols, T is a finite set of compound task symbols, N is a finite set of primitive task symbols, and M is an infinite set of name symbols. All these sets are mutually distinct. To distinguish among these symbols, I will use the following conventions:

- variable symbols begin with a question mark (such as ?x);
- primitive task symbols begin with an exclamation point (e. g., !unstack);
- constant symbols, predicate symbols, function symbols, and compound task symbols begin with a letter;
- square brackets indicate optional parameters or keywords;
- expressions in *italic* denote any arbitrary term. They have no semantic meaning in JSHOP2 but are used for convenience in examples.

Any of the structures defined in the remaining sections are said to be ground if they contain no variable symbols.

2.6.4.2 Term

A term is any one of the following:

- a variable symbol;
- a constant symbol;
- a name symbol;
- a number;
- a *list term*;
- a *call term*.

List Term

A list term is a term of the form

$$(t_1\ t_2\ \ldots\ t_n\ [.\ 1])$$

where each t_i is a term. This specifies that t_1, t_2, ..., and t_n are the items of a list. If the final, optional element is included, the item 1 should evaluate to a list; the "." indicates that all items in 1 are included in the list after t_1 through t_n

Call Term

A call term is an expression of the form

$$(\text{call}\ f\ t_1\ t_2\ \ldots\ t_n)$$

where f is a function symbol and each t_i is a term. A call term tells JSHOP2 that f is an attached procedure, i.e., that whenever JSHOP2 needs to evaluate a structure where a call term appears, JSHOP2 should replace the call term with the result of applying the external function f on the arguments t_1, t_2, ..., and t_n. In JSHOP2, any Java function can be attached as a procedure, as long as it returns a term as a result.

Example 2.5. The following call term has the value 6: (call + (call + 1 2) 3).

2.6.4.3 Logical Atom

A *logical atom* has the form

$$(p\ t_1\ t_2\ \ldots\ t_n)$$

where p is a predicate symbol and each t_i is a term.

Example 2.6. Later in this volume, I will describe the fact that a resource r was inserted in course using the logical atom (inserted r).

2.6.4.4 Logical Expression

A *logical expression* is a logical atom or any of the following complex expressions: *conjunctions, disjunctions, negations, implications, assignments,* or *call expressions.*

Conjunction

A *conjunction* has the form

    ([and] L_1 L_2 ... L_n)

where each L_i is a logical expression.

Disjunction

A *disjunction* has the form

    (or L_1 L_2 ... L_n)

where each L_i is a logical expression.

Negation

A *negation* is an expression of the form

    (not L)

where L is a logical expression.

Implication

A *implication* has the form

    (imply Y Z)

where each Y and Z are logical expressions, and Y has to be ground. An implication is interpreted as (or not(Y) Z).

Assignment

An *assignment expression* has the form

    (assign v t)

where v is a variable symbol and t is a term. An assignment expression binds the value of t to the variable symbol v.

Call Expression

A *call expression* has the same form as a call term but is interpreted as **false** if it evaluates to an empty list and as **true** otherwise.

2.6.4.5 Logical Precondition

A *logical precondition* is either a logical expression or a *first satisfier precondition*.

First Satisfier Precondition

A first satisfier precondition has the form

    (:first L)

where L is a logical expression. Such a precondition causes JSHOP2 to consider only the first binding that satisfies L (similar to the cut operator in Prolog). Alternative binding will not be considered, even if the first binding does not lead to a valid plan.

2.6.4.6 Axiom

An *axiom* in a expression of the form

    (:- a [name$_1$] L$_1$ [name$_2$] L$_2$ ... [name$_n$] L$_n$)

where the axiom's *head* is the logical atom a, and its *tail* is the list [name$_1$] L$_1$ [name$_2$] L$_2$ ... [name$_n$] L$_n$, and each L$_i$ is a logical precondition and each name$_i$ is a symbol called the *name* of L$_i$. The names serve debugging purposes only, and have no semantic meaning. The intended meaning of an axiom is that a is true if L$_1$ is true, or if L$_1$ is false, but L$_2$ is true, ..., or if all of L$_1$, L$_2$, ..., L$_{n-1}$ are false but L$_n$ is true.

2.6.4.7 Task Atom

A *task atom* is an expression of the form

    (s t$_1$ t$_2$ ... t$_n$)

where s is a task symbol and the arguments t$_1$ t$_2$ ... t$_n$ are terms. The task atom is *primitive* if s is a primitive task symbol, and it is *compound* if s is a compound task symbol.

Example 2.7. Lather in this volume, I will use the primitive task (!insert r) to represent the goal that a resource r should be inserted into a course. The compound task (**rehearse r**) represents that a course should be generated that supports the learner is rehearsing r.

2.6.4.8 Task List

A *task list* is either a task atom or an expression of the form

    ([tasklist$_1$ tasklist$_2$ ... tasklist$_n$])

where tasklist$_1$ tasklist$_2$ ... tasklist$_n$ are task lists themselves. n can be zero, resulting in an empty task list.

2.6.4.9 Operator

An *operator* has the form

    (:operator h P D A)

where

- h (the operator's *head*) is a primitive task atom;
- P (the operator's *precondition*) is a logical expression;
- D (the operator's *delete list*) is a list that consists of logical atoms;
- A (the operator's *add list*) is a list that consists of logical atoms.

A planning operator accomplishes a primitive task: the task symbol is the name of the planning operator to use, and the task's arguments are the parameters for the operator. An action is defined as being an instantiated operator.

JSHOP2 allows defining *internal operators*. An internal operator is only used for supporting purposes during the planning process (e. g., to perform calculations which might become useful later during planning) and does not correspond to actions performed in the plan. Internal operators are specially marked (they begin with two exclamation marks), yet they have the same syntax and semantics as other operators. Internal operators serve the purpose that a client that uses plans generated by JSHOP2 can distinguish between operators that are internal to the planning process and those that involve action.

JSHOP2 requires that an operator is designed such that each variable symbol in the add list and delete list can always be bound to a single value when the operator is invoked. Variable symbols can be bound in the head of the operator (by the method that invokes the associated primitive task) or in the precondition of the operator.

2.6.4.10 Method

A *method* is a list of the form

    (:method h [name$_1$] L$_1$ T$_1$ [name$_2$] L$_2$ T$_2$ ...[name$_n$] L$_n$ T$_n$)

where

- h (the method's *head*) is a compound task atom;
- each L$_i$ (a *precondition* for the method) is a logical precondition;
- each T$_i$ (a *tail* or the *subtasks* of the method) is a task list;
- each name$_i$ is the name for the succeeding pair L$_i$ T$_i$.

A method specifies that the task in the method's head can be performed by performing all of the tasks in one of the method's tails, when that tail's precondition is satisfied. Note that the preconditions are considered in the given order, and a later precondition is considered only if all of the earlier preconditions can not be satisfied. If there are multiple methods for a given task available at some point in time, then the methods are considered in the order given in the domain definition.

2.6.4.11 Planning Domain

A *planning domain* has the form

    (defdomain domain-name (d_1 d_2 ...d_n))

where `domain-name` is a symbol and each item d_i is either an operator, a method, or an axiom.

2.6.4.12 Planning Problem

A *planning problem* has the form

    (defproblem problem-name domain-name
                ([a_{1,1} a_{1,2} ... a_{1,n}]) T_1 ...
                ([a_{m,1} a_{m,2} ... a_{m,o}]) T_m)

where `problem-name` and `domain-name` are symbols, each $a_{i,j}$ is a ground logical atom, and each T_i is a task list. This form defines m planning problems in domain `domain-name` each of which may be solved by addressing the tasks in T_i with the initial state defined by the atoms $a_{i,1}$ through $a_{i,j}$.

2.6.4.13 Plan

While the above sections described the input to JSHOP2, this section describes the output that JSHOP2 produces. A *plan* is a list of the form

    (h_1 h_2 ... h_n)

where each h_i is the head of a ground operator instance o_i (an action). If p = (h_1 h_2 ... h_n) is a plan, o_i the operator associated with h_i, and S is a state, then p(S) is the state produced by starting with S and executing o_1, o_2, ... o_n in the given order.

2.6.4.14 Example of an Operator and a Method

Figure 2.4 presents an example of an HTN operator in JSHOP2 syntax (this and the following example are taken from [125]). It uses the conventions defined above: the semicolon indicates the start of a comment, terms starting with a question mark denote variables, primitive HTN tasks are marked with an exclamation mark, and a double exclamation mark denotes a task only relevant for internal purposes.

The operator in the example is applicable given a) that the primitive task (!board ?person ?plane) can be matched against a not yet achieved primitive task (i. e., that there is a person that should board a plane) and b) that the instantiated preconditions in lines 3–4 hold (i. e., atoms exists in the world state that can be matched with the preconditions whose variables are replaced by the value they were bound to in the operator's task). In case an

```
1   (:operator (!board ?person ?plane)   ;; the primitive HTN task
2              ( ;; the precondition
3              (at ?person ?place)
4              (at ?plane ?place)
5              )
6              ( ;; the delete list
7              (at ?person ?place)
8              )
9              ( ;; the add list
10             (in ?person ?plane)
11             )
12             )
```

Fig. 2.4. An HTN operator

operator is applied all atoms contained in the delete list are removed and all atoms contained in the add list are added to the world state respectively. In the example, the person would no longer be at the original place but in the plane.

```
(:method (transport-person ?person ?destination) ;; the HTN task
         ;; the first preconditions
         (
           (at ?person ?current-position)
           (same ?current-position ?destination)
         )
         ;; the corresponding subtask
         ()
         ;; the next preconditions
         (
           (at ?person ?current-position)
           (plane ?p)
         )
         ;; the corresponding subtask
         ((transport-with-plane ?person ?p ?destination)))
```

Fig. 2.5. An HTN method

Figure 2.5 contains an example of a HTN method. The method is applicable in case an open HTN task exists that matches with (transport-person ?person ?destination) and any of the precondition lists holds. The preconditions are tried in the given order. If one of them matches, the method's head is replaced by the corresponding subtasks.

3

Descriptive and Prescriptive Learning Theories

Learning theories describe how people learn, often by reference to a particular model of human cognition or development. Depending on the learning theory, different requirements arise regarding the learning process, e. g., how to structure it, what questions to ask the learner, etc.

Learning theories can be divided into *descriptive* and *prescriptive* theories [162, page 137]. Descriptive learning theories make statements about how learning occurs and devise models that can be used to explain and predict learning results. When describing different descriptive theories of learning below, I will follow the common categorization that distinguishes between *behaviorist*, *cognitive*, and *constructivist* learning theories [151, 162].

Prescriptive learning theories are concerned with guidelines that describe what to do in order to achieve specific outcomes. They are often based on descriptive theories; sometimes they are derived from experience. *Instructional design* is the umbrella which assembles prescriptive theories. I will describe instructional design in Section 3.4.

3.1 Behaviorism

Behaviorism explains human behavior based on observable stimulus-response associations, without referring to mental processes. Behavioristic theories were developed in the beginning of the 19th century as a reaction to the then predominantly used psychological methods of introspection and subjectivity, which behavioral theorists such as John B. Watson qualified as nonscientific [206].

Learning is viewed as the forging of the desired condition-action pairs. Positive reactions have to be reinforced, undesired ones avoided. Behaviorists such as Burrhus F. Skinner applied their research results to technology-supported learning. Skinner [169] provided principles for *programmed instruction*, which is characterized by leading the learner through the learning material in gradual steps, providing immediate feedback, and continuous positive reinforcement.

In the sixties, the US government, especially the Department of Defense invested considerable amounts of money in the development of programmed instruction, with the hope of reducing the costs for civil and military training.[1] One prominent system developed at that time was Plato whose trademark is still used today.[2] Yet, evaluation results of programmed instruction were mixed, and the authoring costs were extremely high, so that educational systems based on pure behavioristic principles became rare.

3.2 Cognitivism

Cognitive psychology makes mental processes the primary object of study. Experiments involving mental operations are designed such that they allow conclusions on the cognitive structures used in the mind during problem solving. These experiments are reproducible, in contrast to the former introspective and subjective experiments.

Learning is viewed as transferring the cognitive structures in long-term memory and being able to use them, when necessary. Learning takes place through organizing, storing and linking the new structures to old knowledge.

Based on cognitive theories, one can devise principles for instruction. In the 1960ties, Gagné [44] published his principles of instruction, an effort to collect the existing theories and to put them into a common framework. He distinguishes nine cognitive processes and assigns specific instructional events to the objectives, e. g., the process "retrieval", with the instructional event "stimulating recall of prior learning".

In technology-supported learning, the research in cognitive psychology led to the new field of *Intelligent Tutoring Systems* (ITS). ITS were designed to support the learner during problem solving in his creation of the appropriate cognitive structures. One of the most prominent ITS, the PACT-tutors were originally based on Anderson's ACT-* theory [3, 4, 5].

3.3 Constructivism

Constructivism is based on the premise that knowledge can not be transmitted but has to be constructed by the individual. Therefore, learning is an active process of integrating information with pre-existing knowledge.

---

[1] The ratio between military and civilian investment in education is astonishing: "within government agencies, the military spends seven dollars for every civilian dollar spent on educational technology research. Each year, for example, the military spends as much on educational technology research and development as the Department ... of Education has spent in a quarter century" [132].

[2] http://www.plato.com [145].

Cognitively oriented constructivist theories such as discovery learning (e. g., [17]) and microworlds [140] emphasize exploration and discovery. Socially oriented constructivist theories, such as social constructivism [201] and cognitive apprenticeships [16] stress the collaborative efforts of groups of learners as sources of learning.

In constructivism, the control over the learning process shifts from the teacher to student. The learner plays the active role in the learning process. He is regarded to be an information-processing individual; the external stimulus is processed actively and independently. The kind and quality of the processing varies between the learners, depending on the account of different experiences, previous knowledge and levels of development of the learners. Learning takes place in context and in collaboration and provides opportunities to solve realistic and meaningful problems. In contrast, the teachers focus mainly on preparatory activities and provide support in case assistance is needed. Consequently, the teacher is an initiator of and an adviser in the learning process.

Papert's Turtle microworld in LOGO [140] is one of the best known examples of technology-supported learning based on constructivist principles.

The last years have seen an increasing research in and appliance of constructivist approaches. Pure constructivist approaches, however, are not unchallenged. Authors such as Mantyka [94] point out that it is not possible to completely abandon instructions and drill from lessons. Hence, the moderate constructivist theory has been developed as a pragmatic approach which integrates instructions into a theory that has a clear constructivist tendency.

3.4 Instructional Design

According to Reigeluth [150], *instructional design* describes how to design teaching materials that are effective (how well a topic is learned), efficient (ratio of effectivity and the time required for learning), and appealing to the learner. Instructional design being a prescriptive learning theory is orthogonal to descriptive theories. The work by Gagné [44] counts as one of the first examples of instructional design.

Usage of instructional design is wide-spread. However, it is not unquestioned. Some authors [211, 150, 115] claim that instructional design can encompass cognitive and even constructivist elements. Others, e. g., Schulmeister, classify instructional design as behavioristic ([162], pages 142–166). There, Schulmeister documents an intensive debate in the journal "Educational Technology" between supporters of instructional design and constructivism. He provides the following quote by Jones, Li, and Merrill [69], which convincingly illustrates the principal differences between the traditional instructional design and the constructivist approach:

Instruction, in large measure, communicates accepted meaning. The developer of instruction explicitly desires that the learner adopt the meaning intended by the developer, and not reach a separate and personal interpretation of that meaning. ... [M]ost instruction ... concerns transferring, as effectively and efficiently as possible, determined interpretations.

No matter what, the debate between the protagonists of instructional design and constructivist is not subject of this volume. However, what this debate illustrates is that different views exist on the "best" way of teaching. Therefore, PAIGOS was designed to be educational neutral, that is, as such, it is independent of any learning theory, but can be instantiated to the required learning theory at hand. In Chapter 5, I will describe course generation based on moderate constructivist as well as on instructional design principles.

Throughout this volume, I use the term "instruction" in a manner that reflects this educational neutrality. Following the Random House Unabridged Dictionary [148], in this work, instruction denotes "the act or practice of instructing or teaching".

3.5 Competency-Based Learning

3.5.1 Mathematical Competencies

In the late nineties, the OECD (Organisation for Economic Co-operation and Development) started the *PISA* studies (Programme for International Student Assessment), which "aim to measure how far students approaching the end of compulsory education have acquired some of the knowledge and skills essential for full participation in the knowledge society" [139].

From early on, PISA considered mathematics as one of the central subjects to be tested. PISA is based on the notion of *competency-based learning* [138]: learning mathematics should not only aim at solving a problem but also at thinking mathematically and arguing about the correctness or incorrectness of the problem solving steps and involved methods, to perform simple and complex computations, etc.

The competency approach is based on the *literacy* concept. The general assumption is that different competencies together build up mathematical literacy. One can only become mathematically literate by sufficiently high achievement over the complete set of competencies.

The competency approach can be considered as a way to support the presentation of concepts from different perspectives by giving varying tasks to the students. The tasks differ in the required mathematical activities, the competencies.

Based on the PISA studies and related work by the (American) *National Council of Teachers of Mathematics*, the European FP6 project LEACTIVE-MATH investigated employing mathematical competencies for technology-supported learning.

The competencies in LeActiveMath describe high level learning objectives and can be characterized as following (see also [131] and [81]):

Think mathematically. Includes the ability to
- pose questions that are characteristic for mathematics (e. g., "Are there ... ?", "How does ... change?", "Are there exceptions?")
- understand and handle the scope and limitations of a given concept
- make assumptions (e.g. extend the scope by changing conditions, generalize or specify, with reasons)
- distinguish between different kinds of mathematical statements (e.g. conditional assertions, propositional logic)

Argue mathematically. Includes the ability to
- develop and assess chains of arguments (explanations, reasons, proofs)
- know what a mathematical proof is and what not
- describe solutions and give reasons for their correctness or incorrectness
- uncover the basic ideas in a given line of arguments
- understand reasoning and proof as fundamental aspects of mathematics

Solve problems mathematically. Includes the ability to
- identify, pose and specify problems
- self-constitute problems
- monitor and reflect on the process of problem solving
- endue strategies / heuristics
- solve different kinds of problems (with various contexts outside of mathematics, open-ended exercises)

Model mathematically. Includes the ability to
- translate special areas and contents into mathematical terms
- work in the model
- interpret and verify the results in the situational context
- point out the difference between the situation and the model

Use mathematical representations. Includes the ability to
- understand and utilize (decode, interpret, distinguish between) different sorts of representation (e.g., diagrams and tables) of mathematical objects, phenomena, and situations
- find relations between different kinds of representation
- choose the appropriate representation for the special purpose

Deal with symbolic and formal elements of mathematics. Includes to
- use parameters, terms, equations and functions to model and interpret
- translate from symbolic and formal language into natural language and the other way round
- decode and interpret symbolic and formal mathematical language and understand its relations to natural language

Communicate. Includes the ability to
- explain solutions

- use a special terminology,
- work in groups, including to explain at the adequate level
- understand and verify mathematical statements of others

Use tools and aids. Includes the ability to

- know about the existence of various tools and aids for mathematical activities, and their range and limitations;
- to reflectively use such tools and aids

3.5.2 Competency Levels

Competency levels of exercises are intervals of difficulty labeling. They serve the purpose to measure to what extent a specific competency has to be developed by the student in order to solve the particular exercise with a certain probability. The competency levels are characterized as follows [81]:

Level I: Computation at an elementary level. To achieve this level, students have to apply arithmetic knowledge (factual knowledge, schematic applicable procedures). This level comprises knowledge learned by heart that is easy to recall and can be applied directly in a standard situation without requiring conceptual modeling.

Level II: Simple conceptual solutions. This competency level involves simple forms of conceptual modeling, solutions that require only a limited amount of problem solving steps, and factual knowledge. In exercises on this level, either the task is to select the correct solution from several alternatives or the student is provided with structural aids and graphical hints to develop her own solution.

Level III: Challenging multi-step-solutions. This competency level requires to perform more extensive operations and to solve a problem in several intermediate steps. Additionally, it includes dealing with open-ended modeling tasks that can be solved in various ways, but that require to find a solution of their own. High level modeling on inner-mathematical connections can also be required.

Level IV: Complex processing (modeling, argumentation). Students who successfully solve exercises of this competency level are able to work on open-ended tasks, choose adequate models and construct models themselves where necessary. Conceptual modeling at this highest level often includes mathematical justification and proof as well as reflection on the modeling process itself.

The scenarios described in this work (Section 5) are based on the notion of competencies and competency levels.

Part II

PAIGOS

4

General Principles

In this chapter, I will identify and describe general principles that apply to course generation as formalized in PAIGOS, independent of both the underlying learning theory and the learning goals the course is generated for.

The chapter starts with metadata. In Section 4.1, I show that existing learning object metadata standards fail to describe educational resources sufficiently precise for their automatic integration into learning processes by intelligent components. I then describe an ontology of instructional objects that contains specifically this previously missing information. The ontology facilitates the process of making repositories available to the course generator. On the one hand, this process helps to assemble a course from resources of different repositories. On the other hand, the course generator can provide its functionalities as a service to other systems that plug-in their repositories. The mediator architecture that was developed for this purpose is described in Section 4.2. A further question concerns the learning goals that PAIGOS processes. In traditional course generation systems, learning goals consist only of educational resources, which represent the target content that is to be learned. Such an approach ignores that different purposes require different course of actions. For instance, a course for preparing an exam should consist of different educational resources from a course that provides a guided tour. Section 4.3 tackles this question and provides a general representation of learning goals. The subsequent sections form the main part of this chapter. They explain how course generation knowledge can be formalized as an HTN planning domain. This chapter describes general axioms, operators and methods used in that domain (Chapter 5 describes how these general techniques are used to generate course for different learning goals in different learning theories). The remaining sections of this chapter cover additional features that arise from the need of the application and are possible in PAIGOS: Section 4.8 describes how to generate a complete course and still allow for adaptive selection of resources when needed. Section 4.9 focuses on the problem that automatically generated sequences of educational resources can lack coherence and explanations about the learning goals, and describes how to use the information about the learning goals available during course generation to generate such information.

4.1 An Ontology of Instructional Objects

According to Gruber [53] an "ontology is an explicit specification of a conceptualization". He continues: "when the knowledge of a domain is represented in a declarative formalism, the set of objects that can be represented is called the universe of discourse. This set of objects, and the describable relationships among them, are reflected in the representational vocabulary with which a knowledge-based program represents knowledge." The set of objects is also called concepts or classes.

Mizoguchi and Bourdeau [117] stress that a first step towards intelligent services is to define the terms used in the application domain. For educational services such as course generation the terms need to describe the educational resources as well as the learning goals.[1] This section describes an ontology of instructional objects (OIO) that was developed in order to characterize educational resources. Although originally developed for mathematical resources, it can also be used for describing other subject domains, as long as the domain can be structured in distinct elements with relations (e. g., physics, future work will investigate applicability to domains such as language learning). The OIO describes resources sufficiently precise for a pedagogically complex functionality such as course generation.

Seminal work on using ontologies for e-learning was done in the ISIR lab, headed by Mizoguchi: Mizoguchi and Bourdeau [117] lay out how ontologies can help to overcome problems in artificial intelligence in education; Aroyo and Mizoguchi [8] and Hayashi et al. [55] describe how an assistant layer uses an ontology to support the complete authoring process, for instance by giving hints on the course structure (see also the description of related work in Chapter 8. The following ontology has a more specific scope; instead of describing the authoring process during which the educational resources are developed, the ontology is focused on describing the resources. It thus defines a set of types (or classes) that is used to annotate educational resources.[2]

---

[1] Equally important is information about the learner and her current learning context. However, this is outside the scope of this volume. We will assume that there exists a component that contains the necessary information about the learner (a learner model).

[2] Part of the work described in this section was published in the following publications: [184, 185, 113, 186, 110].

4.1.1 Motivation

The requirements that influenced the design of the ontology are the following (partly based on [86]):

Domain independence. The types represented in the ontology should be independent of the domain that is being taught as long as the domain can be structured in distinct entities connected by relations. Ideally, the types should characterize educational resources about mathematics as well as physics or chemistry.

Pedagogical flexibility. The types should be independent of the learning theory underlying the educational resources, i. e., they should describe constructivist as well as more traditional didactic approaches.

Completeness. The types should cover the range of educational resources as much as possible.

Compatibility. Mapping the ontology onto existing standards and learning object metadata should be as easy as possible.

Applicability. Users should be able to understand and apply the ontology using terms that reflect their needs. LOM, for instance, is notorious for putting a heavy load on content developers due to its vast amount of properties. [39].

Machine processability. The types (together with additional metadata) should enable intelligent applications to find and reuse learning objects without human guidance or intervention.

In order to design an ontology that complies with these goals as much as possible, I analyzed sources ranging from text classification [92], over instructional design [e. g., 149, 150, 45, 178, 34, 209, 102] to knowledge representations of structured texts [22, 204, 65] and representations used for technology-supported learning [e. g., 197, 172, 141, 107, 90, 25, 48]. Whenever applicable, these sources were taken into account in the ontology.

A concrete example illustrates best the entities described by the ontology. Figure 4.1 includes several learning resources (taken from the textbook [10]), clearly divided into several distinct paragraphs. Each paragraph serves a particular *instructional role*. The first two paragraphs introduce two concepts (a *definition* and a *theorem*), the third provides *examples of applications* of a concept, and the last one offers *activities to apply* the concept. The example is taken from a traditional textbook in order to illustrate that the ontology applies to other resources than digital ones.

Currently, the most established standard for describing educational resources is LOM. It is a common and exhaustive, yet easily extensible description of learning objects, which allows describing, finding, and using educational resources across any learning environment. LOM's educational categories partially describe resources from an pedagogical perspective, in particular the slot `learningResourceType`. Its possible values are `Exercise`, `Simulation`, `Questionnaire`, `Diagram`, `Figure`, `Graph`, `Index`, `Slide`, `Table`,

2.3.7 Definition Let $a \in R$ and $\varepsilon > 0$. Then the ε-neighborhood of a is the set $V_\varepsilon(a) := \{x \in R: |x - a| < \varepsilon\}$.

For $a \in R$, the statement that x belongs to $V_\varepsilon(a)$ is equivalent to either of the statements

$$-\varepsilon < x - a < \varepsilon \quad \Longleftrightarrow \quad a - \varepsilon < x < a + \varepsilon.$$

(See Figure 2.3.2.)

FIGURE 2.3.2   An ε-neighborhood of a.

2.3.8 Theorem Let $a \in R$. If x belongs to the neighborhood $V_\varepsilon(a)$ for every $\varepsilon > 0$, then $x = a$.

Proof. If a particular x satisfies $|x - a| < \varepsilon$ for every $\varepsilon > 0$, then it follows from 2.2.9 that $|x - a| = 0$, and hence $x = a$.   Q.E.D.

2.3.9 Examples (a) Let $U := \{x: 0 < x < 1\}$. If $a \in U$, then let ε be the smaller of the two numbers a and $1 - a$. Then $V_\varepsilon(a)$ is contained in U. Thus each element of U has some ε-neighborhood of it contained in U.

(b) If $I := \{x: 0 \leq x \leq 1\}$, then for any $\varepsilon > 0$, the ε-neighborhood $V_\varepsilon(0)$ of 0 contains points not in I, and so $V_\varepsilon(0)$ is not contained in I. For example, the number $x_\varepsilon := -\varepsilon/2$ is in $V_\varepsilon(0)$ but not in I.

(c) If $|x - a| < \varepsilon$ and $|y - b| < \varepsilon$, then the Triangle Inequality implies that

$$|(x + y) - (a + b)| = |(x - a) + (y - b)|$$

$$\leq |x - a| + |y - b| < 2\varepsilon.$$

Thus if x, y belong to the ε-neighborhoods of a, b, respectively, then $x + y$ belongs to the 2ε-neighborhood of $a + b$ (but not necessarily to the ε-neighborhood of $a + b$).

Exercises for Section 2.3

1. Let $a \in R$. Show that we have:
   (a) $|a| = \sqrt{a^2}$,   (b) $|a^2| = a^2$.
2. If $a, b \in R$ and $b \neq 0$, show that $|a/b| = |a|/|b|$.
3. If $a, b \in R$, show that $|a + b| = |a| + |b|$ if and only if $ab \geq 0$.

Fig. 4.1. A page that contains several types of instructional objects (from the mathematics textbook [10], marginally modified)

NarrativeText, Exam, Experiment, ProblemStatement, and SelfAssesment. The problem with these values is that they mix pedagogical and technical or presentation information: while Graph, Slide and Table describe the format of a resource, other values such as Exercise, Simulation and Experiment cover the instructional type. They represent different dimensions, hence need to be separated for an improved decision-making. Furthermore, several instructional objects are not covered by LOM (e. g., definition, example). As a result, LOM fails to represent the instructional type sufficiently precise to allow for *automatic* usage of educational resources, in particular if the usage involves complex pedagogical knowledge necessary for effective learning support. For instance, LOM has no easy way to determine to what extent a resource annotated with Graph can be used as an example. Related metadata standards, e. g., GEM [46], exhibit similar problems.

Other relevant e-learning standards in this context are IMS LD and IMS Question and Test Interoperability (IMS QTI [50]). IMS LD describes ordered activities in learning and the roles of the involved parties. It does not represent single learning resources and their instructional functions. IMS QTI specifies a representation of exercises which encodes common exercise types, such as multiple choice, image hot-spot, and fill-in-blank. It specifies the functionality of an exercise rather than its pedagogical purpose.

Since no existing standard could fulfill the above requirements, I designed an ontology of instructional objects (OIO) that describes learning resources from an instructional perspective. Note that each of the classes of the ontology stands for a particular instructional role an educational resource can play – they do not describe the content taught by the educational resources, e. g., concepts in mathematics and their relationships.

4.1.2 Description of the Ontology

An overview of the OIO is shown in Figure 4.2. In the following, I will describe the classes and relations in detail.[3]

Instructional Object

The root class of the ontology is instructionalObject. At this class, several properties are defined that are used in all classes of the ontology. They include Dublin Core Metadata for administrative data, an unique identifier, and some values adopted from LOM such as difficulty and learningContext (the educational context of the typical target audience). Dependencies between instructional objects are represented using the relation requires. In the current version of PAIGOS it proved to be not necessary to distinguish between educational and content-based dependencies, as done, e. g., in the learning environment ACTIVEMATH [109]. The relation isVariantOf is used

---

[3] The ontology is publicly available at http://semanticweb.dfki.de/Wiki.jsp?page= Ontologies.

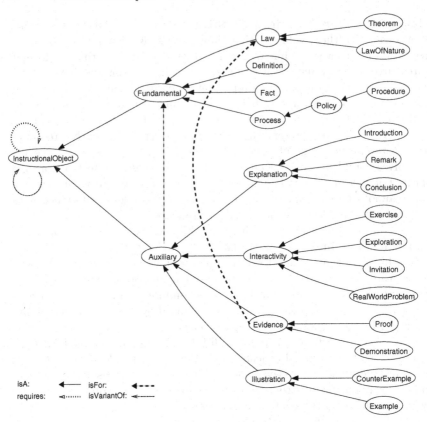

Fig. 4.2. Overview of the Ontology of Instructional Objects

to indicate that an instructional object is a variant of another one, e. g., that an exercise e is a simpler version of an exercise f. In the current version of PAIGOS, handling variants of fundamentals is limited to the learning context, i. e., all definitions for the same learning context are assumed to be different. This is due to the way how fundamentals are processed in the learning environment ACTIVEMATH in which PAIGOS was implemented. It poses no principal difficulties to extend PAIGOS to take this kind of variants into account.

Central to the ontology is the distinction between the classes **fundamental** and **auxiliary**. The class **fundamental** subsumes instructional objects that describe the central pieces of domain knowledge (concepts). Auxiliary elements include instructional objects which contain additional information about the fundamentals as well as training and learning experience.

Fundamental

More specifically, an educational resource of type **fundamental** conveys the central pieces of information about a domain that the learner should learn during the learning process. Pure fundamentals are seldom found in educational resources. Most of the time, they come in the form of one of their specializations. Albeit fundamentals are not necessarily instruction-specific because they cover types of knowledge in general, they are included in the ontology because they are necessary for instruction: educational resources often have the instructional function of presenting a fundamental.

Fact

An educational resource of type `fact` contains information based on real occurrences; it describes an event or something that holds without being a general rule.

Definition

A `definition` states the meaning of, e. g., a word, term, expression, phrase, symbol or class. In addition, it can describe the conditions or circumstances that an entity must fulfill in order to count as an instance of a class.

Law, Law of Nature, Theorem

A `law` describes a general principle between phenomena or expressions that has been proven to hold or is based on consistent experience. Two sub-classes allow a more precise characterization: `lawOfNature` describes a scientific generalization based on observation; `theorem` describes an idea that has been demonstrated to be true. In mathematics, it describes a statement which can be proven true on the basis of explicit assumptions.

Process, Policy, Procedure

`Process` and its subclasses describe a sequence of events. The deeper in the class hierarchy, the more formal and specialized they become. An educational resource of type `process` contains information on a flow of events that describes how something works and can involve several actors. A `policy` describes a fixed or predetermined policy or mode of action. One principal actor can employ it as an informal direction for tasks or as a guideline. A `procedure` consists of a specified sequence of steps or formal instructions to achieve an end. It can be as formal as an algorithm or a proof planning method [104].

Auxiliary

An educational resource of type `auxiliary` contains information about fundamentals that, in theory, is not necessary for understanding the domain but supports the learning process and often is crucial for it. They motivate the learner and offer engaging and challenging learning opportunities. Every auxiliary object contains information about one or several fundamentals. The identifiers of these fundamentals are enumerated in the property `isFor`.

Interactivity

An **interactivity** requires the learner to give active feedback. It is more general than an exercise as it does not necessarily have a defined goal that the learner has to achieve. It is designed to develop or train a skill or ability related to a fundamental. The subclasses of **interactivity** do not capture technical aspects. In general, the way an interactivity is realized, for instance as a multiple choice question, is independent of its instructional function. As illustrated by [15] for the "taxonomy of educational objectives", well-designed multiple choice questions can address different educational objectives.

Exploration, Real World Problem, Invitation, Exercise

Using an educational resource of type **exploration**, the user can freely explore aspects of a fundamental without a specified goal or with a goal but no predefined solution path. A **realWorldProblem** describes a situation from the learner's daily private or professional life that involves open questions or problems. An **invitation** is a request to the learner to perform a meta-cognitive activity, for instance by using a tool. An educational resource of type **exercise** is an interactive object that requires the learner's response/action. The response can be evaluated (either automatically or manually) and an success ratio can be assigned to it.

Illustration, Counter Example, Example

Educational resources of type **illustration** illustrate a fundamental or parts of it. A **counterExample** is an instructional object that is exception to a proposed general fundamental. An educational resource of the type **example** positively illustrates the fundamental or parts of a fundamental.

Evidence, Demonstration, Proof

An **evidence** contains supporting claims made for a law or one of its subclasses, hence the **isFor**-property of an evidence has as range the class **law**. A **demonstration** provides informal evidence that a law holds, e. g., experiments in physics or chemistry. A **proof** contains formal evidence, i. e., a test or a formal derivation of a law.

Explanation Conclusion, Introduction, Remark

An **explanation** contains additional information about a fundamental. It elaborates certain aspects or points out important properties. Its sub-class **conclusion** sums up the main points of a fundamental. An **introduction** contains information that leads the way to a fundamental. A **remark** provides additional, not strictly mandatory information about an aspect of a fundamental. It can contain interesting side information, or details about how the fundamental is related to other fundamentals.

To summarize, this vocabulary was designed to describe educational resources such that they can be automatically re-used for educational purposes such as course generation.

The OIO is used in the ACTIVEMATH environment and has also been used for a revised version of the ALOCoM ontology, an effort in the European Network of Excellence ProLearn [82], in the e-learning platform e-aula [159], and in the CampusContent project of the Distant University Hagen [87]. Section 7.1.1 describes the evaluations performed with the ontology. The following sections motivate why it makes sense to represent the instructional vocabulary in an ontology and gives examples of applications of the OIO in areas other than course generation.

4.1.3 Why an Ontology?

Why is the information about the instructional types represented in an ontology rather than in a flat list as e. g., the learning-resource-type of LOM or in a taxonomy? The need for ontologies, that is, for a common understanding of a domain that serves as a basis for communication between people or systems, has been widely recognized (for a recent discussion see Heflin 57); in the following, I will only summarize the most relevant points.

First of all, one needs to be able to express relations between educational resources, i. e., that an exercise is *for* a definition. In addition, as we will see in Section 4.2, the sub-class information contained in the ontology contains valuable information when searching for educational resources.

Benefits of a formal description of the domain for human users include the following. For technology-supported learning, the usage of such a shared instructional vocabulary offers advantages for teachers and learners. The explicit instructional function represented in the ontology enables a more accurate search for learning resources, which leads to better reuse and less duplication. This enables a faster authoring of courses by teachers and tutors. Learners can bridge knowledge gaps more efficiently by seeking instructionally appropriate educational resources.

The pedagogically relevant information of the ontology might also bring forth better pedagogical Web-services. It can increase the accuracy of a service because at design time, a Web-service developer can foresee different functionalities depending on the type of the resource. For most pedagogical services, the information whether, say, a resource contains a definition or an example will be of use, since it can react differently depending on the type. Similarly, service composition is enhanced. For instance, a requester service can require different actions from a provider depending on the instructional type of a resource. Furthermore, interoperability is eased, and at least in theory, each system can provide its own specialized service and make use of the services offered by others.

4.1.4 Applications of the Ontology

This section describes services other than course generation that might profit from the ontology of instructional objects.

Learner modeling. A learner model stores personal preferences and information about the learner's mastery of domain concepts etc. The information is regularly updated according to the learner's interactions. A user model server such as Personis [76] can use the information about the instructional function of a learning resource for more precise updating. For instance, reading an example should trigger a different updating than solving an exercise.

Interactive exercises. In interactive exercises, feedback to the learner is crucial. Using an ontology of instructional objects, an exercise system can generate links to educational resources that additionally support the learner in problem solving, e.g. (counter) examples or definition of the important fundamentals.

Suggestion mechanism/Intelligent assistant. Feedback is not restricted to exercises. During the whole interaction of a learner with educational resources, a suggestion mechanism [103] or intelligent assistant [161] can analyze the student's actions and provide hints of what to do next, which content to read additionally, etc. An ontology of instructional objects can be used by such tools to analyze actions and to make specific suggestions. Section 6.2.5.1 describes how this was realized in the learning environment ACTIVEMATH.

Browsing services. Services that support the user's navigation through the hypertext-space (or, generally speaking, the space opened by the resources and their relations) benefit when the instructional function of a learning resource is made explicit. They can better classify and select the presented objects. Systems that adaptively add links to content [21] can decide what links to add and how to classify them appropriately. Similarly, tools that generate concept maps can better adapt the maps to the intended learning goal, both with respect to the selection and the graphical appearance of the elements. A search tool that provides a view on the dependencies of the domain elements can sort the element with respect to their instructional type, which can be useful for authors and learners alike.

Authoring support. An ontology of instructional objects assists authors by enabling enhanced search facilities and by describing an conceptual model of the content structure. It equips authors with a set of concepts at an adequate abstractness level to talk about instructional strategies, thus allowing them to describe their teaching strategies at a level abstracted from the concrete learning resources. Hence, instructional scenarios can be exchanged and re-used. An ontology of instructional objects can additionally support the author by providing an operational model in the sense of Aroyo and Mizoguchi [8] and Hayashi et al. [55, 56] that gives hints to the author, e. g., what instructional objects are missing in his course.

Data mining. In a joint work in the European Network of Excellence Kaleidoscope, Merceron, Oliveira, Scholl, and Ullrich [113] investigated applications of the OIO for data mining of learning paths. There, a data mining tool extracts pedagogically relevant information from the paths of a learner through the educational resources. The data-mining can include the specific information about the instructional type of the learning resource. For instance, if a learner regularly skips introductions and directly tries to solve exercises, a system can infer what Merceron and Yacef [112] call a practical instead of a theoretical learning style.

In the following section, I describe how the OIO is used for accessing educational resources stored in distinct repositories.

4.2 A Mediator for Accessing Learning Object Repositories

The ontology described in the previous section allows specifying the instructional function of educational resources and contains necessary information required for automatic, intelligent course generation. However, as a matter of fact, most of the repositories available today use their own metadata schema rather than the terms defined in the OIO. Yet, the pedagogical knowledge formalized in the course generator should be independent of the concrete metadata used in the repositories, as one wants to avoid designing separate methods for each repository. In this section, I describe how a *mediator*, an architecture from the field of distributed information systems, enables the course generator to abstract from the specific metadata schemas and repository accesses.[4]

4.2.1 Related Work

The challenge of providing uniform access to resources has been recognized since long. Mediation information systems as proposed by Wiederhold [208] are a well-known solution to this challenge. Its main component, called *mediator*, offers a uniform interface for accessing multiple heterogeneous data stores (e. g., file systems, different databases, . . .). The mediator uses mappings between the data representation used in the mediator and those used in the repository to translate queries. Each repository is enhanced with a wrapper,

---

[4] The work described in this section was jointly developed by Philipp Kärger, Erica Melis, Tianxiang Lu and myself [74, 75, 73, 89]. Therefore, I will use the personal pronoun "we" in this section.

which can be integrated into the repository itself or into the mediator. This way, the query component does not have to know the specification of the data sources and their query languages

4.2.1.1 Edutella

An example of a mediator architecture in the domain of technology-enhanced learning is EDUTELLA [127]. EDUTELLA is a Peer-To-Peer approach for sharing information in the Semantic Web. One of its first applications was the federation of learning objects. A peer that encodes its metadata in RDF format can be connected to the EDUTELLA services by specifying a wrapper. A query service offers a uniform query language with different levels of expressiveness. EDUTELLA is a general purpose infrastructure and connecting a peer is rather complex. In EDUTELLA, a client (a human or a system) can pose queries that are answered by all repositories connected to the P2P network. Queries can be quite sophisticated and return single objects as well as sequences of learning objects, for instance using a prerequisite relationship. Since these systems provide a generic, technical infrastructure for repository integration, they do not aim at specifying the educational semantics of resources. This, however, is needed by clients who wish to automatically retrieve resources based on their instructional function (e. g., definition, example, etc.).

4.2.1.2 Ontology Mapping Languages

Structured representations of data can be represented as ontologies. For ontology mapping, expressive mapping languages have been developed, e. g., de Bruijn et al. [33] propose a mapping language as well as a set of pattern templates; Pazienza et al. [142] introduce the XML-based mapping language XEOML. Both mapping languages are very expressive but were not implemented at the time of writing.

4.2.1.3 SQI

Simon et al. [168] specify an interface called SQI (Simple Query Interface) for interoperable repositories of educational resources. The aim of SQI is to create a standardized interface for repository access and thus SQI specifies only the interface. It does not prescribe any implementation and therefore it does not offer a framework for query rewriting.

4.2.1.4 Triple

An approach based on the Semantic Web rule language TRIPLE is introduced by Miklos et al. [116]. They describe an architecture which queries for resources in the Semantic Web by specifying their metadata. TRIPLE is based on RDF and mainly used for data manipulation, which makes parsing, translating and processing of simple queries rather expensive.

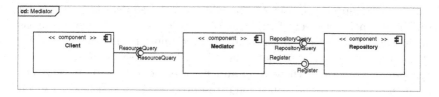

Fig. 4.3. Overview of the mediator

4.2.1.5 Reinventing the Wheel but Making It Faster

Any mediator used for course generation needs to answer queries extremely quickly: as the evaluation in Chapter 7 will show, generating an expanded course for a single fundamental results in about 1 500 mediator queries that are expanded to more than 11 000 queries to the repository.

Existing ontology-based query rewriting approaches are very expressive, but, in consequence, complicated to use and not optimized for efficiency. Therefore, we decided to develop a query rewriting approach which is less powerful than other systems but expressive enough for our translation purposes. This specialization allows for optimizations, e. g., during query processing.

Additionally, in the developed framework it is easy to integrate new repositories, by specifying a mapping between the OIO and the representation used in the repositories and implementing a small set of interfaces.

4.2.2 Overview of the Mediator Architecture

The mediator described in this section answers queries about the existence of specific educational resources. It is illustrated in Figure 4.3. Its interfaces[5] are Web-service interfaces. A repository can register (interface **Register**), passing an OWL representation of its metadata structure as well as a mapping of the OIO onto this representation to the mediator. Additionally, each repository needs to implement the interface **RepositoryQuery** that allows the mediator to query the existence of educational resources. Clients access the mediator using the interface **ResourceQuery**.

4.2.3 Querying the Mediator

The interface **ResourceQuery** takes a partial metadata description as input and returns the set of identifiers of the educational resources that meet the description. The metadata used in a query sent to the mediator must comply to the OIO. It can consist of three parts:

---

[5] The figure uses UML ball-and-socket icons. A ball represents a provided interface, a socket a required interface.

- Class queries specify the classes the educational resources have to belong to. They consist of a set of tuples (class *c*) in which *c* denotes the class of the OIO the returned educational resources must belong to.
- Property queries specify property metadata. They consist of a set of triples (property *prop val*), where *prop* and *val* are property and value names from the OIO. Retrieved educational resources have to satisfy each given property-value pair.
- Relation queries specify the relational metadata the educational resources have to meet. They consist of a set of triples (relation *rel id*) in which *rel* specifies the relation that must hold between the resource referenced by the identifier *id* and the educational resources to be retrieved. *rel* is a relation name of the OIO.

Example 4.1. A query asking for all resources with an easy difficulty level illustrating the definition def_slope looks as follows:

```
(relation isFor def_slope) (class illustration)
(property hasDifficulty
easy)
```

While processing a query, the mediator uses the information of the OIO to expand a query to subclasses. Hence, if asked for class *c*, the mediator returns resources belonging to *c* and to its subclasses.

Example 4.2. Continuing the above example, the expanded query is shown below:

```
(relation isFor def_slope) (class example)
    (property hasDifficulty easy)
(relation isFor def_slope) (class counterExample)
    (property hasDifficulty easy)
```

4.2.4 Ontology Mapping and Query Rewriting

A repository that registers itself using the interface Register must provide sufficient information to enable the mediator to translate the metadata of an incoming query to the metadata used by the repository.

The translation is performed by an ontology-based query-rewriting mechanism. The mechanism requires an ontological representation *O* of the metadata structure used by the repository and an ontology mapping *M*. It uses *O* and *M* to compute the rewriting steps for translating the queries it receives. A registration time, a repository passes both the ontology and the mapping to the mediator. The mappings currently used by the mediator were produced beforehand by the developers.

We designed an XML-based ontology mapping language that represents the mappings between the OIO and the target ontologies. An ontology mapping contains a set of mapping patterns, where each mapping pattern m consists of a matching pattern mp and a set of replacement patterns $RP = \{rp_1, \ldots, rp_n\}$. mp and RP consist of terms of the OIO and the ontology of the repository, respectively. A mapping pattern $m_1 = (mp_1, RP_1)$ is more specific than a pattern $m_2 = (mp_2, RP_2)$ if $mp_2 \subset mp_1$.

The idea of the ontology mapping is that every part of a query that matches a matching pattern is replaced by the replacement patterns. More formally, we say a mapping pattern $m = (mp, \{rp_1, \ldots, rp_n\})$ matches a query q if q contains each term specified in mp. Applying m to q results in new queries $q_1, \ldots, q_n$, which are derived by replacing each term of mp by the terms of $rp_1, \ldots, rp_n$, respectively.

The ontology mapping procedure applies the most specific mapping pattern to a query q. Currently, the author of an ontology mapping has to ensure manually that there is only one such pattern; future work will investigate how to support this automatically. A term for which no matching pattern is found is left as it is. This approach avoids writing mapping patterns that express the identity of terms (the use cases have shown that this is the most frequently occurring case).

Example 4.3. To illustrate the rewriting, we assume that a repository registers with the mapping patterns (example, {exa}), (isFor, {for}), and (hasDifficulty=easy, {difficulty_level=1}). The queries from Example 4.2 will be translated to

```
(relation for def_slope) (class illustration)
    (property difficulty_level 1)
(relation for def_slope) (class exa)
    (property difficulty_level 1)
(relation for def_slope) (class counterExample)
    (property difficulty_level 1)
```

4.2.5 Repository Interface and Caching

In order to be accessible from the mediator, a repository must implement the following interface that provides information about each of the above query types:

- `public Set queryClass(String id)` returns the classes a given resource belongs to.
- `public Set queryRelation(String rel, String id)` returns the set of identifiers of those educational resources the resource `id` is related to via the relation `rel`.
- `public Set queryProperty(String id)` returns the set of property-value pairs the given resource has.

In real use, performance matters and query processing is often time consuming mostly because of latency of the Web. For instance, course generation involves a significant amount of queries (about 30 000 for a course consisting of about 100 educational resources). Therefore, the amount of processed queries has to be reduced. We tackled this problem by integrating a caching mechanism into the mediator. If the same query (or sub-query) is sent repeatedly, the mediator does not query each connected repository again. Instead, it returns the cached set of identifiers, which increases run-time performance dramatically. The results of partial queries are cached, too. Section 7.1.4 provides details about evaluations of the cache.

Please note that our approach focuses on mapping of pedagogical concepts and not on mapping of instances of the subject domain. Thus, the mediator cannot yet use the information that fundamental c_1 in repository r_1 represents the same domain entity as fundamental c_2 in repository r_2, say def_group in r_1 and definition_gruppe in r_2 both define the same mathematical concept *group*. In future work, we will integrate an instance mapping technology that maps domain ontologies.

4.2.6 Limitations of the Mediator as an Educational Service

The mediator allows access to resources based on their instructional function: a service generates partial metadata, and the mediator retrieves a list of corresponding educational resources. However, this is a basic service, which has some limitations:

- How to come up with the metadata? Determining the appropriate metadata for finding educational resources is not trivial. Assume a service wants to present an example of "average slope" to the learner. Is the learning context relevant? Should it be an easy or a difficult example? These decisions depend on the current learning goal, i.e., the current pedagogical task.
- Which precise educational resources to select? Typically, the mediator returns a list of resources. Which one is the most appropriate? Are they all equivalent? A too large set might indicate that the metadata was too general. However, narrowing it down might result in an over-specification and hence in an empty set.
- A single educational resource might not be sufficient to achieve learning progress. For instance, understanding content in depth requires a sequence of carefully selected educational resources. Again, the precise resources to select depend on the learning goal.

These limitations motivate the need for a course generator, i.e., a component that operationalizes the educational knowledge and provides services on a higher level of abstraction. The following sections describe the course generator.

4.3 Pedagogical Tasks, Methods and Strategies

The mediator architecture allows finding educational resources that fulfill given criteria. Typically, an agent (a learner or a machine) searches for the resources in order to achieve a learning goal. In this section, I describe an explicit and declarative representation that can be used to encode such learning goals.

A declarative representation of goals offers several advantages. First of all, it allows a system to autonomously generate actions to achieve the goal if the system uses an appropriate framework. Secondly, it provides an abstract layer that can be used for communication between systems. Instead of only being able to talk about the resources used in the learning process, systems can communicate about the purposes of the learning process. Third, it can be used to describe precisely the functionalities that the course generator offers: for each learning goal, PAIGOS can calculate a sequence of educational resources (if available) that help the learner to achieve this goal.

As I will describe in Related Work (Section 8), existing course generators often use the domain concepts to represent learning goals. There, the generated course provides a sequence of educational resources that leads to these concepts and includes prerequisites and other resources. However, such an approach that restricts goals to resources is too limited. Depending on their current situation, learners want to achieve different objectives with the same target fundamentals, and a course should reflect the different needs associated with the objectives. For instance, a course that helps students to discover new content should differ different from a course that supports rehearsal.

Van Marcke [197] introduced the concept of an *instructional tasks*, which helps to define learning goals in more details: an instructional task represents an activity that can be accomplished during the learning process.

Both, the content and the instructional task are essential aspects of a learning goal. Therefore, I define learning goals as a combination of the two dimensions *content* and *task*. In the remainder of this volume, I will refer to instructional tasks as *pedagogical objectives*, in order to distinguish them from the declarative representation of learning goals, which I will call *pedagogical tasks*:

Pedagogical Task

A *pedagogical task* is a tuple $t = (p, L)$, where p is an identifier of the pedagogical objective and L is a list of educational resource identifiers. L specifies the course's target fundamentals, and p influences the structure of the course and the educational resources selected. The order of the resources in L is relevant and the same task with L's elements ordered differently can result in a different course.

Example 4.4. The educational objective to discover and understand content in depth called `discover`. Let's assume that `def_slope` and `def_diff` are the identifiers of the educational resources that contain the definition of the mathematical fundamental "average slope of a function" and "definition of the derivative, resp., differential quotient", respectively. We can now write the learning goal of a learner who wants to discover and understand these two fundamentals as the educational task $t = (\texttt{discover}, (\texttt{def\_slope}, \texttt{def\_diff}))$. The fundamentals are processed in the given order: first $\texttt{def\_slope}$, followed by $\texttt{def\_diff}$.

Table 4.1. A selection of pedagogical objectives used in PAIGOS

Identifier	Description
discover	Discover and understand fundamentals in depth
rehearse	Address weak points
trainSet	Increase mastery of a set of fundamentals by training
guidedTour	Detailed information, including prerequisites
trainWithSingleExercice	Increase mastery using a single exercise
illustrate	Improve understanding by a sequence of examples
illustrateWithSingleExample	Improve understanding using a single example

Table 4.1 contains a selection of pedagogical tasks formalized within this volume, partly designed in cooperation with pedagogical experts. Chapter 5 provides the worked-out pedagogical tasks and methods.

It is important to note that tasks correspond to goals, not to methods that achieve these goals. The distinction between *task* and *methods*, i. e., between *what* to achieve and *how* to achieve it [174] is important in this context since tasks and methods represent different kinds of knowledge.

Pedagogical Method

Methods that are applicable to pedagogical tasks and decompose them are called *pedagogical methods.*

Scenario

Pedagogical objectives exist on different levels of abstraction: the highest-level objectives correspond to different types of courses that can be assembled. These types of courses are called *scenarios*. The first four tasks in Table 4.1 are examples of scenarios.

Public Task

Pedagogical tasks can be "internal" tasks, used for internal course generation purposes only, or tasks that are of potential interest for other services. The second category of tasks is called *public tasks*. Public tasks need to be described sufficiently precise in order to enable a communication between components as described above. The description designed for PAIGOS contains the following information:

- the identifier of the pedagogical objective;
- the number of concepts the pedagogical objective can be applied to. A task can either be applied to a single concept (cardinality 1) or multiple concepts (cardinality n).
- the type of educational resource (as defined in the OIO) that the task can be applied to;
- the type of course to expect as a result. Possible values are either `course` in case a complete course is generated or `section` in case a single section is returned. Even in case the course generator selects only a single educational resource, the resource is included in a section. This is due to requirements from standards like IMS CP which is used by the course generator Webservice.
- an optional element `condition` that is evaluated in order to determine whether a task can be achieved. In some situations, a service only needs to know whether a task can be achieved but not by which educational resources. In that case, the condition can be passed to the mediator, and if the return value is different from `null`, the task can be achieved. An example is the item menu (Section 6.2.5.3) that allows the learner to request additional content. Menu entries are displayed only if the corresponding tasks can be achieved. For instance if there are no examples available for `def_slope`, then the task (`illustrate`, (`def_slope`)) cannot be achieved. Most of the time, the condition element corresponds to a subset of the preconditions of the least constrained pedagogical method applicable to the task. This way, the course generator can guarantee that a learning object that fulfills these conditions will be returned but the exact elements will be determined only on-demand.
- a concise natural language description of the purpose that is used for display in menus.

Figure 4.4 contains a selection of pedagogical tasks. In the figure, all keywords in the `condition` element that start with ? are variables which are instantiated by the corresponding value at the time the condition is sent to the mediator. The top element in Figure 4.4 describes the pedagogical task `discover`. It is applicable to several educational resources of type `fundamental`. The bottom element specifies the task `trainWithSingleExercise!`. It is applicable to a single educational resource of the type `fundamental` and returns a result in case the condition holds.

```
<tasks>
   <task>
      <pedObj id="discover"/>
      <contentIDs cardinality="n"/>
      <applicableOn type="fundamental"/>
      <result type="course"/>
      <condition></condition>
      <description>
         <text xml:lang="en">Generate a book that helps a learner to
            understand the selected topics in depth.</text>
         <text xml:lang="de">Erstelle ein Buch das hilft die
            ausgewählten Begriffe grundlegend zu verstehen</text>
      </description>
   </task>
   <task>
      <pedObj id="illustrateWithSingleExample!"/>
      <contentIDs cardinality="1"/>
      <condition>(class Example)(relation isFor ?c)
                 (property hasLearningContext ?learningContext)
      </condition>
      <applicableOn type="fundamental"/>
      <result type="section"/>
      <description>
         <text xml:lang="en">Illustrate the concept.</text>
         <text xml:lang="de">Veranschauliche den Inhalt.</text>
      </description>
   </task>
   <task>
      <pedObj id="trainWithSingleExercise!"/>
      <contentIDs cardinality="1"/>
      <applicableOn type="fundamental"/>
      <result type="section"/>
      <condition>(class Exercise)(relation isFor ?c)
                 (property hasLearningContext ?learningContext)
      </condition>
      <description>
         <text xml:lang="en">Train the concept.</text>
         <text xml:lang="de">Übe den Inhalt.</text>
      </description>
   </task>
   ...
</tasks>
```

Fig. 4.4. A selection of pedagogical task descriptions

Educational tasks together with the ontology of instructional objects allow representing learning goals and the instructionally relevant aspects of resources used to achieve those goals. In the next section, I describe how the course generator PAIGOS uses these representations in order to assemble personalized sequences of educational resources that support the learner in achieving her learning goals.

4.4 Representing Course Generation Knowledge in an HTN Planner

In this section, I describe how course generation knowledge is formalized as an hierarchical task network planning problem. I start by motivating why planning in general and HTN planning in particular is an adequate choice for the formalization of course generation knowledge. Then, in Section 4.4.2, I describe how to join the notion of HTN task and pedagogical task. The course generation domain as formalized in this volume contains several basic operators and methods which are reused throughout the domain. Those are described in Section 4.5.

Part of the work described in this section was developed jointly with Okhtay Ilghami, a member of the Automated Planning Group of the University of Maryland, led by Dana Nau and James Hendler.[6]

4.4.1 Motivation

The central principle of knowledge representation consists of having a formal and explicit representation of the world, including how the actions of an agent affect the world ([157], p. 19). Such a representation allows modeling manipulations of the world. As a consequence, deductive processes can be used to reason about actions, e. g., whether an action helps to achieve a goal of the agent. Different frameworks for knowledge representation and reasoning exist, e. g., planning, multi-agent systems and expert systems.

For technology-supported learning, Murray [121] concisely summarizes: "a system should have a plan and should be able to plan". Generally speaking, a system should be able to plan, since it is practically impossible to cater for individual learning goals and characteristics by providing manually authored courses. It should have a plan in order to ensure global coherence, where resources are sequenced in a manner that supports the overall learning goal and respects the learner's characteristics, such as competencies, motivation, and interests.

Arguments in favor of hierarchical planning methods include that non-AI experts quickly grasp the principal mechanism. The hierarchical decomposition of the HTN framework provides a quite natural way for formalizing the

---

[6] The work described in this section was published in the following publications: [183, 187, 109, 189].

pedagogical knowledge: the pedagogical experts I cooperated with while designing the course generation knowledge felt comfortable with the approach, despite having no experience in computer science.

Additionally, HTN is efficient in planning. HTN can result in linear-time instead of exponential-time planning algorithms if the high-level solutions formulated in the methods always result in good low-level implementations ([157], p. 422).

The practical relevance of HTN is also "proved by demonstration" by its wide-spread use in real-life applications. According to ([157], p. 430), most of the large-scale planning applications are HTN planners. The primary reason is that HTN allows human experts to encode the knowledge how to perform complex tasks in a manner that can be executed with little computational effort.

However, using a planning approach also brings forth some difficulties. During course generation, educational resources serve as a basis for the reasoning process of the planner: different methods will be applied depending on whether specific educational resources exist that fulfill given criteria. Say, an introduction to the mathematical concept "Definition of Derivation" needs to be generated. If no resource that is a textual introduction to the concept exists, then an alternative is to use an educational resource that is an easy example for the concept. However, taking into consideration such information about available resources involves the difficulty that traditional AI planning requires evaluating a method's precondition against the planner's world state. In a naive approach, this would require mirroring in the world state all the information available about the resources in all the repositories. In real world applications, this is simply infeasible. Usually, only a subset of all the stored resources may be relevant for the planning, but which subset is unknown beforehand.

JSHOP2's planning algorithm allows overcoming this problem. JSHOP2's planning algorithm is based on *ordered task decomposition*. There, tasks are expanded in the order in which they will be performed, when the plan is executed. According to [122], this approach has the advantage that when the planner plans for tasks, it knows all that is to know about the world state at the time when task will be executed. This enables performing doing complex numeric calculations and using external knowledge sources to retrieving information. In the case of the course generation domain, this allows accessing the repositories that contain the educational resources as well as the learner model.

4.4.2 Mapping Pedagogical Tasks onto HTN Tasks

In the following sections, I describe the course generation planning domain. In a first step, I explain the relationship between the notion of a pedagogical task and HTN task.

Section 4.3 defined a pedagogical task as a tuple $t = (p, L)$, where p is an identifier of pedagogical objective and $L = \{l_1, \ldots, l_m\}$ is a list of educational resource identifiers. This definition is now mapped onto the definition of HTN task as given in Section 2.6.4.7: there, a task atom was defined as an expression of the form $(s\ t_1\ t_2\ \ldots\ t_n)$ where s is a task symbol and the arguments $t_1\ t_2 \ldots t_n$ are terms.

Let $P = \{p_1, \ldots, p_n\}$ be the set of all pedagogical objectives. For each $p_i \in P$, we define a corresponding task symbol t_j. Let $T = \bigcup_{i=1}^{n} t_i$ and $f : P \to T$ be a function that maps each p_i onto the corresponding task symbol t_j. Furthermore, let g be a function that assigns each educational resources identifier a unique name symbol $s \in M$, with M being the infinite set of name symbols as defined in Section 2.6.4. Then, for a pedagogical task $t = (p, l_1, \ldots, l_m)$ the corresponding HTN task atom is given by $(f(p)\ g(l_1)\ \ldots\ g(l_m))$.

4.4.3 Course Generation Planning Problems

The general form of planning problems in the course generation domain is shown in Figure 4.5. The first line defines a problem with the name *Problem* to be solved in the domain CourseGeneration. The problem itself is quite small: the initial state consists of the user identifier and a logical atom that represents the pedagogical task to be achieved (line 3–4). The task to be solved by the problem is a task without parameters, called (generateCourse) (line 7). This task starts the initialization process (described in detail in Section 4.6.9) that performs conceptually irrelevant but technically required processing. Once the initialization is complete, the pedagogical task is the goal task of the planning problem.

Notably, the world state contains neither information about the resources nor about the learner (besides her identifier). All this information is retrieved dynamically, when required.

```
1   (defproblem Problem CourseGeneration
2     (
3       (user userId)
4       (goalTask task)
5     )
6
7     ((generateCourse))
8   )
```

Fig. 4.5. A schema of a course generation planning problem

4.4.4 Critical and Optional Tasks

A feature that distinguishes the course generation planning domain from other domains is that there exist a number of tasks that should be achieved if possible, but failing to do so should not cause backtracking. These tasks are called *optional* tasks. An example is the motivation of a fundamental. If there exist educational resources that can serve as a motivation, then they should be included in the course. If no suited resource can be found, the course generation should continue anyway. In contrast, other tasks are *critical*, and have to be achieved. In the following, critical task symbols are marked with the suffix "!". Whether a specific task is critical or optional depends on the scenario. Therefore, in PAIGOS, for almost each critical task there exists an equivalent optional task.

Technically speaking, optional tasks are realized by encapsulating critical tasks in *fallback* methods. Figure 4.4.4 illustrates the general approach. The first method in the Figure (lines 1–4) is an exemplary method for a critical task. The second method (lines 6–9) encapsulates the critical task in an optional task. In case this method cannot be applied (due to the critical task not being achievable), the fallback method in lines 11–15 is applied. It has no preconditions and not subtasks, hence achieves the task immediately.

```
1   (:method (taskSymbol ! term)
2            (preconditions )
3            (subtasks )
4            )
5
6   (:method (taskSymbol  term)
7            ()
8            (taskSymbol ! term)
9            )
10
11  (:method (taskSymbol  term)
12           ;; fallback method
13           ()
14           ()
15           )
```

Fig. 4.6. Implementing optional tasks by encapsulating critical tasks in fallback methods

In the following, I will assume that a) there exists an optional task for each critical task, and b) for each optional task there exists a set of methods like described above. Due to length reasons, I will not include them explicitly in this document.

4.5 Basic General Purpose Axioms and Operators

In this section, I describe the basic axioms that are used in the course generation domain but serve general purposes, such as list manipulation.

4.5.1 Testing for Equality

The axiom in Figure 4.7 tests the equality of two given terms: it matches only if the terms passed as arguments are the same. In that case, the axiom's body is evaluated. Since it is empty, the axiom is satisfied.

```
(:- (same ?x ?x) ())
```

Fig. 4.7. same tests the equality of two terms

Example 4.5. The axiom (same a a) is satisfiable; the axiom (same a b) is not.

4.5.2 List Manipulation

Figure 4.8 contains a list of axioms that perform basic list operations. The first axiom with the head **first** either checks whether the first parameter (head) is the first element of the given list or, if the first parameter is a variable, returns the first element of the list given as parameter. The second axiom with head **first** specifies that the first element of the empty list (nil) is the empty list.

Example 4.6. The axiom (first a (a b c)) is satisfiable because ?head can be instantiated with a and ?tail can be instantiated with (b c).

Example 4.7. The axiom (first ?p (a b c)) is satisfiable and binds ?p to a.

Analogously, the axioms in line 4 and 5 in Figure 4.8 check whether the first parameter is the rest of the list given as parameter or, if the first parameter is a variable, return the rest of the given list. The rest of the empty list is defined to be the empty list.

Example 4.8. The axiom (rest (b c) (a b c)) is satisfiable because ?head (see Figure 4.8) can be instantiated with a and ?tail can be instantiated with (b c).

Example 4.9. The axiom (rest ?p (a b c)) results in binding ?p to (b c).

```
1   (:- (first ?head (?head . ?tail)) ())
2   (:- (first nil nil) ())
3
4   (:- (rest ?tail (?head . ?tail)) ())
5   (:- (rest nil nil) ())
6
7   (:- (restrict ?result ?list1 ?list2)
8       (assign ?result (call Restrict ?list1 ?list2)))
9
10  (:- (removeElement ?result ?element ?list)
11      (removeH ?result nil ?element ?list))
12
13  (:- (removeH ?result ?tempResult ?element nil)
14      (assign ?result (call Reverse ?tempResult)))
15
16  (:- (removeH ?result ?tempResult ?first (?first . ?tail))
17      (removeH ?result ?tempResult ?first ?tail))
18
19  (:- (removeH ?result ?tempResult ?element (?first . ?tail))
20      (
21      (not (same ?first ?element))
22      (removeH ?result (?first . ?tempResult) ?element ?tail)
23      ))
```

Fig. 4.8. Axioms for basic list operations

The intent of the axiom with head **restrict** (lines 7–8) is to remove all elements from the term list bound to **list1** that do not occur in the term list bound to **list2** and to bind the result to the variable **?result**. This axiom uses the external function **Restrict** (line 8), a Java function that implements the above described functionality (since external functions are Java functions, they are written with an initial capital). There is no difference between embedding an external function in an axiom or calling it directly and binding the resulting value to a variable.

Example 4.10. Using the axiom (**restrict** ?r (a b c d) (a c e)), the variable ?r is bound to the term list (a c). Similarly, the call term (**assign** ?r (**call** Restrict (a b c d) (a c e))) binds the variable ?r to the term list (a c).

Similar functions are **Concat** (concatenates the given term lists or name symbols), **Length** (returns the length of a given term list as an integer value), and **Reverse** (reverse a given term list).

Example 4.11. The call term (**call** Concat (a b c) (d e) (f g h)) returns the list (a b c d e f g h); (**call** Length (a b c)) returns 3; (**call** Reverse (a b c)) returns (c b a).

The axioms in lines 10–23 of Figure 4.8 serve to illustrate that in principle such functions can be realized without resorting to call terms. These lines define the axiom `removeElement` which removes the term bound to `?element` from the term list bound to `?list` and binds the result to the variable `?result`. The advantage of using call terms that access Java functions instead of defining a set of axioms is efficiency: in general, the Java function is evaluated much faster then the corresponding axioms.

Example 4.12. The axiom (`removeElement` `?var` (a b c) c) binds `?var` to (a b).

4.5.3 Binding a Variable to All Terms of a Term List

An assignment expression (`assign` `?var` t) as defined in Section 2.6.4 binds `?var` to the term t. The axioms illustrated in Figure 4.9 extend this behavior to a list: if the precondition of an operator or method contains (`assignIterator` `?var` termList), all bindings of `?var` to the elements of the list termList will be generated. The first axiom binds `?var` to the first value of the list; if the planning process fails at any later time, backtracking causes the second axiom to be applied, which recurses into the list and thus applies the first axiom to bind `?var` to the next value. This process is repeated until the list is empty. In that case, the axiom cannot be satisfied and the planning process backtracks.

```
(:- (assignIterator ?var (?head . ?tail))
    (assign ?var ?head))

(:- (assignIterator ?var (?head . ?tail))
    (assignIterator ?var ?tail))
```

Fig. 4.9. `assignIterator` binds a variable to all terms of a list

Example 4.13. (`assignIterator` `?var` (a b c)) first binds `?var` to the term a. Backtracking can later cause binding `?var` to b and finally to c.

4.5.4 Manipulating the World State

Methods cannot change the world state, unlike operators. Therefore, a method that requires changes to the world state has to resort to operators. The operators illustrated in Figure 4.10 provide a generic means to achieve this functionality. `!!addInWorldState` adds the given parameter as an atom to the world state, while `!!removeFromWorldState` removes it. The two exclamation marks denote the operators as being internal operators, that is, not corresponding to

```
(:operator (!!addInWorldState ?atom)
           ;; precondition
           ()
           ;; delete list
           ()
           ;; add list
           (?atom)
           )

(:operator (!!removeFromWorldState ?atom)
           ;; precondition
           ()
           ;; delete list
           (?atom)
           ;; add list
           ()
           )
```

Fig. 4.10. !!addInWorldState and !!removeFromWorldState change the world state

actions performed in a plan. Examples of methods using these two operators are, e. g., initializing methods that add information about the user and her learning goals to the world state (see Section 4.6.9).

4.6 Basic Operators and Methods of the Course Generation Domain

The above axioms, operators and methods might be of use in any planning domain. The operators and methods describe in the subsequent sections are domain-specific: they insert educational resources into a course, access information about the learner, etc. In the following, whenever I use the term "resource" (e. g., a resource is given as parameter, added to the world state, etc.) I used it as abbreviation for "resource identifier".

4.6.1 Inserting References to Educational Resources

The result of a planning process in the course generation domain is a plan consisting of a sequence of operators that, when applied, generates a structured list of references to educational resources and learning-support services. These "inserting" operators and methods are described below and in the following two sections.

Several operators and methods handle the insertion of references to educational resources in a course. The basic operator is shown in Figure 4.11. The

```
(:operator (!insertResource ?r)
           ;; precondition
           ()
           ;; delete list
           ()
           ;; add list
           ((inserted ?r))
           )
```

Fig. 4.11. !insertResource inserts references to an educational resource in a course

operator has no precondition and delete list, and adds a logical atom to the world state that describes that a resource ?r was inserted into the course.

Note that the basic operators in the course generation domain have neither preconditions nor delete or add lists. This is one peculiarity of the course generation domain as formalized in PAIGOS: in general, resources are not consumed in the sense that they are no longer available, like, say, fuel that is consumed in the travel domains. An educational resource that is added into a course can be added again at a later time (the only potential constraint being that it makes sense from a pedagogical point of view). Similarly, starting/ending a section can be realized at any time and repeatedly without consuming any resources.

```
1   (:method (insertResourceOnce! ?r)
2            ((not (inserted ?r)))
3            ((!insertResource ?r))
4            )
5
6   (:method (insertResource ?r)
7            ((not (inserted ?r)))
8            ((!insertResource ?r))
9
10           ()
11           ()
12           )
```

Fig. 4.12. insertResourceOnce! and insertResource insert a resource in a course once

The operator !insertResource is used by the methods in Figure 4.12. The first method (lines 1–4) is applicable only if the given resource was not yet inserted into the course and in that case inserts the resource: it "decomposes" the task atom (insertResourceOnce! ?r) into the primitive task atom (!insertResource ?r), otherwise it fails. The second method inserts a given resource if it was not yet inserted (line 7–8), otherwise achieves the task directly since it has no subtasks (lines 10–11).

Example 4.14. Let

$T =$((insertResourceOnce! a) (insertResource b)
(insertResource c) (!insertResource d)
(insertResourceOnce! a))

be a task list and $S =$((inserted c) (inserted d)) be the current world state. Then, the first two tasks can be achieved by applying the methods of Figure 4.12 and the operator of Figure 4.11, resulting in the plan

((!insertResource a) (!insertResource b)).

Since c was already inserted, the third subtask is achieved by the second precondition-subtask pair of the bottom method in Figure 4.12 (lines 10–11): there, the subtask consist of the empty list, thus the task is achieved without applying an operator. The fourth task (!insertResource d) (different from the previous ones, note the !) is directly achieved by the operator of Figure 4.11, and hence d is inserted although the world state indicates it was already inserted. At this time, the resulting plan is

((!insertResource a) (!insertResource b)
(!insertResource d)).

However, the final task (insertResourceOnce! a) cannot be achieved: it was already inserted and no method other than the upper method of Figure 4.12 (lines 1–4) is applicable on it. Hence, the planning process backtracks.

```
(:method (insertAllResources (?head . ?tail))
         MethodInsertAllResources
         ()
         (
          (insertResource ?head)
          (insertAllResources ?tail)
         )
         )

(:method (insertAllResources nil)
         MethodInsertAllResourcesFallback
         ()
         ()
         )
```

Fig. 4.13. insertAllResources inserts in a course all resources of a given list

The methods illustrated in Figure 4.13 insert into a course all resources from the given list. The bottom method makes sure that the recursion performed in the top method terminates in case the list has no (more) elements.

```
(:- (allInserted (?head . ?tail))
     (
      (inserted ?head)
      (allInserted ?tail)
      )
     )

(:- (allInserted nil)
     ()
     )
```

Fig. 4.14. `allInserted` tests whether the given resources are contained in the course

Figure 4.14 contains the axiom `allInserted` that is used to test whether all resources of a given term list are contained in the current course. The upper axiom tests whether the first element is inserted, and if it is, recurses into the rest of the list. The bottom axiom ends the recursion.

```
(:method (addInWorldStateAsInserted (?head . ?tail))
         MethodAddInWorldStateAsInserted
         ()
         (
          (!!addInWorldState (inserted ?head))
          (addInWorldStateAsInserted ?tail)
          )
         )

(:method (addInWorldStateAsInserted nil)
         MethodAddInWorldStateAsInsertedEmptyList
         ()
         ()
         )
```

Fig. 4.15. `addInWorldStateAsInserted` marks a list of resources as inserted

Under some circumstances, resources need to be marked as inserted without actually being inserted into a course. Figure 4.15 illustrates the methods that achieve this functionality. The upper method recurses into a list of references and adds in the world state the fact that the references were inserted. Yet, since the method does not involve the operator !insertResource, the references are not inserted into the course, but only marked as such. The lower method ends the recursion as soon as the list has become empty.

```
(:- (getNonInserted ?result ?resources)
    (getNIH ?result (call Reverse ?resources) nil))

(:- (getNIH ?result ?resources ?temp)
    ((same ?resources nil)
     (assign ?result ?temp)

    ((first ?el ?resources)
     (inserted ?el)
     (rest ?tail ?resources)
     (getNIH ?result ?tail ?temp))

    ((first ?el ?resources)
     (rest ?tail ?resources)
     (getNIH ?result ?tail (?el . ?temp)))
    )
```

Fig. 4.16. getNonInserted selects those resources from a list that were not inserted

The axiom getNonInserted displayed in Figure 4.16 is used to select those resources from a given list that were not yet inserted into the course. It uses a helper axiom (getNIH) that recurses into the list and tests whether the current resource is marked as inserted into the world state. The result is then bound to ?result.

4.6.2 Starting and Ending Sections

Figure 4.17 contains the four operators that are used for creating structure within a course. The top three operators applicable to !startSection begin a section. They vary only in the number of arguments. The lower operator ends a section. The intended meaning is that all references that are inserted between a !startSection and an !endSection operator are contained within the same section. Sections can be nested.

The !startSection operators require additional information to be passed by the parameters. This information is used later to generate the section titles, which is described in detail later in Section 4.9. For the time being, it suffice to know that the parameter ?type is used to provide information about the type of the section, say an introduction or a training section. The parameter ?parameters contains the list of identifiers of the fundamentals the section

```
(:operator (!startSection ?type)
           ()
           ()
           ()
           )

(:operator (!startSection ?type ?parameters)
           ()
           ()
           ()
           )

(:operator (!startSection ?type ?parameters ?task)
           ()
           ()
           ()
           )

(:operator (!endSection)
           ()
           ()
           ()
           )
```

Fig. 4.17. !startSection and !endSection create structure

is for. In addition, sections can contain information about the pedagogical task for which they were generated: the third !startSection operator allows passing a task as an argument. When the course is generated after the planning process by applying the operators, the task is added as metadata of the section. This allows preserving the information about the pedagogical context that was available during the planning process. Other components can later use this information. For instance, a suggestion mechanism could interpret the fact that a students fails to solve an exercise taking into consideration whether the exercise occurs in the context of learning the prerequisites or whether it occurs during training the goal fundamentals. The task information could also be used for re-planning a section by passing the task to the course generation service.

For most pedagogical tasks t in PAIGOS there exists a task that embeds the task t into a section. These tasks are marked with the suffix Section. It depends on the scenario whether the "original" task or the embedded variant is used.

Figure 4.18 illustrates the general approach used for creating sections. For every task atom whose head has the suffix Section (for instance *taskSymbol*-Section), there exists a method as shown in the Figure. This method starts

```
(:method (taskSymbol Section ?parameters ?type
                            ?sectionParameters ?task)
       ()
       (
       (!startSection ?type ?sectionParameters ?task)
       (taskSymbol ?parameters)
       (!endSection)
       )
)
```

Fig. 4.18. Embedding tasks into sections

a section with the given parameters, tries to achieve the task *taskSymbol*, and then closes the section. In the following descriptions, I will omit most of these "section" tasks in order to keep the number of methods limited.

4.6.3 Inserting References to Learning-Support Services

Section 2.1 defined a learning-support tool as any application that supports the learner during her learning process in a targeted way and that can be integrated within the learning process automatically.

```
(:- (learningServiceAvailable ?serviceName)
    (call LearningServiceAvailable ?serviceName))
```

Fig. 4.19. The axiom `learningServiceAvailable` tests whether a learning-support service is available

Whether such a service is available or not can vary depending on the actual configuration of the environment in which the course generator is used. PAIGOS offers an axiom to check the availability of service (illustrated in Figure 4.19) using an external function for the query. This way, a method's preconditions can test for the availability of a service.

In case the service is available, methods can use the operators illustrated in Figure 4.20 to insert into the course references to the services. Later, when the course is presented to the learner, these references can be rendered as links. The variables of the operators specify the type of service to be used (`?serviceName`), the method of the service (`?methodName`), the resources potentially required by the method `?resources`, and additional parameters if necessary (`?parameters`). The names and semantics of the parameters of these two operators are based on the requirements of the XML-RPC-protocol, a standard for remote procedure calls over the Internet [212].

```
(:operator (!insertLearningService
                    ?serviceName ?methodName ?resources)
            ()
            ()
            ()
            )

(:operator (!insertLearningService
                    ?serviceName ?methodName ?resources
                    ?parameters)
            ()
            ()
            ()
            )
```

Fig. 4.20. insertLearningService inserts references to learning-support services

Methods that potentially insert references to learning-support services should encode a fallback branch that is applied if the service is not available. This way, the pedagogical knowledge remains reusable, regardless of the actual configuration of the learning environment.

4.6.4 An Operator for Dynamic Text Generation

Courses generated by PAIGOS can include templates used for dynamic text generation. These generated texts augment the dynamically generated courses with texts that set the student's mind, support the students' understanding of the structure and of the learning goals, and make transitions between educational resources smoother. The precise mechanism is described in Section 4.9; here, the basic operators is only briefly mentioned since it will be used in several of the following methods.

```
(:operator (!text ?type ?parameters)
            ()
            ()
            ()
            )
```

Fig. 4.21. !text generates symbolic text representations

The operator (illustrate in Figure 4.21 is used to create a representation of text of a given type and possibly further specified by the additional parameters.

```
(:operator (!dynamicTask ?educationalObjective ?contentIds)
           ()
           ()
           ()
           )
```

Fig. 4.22. !dynamicTask enables dynamic subtask expansion

4.6.5 Dynamic Subtask Expansion

The operator in Figure 4.22 is used to achieve dynamic subtask expansion, i. e., to stop the course generation process even though not all resources are selected and to continue the process at a later time. The advantages of this stop-and-continue are described in detail in Section 4.8; here I will only explain the technical realization.

Since dynamic subtask expansion is not implemented in JSHOP2's planning algorithm, it is simulated in PAIGOS in the following way: if a subtask t of a method is not to be expanded, then t is given as parameter to the primitive task atom !dynamicTask. Since the operator that performs this task atom has no preconditions, it can be performed directly. When the operator is applied during plan execution, it creates a special element called *dynamic item*. At a later time, when the course is presented to the learner and the server that handles the presentation detects a dynamic item on the page, it passes the associated dynamic task to the course generator. Then, the course generator assembles the educational resources that achieve the task. In a final step, these resources replace the dynamic item and are presented to the learner.

4.6.6 Accessing Information about Educational Resources

This section describes the call terms, i. e., the Java functions that PAIGOS uses to access information about educational resources. As explained in Section 4.2, the course generator does not directly access the repositories in which the resources are stored but uses a mediator.

GetResources

The call term (GetResources (*mediatorQuery*)) returns the list of identifiers of those educational resources that fulfill the given mediator query.

Example 4.15. The call term

```
(call GetResources
      ((class Exercise) (relation isFor def_slope)))
```

returns the list of all exercises for the educational resource with the identifier def_slope.

GetMetadata

The call term (GetMetadata *property identifier*) returns the value of
the given property of the educational resources with the given identifier.

```
(:- (typicalLearningTime ?id ?time)
    ((assign ?time (call GetMetadata typicalLearningTime ?id))))
```

Fig. 4.23. typicalLearningTime retrieves the typical learning time of a resource

In the current version of PAIGOS, GetMetadata is only used in the axiom
displayed in Figure 4.23. The axiom binds the variable ?time to the typical
learning time of the resource with the given identifier. This information is required for the scenario "exam preparation", which assembles a list of exercises
that can be solved by the learner within a specified time-frame.

GetRelated

During course generation, it is often required to find educational resources
which are connected to a given resource by some relation. A typical example is to find the prerequisites of a fundamental. In PAIGOS, the function GetRelated provides this functionality: the call term (GetRelated
startingSet distance relation) returns a list of all identifiers of educational resources which are connected to the elements of the starting set by
the given relation up to the given distance. If the distance equals −1, then
the relation is followed without any limit. The returned list of identifiers is
unsorted. Note that this behavior is only reasonable for transitive relations.
PAIGOS does not check whether the given relation is transitive; this has to be
ensured by the developer of the pedagogical knowledge.

The relation is followed using the mediator. Therefore, the relation is evaluated from the perspective of the resource to be tested, not from the resources
in the starting set. This may be confusing at first glance, since the relation
seems to be "reversed":

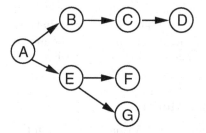

Fig. 4.24. A graph illustrating dependencies between resources

Example 4.16. Let's assume that the graph shown in Figure 4.24 illustrates the relationship `requires` between a set of fundamentals, e. g., A requires B. Then, (`GetRelated` (A) 2 `isRequiredBy`) returns all fundamentals that are connected to A by the relation `requires` up to a distance of two, which are the elements (E G C F B) (or in any other permutation since the result is not sorted). (`GetRelated` (A E) 1 `isRequiredBy`) returns the result (B E G F); (`GetRelated` (D) -1 `requires`) returns (A B C) (or any other permutation).

Sort

Sorting a set of resources with respect to a given relation is done using the function `sort`: the call term (`Sort` *resources relation*) returns the element of *resources* in topological order, sorted with respect to the graph that spanned by the fundamentals as nodes and the relations between the elements of *resources* as edges.

Example 4.17. Referring to the graph in Figure 4.24 (`Sort` (B D C A) `isRequiredBy`) returns (A B C D); (`Sort` (C B E F G) `isRequiredBy`) can return (B C E F G), (B C E G F), (E F G B C), or (E G F B C).

The implementation of `GetRelated` and `Sort` in PAIGOS allows for an additional feature: it is possible to annotate the relation with constraints about metadata. In order for such an "extended" relation to hold between two resources, both resources have to fulfill the metadata constraints. For instance, if the metadata constraint specifies a learning context, then the two resources have to have this learning context. A list of constraints is interpreted as a disjunction: any of the constraints need to hold for the extended relation to hold.

The method in Figure 4.25 illustrates the use of "extended" relations. The task atom `insertWithVariantsIfReady!` serves to insert an auxiliary in a course and at the same time to mark all its variants as inserted. The relation `isVariantOf` represents the fact that two educational resources are almost equivalent and differ only in a minor aspect. For instances, two exercises a and b are marked as being variants if they present the same problem but a uses a graph in addition to the text. More often than not, only a either a or b should be contained in a course.

The method works as follows: if the resource r given as parameter was not yet inserted into the course (line 3) and the learner is ready to see r (line 4, `readyAux` is explained in detail in Section 4.6.8), then all resources that are variants of r and of the adequate learning context (line 6–11) are bound to `?variants`. Finally, r is inserted into the course (line 14) and its variants are marked as inserted (line 15).

4.6.7 Axioms for Accessing the Learner Model

The axioms displayed in Figure 4.26 allow querying information stored in the learner model. The queries are evaluated for the current user, whose identifier

```
1    (:method (insertWithVariantsIfReady! ?r ?resource)
2        (
3        (not (inserted ?r))
4        (readyAux ?r ?resource)
5        (learnerProperty hasEducationalLevel ?el)
6        (assign ?variants
7                (call GetRelated (?r) -1
8                        (((class InstructionalObject)
9                        (relation isVariantOf ?r)
10                       (property hasLearningContext ?el)
11                       ))))
12       )
13       (
14       (!insertResource ?r)
15       (addInWorldStateAsInserted ?variants)
16       )
17       )
```

Fig. 4.25. !insertWithVariantsIfReady inserts a resource and all its variants

is stored in the world state in the atom (user *identifier*). The upper axiom takes a property as input and binds the variable ?value to the value stored in the learner model for this property and for the user identified by ?userId. The lower axiom takes as additional input the identifier of a resource. This allows querying information about the user with respect to a given resource. Both axioms use the Java function LearnerProperty to connect the course generator to the learner model.

```
(:- (learnerProperty ?property ?value)
    (
    (user ?userId)
    (assign ?value (call LearnerProperty ?userId ?property))
    )
    )

(:- (learnerProperty ?property ?r ?value)
    (
    (user ?userId)
    (assign ?value (call LearnerProperty ?userId ?property ?r))
    )
    )
```

Fig. 4.26. learnerProperty accesses information about the learner

Example 4.18. Let `Eva` be the identifier of the user for whom the course is currently generated. Then, (`learnerProperty hasEducationalLevel ?edlev`) binds `?edlev` to the educational level of the learner, e. g., `universityFirst-Year` for a first year university student. (`learnerProperty hasCompetency-Level def_slope ?cl`) binds `?cl` to the current competency level that the learner has reached with respect to the fundamental `def_slope`, e. g., 3.

Table 4.2. Learner properties used during course generation

Identifier	Description
hasEducationalLevel	The current level of education (e. g., high school and university first year) of the user
hasAllowedEducationalLevel	The levels of education the user is able to handle
hasField	The fields of interest of the user

Table 4.3. Learner properties evaluated with respect to a resource

Identifier	Description
hasAlreadySeen	Whether the user has already seen the given resource (**true/false**)
hasCompetencyLevel	The agglomerated competency level of the learner
hasCompetencyArgue	The competency level of the competency "argue" of the learner
hasCompetencyCommunicate	The competency level of the competency "communicate" of the learner
hasCompetencyLanguage	The competency level of the competency "language" of the learner
hasCompetencyModel	The competency level of the competency "model" of the learner
hasCompetencyRepresent	The competency level of the competency "represents" of the learner
hasCompetencySolve	The competency level of the competency "solve" of the learner
hasCompetencyThink	The competency level of the competency "think" of the learner
hasCompetencyTools	The competency level of the competency "tools" of the learner
hasAnxiety	The anxiety the learner exhibits (experimental)
hasMotivation	The motivation the learner exhibits (experimental)

Tables 4.2 and 4.3 list the learner properties that can be used during course generation. All the properties are based on the learner model that is currently used by PAIGOS, called SLM. SLM is based on the PISA competency framework (see Section 3.5). The SLM represents all information about the learner's "mastery" and his anxiety and motivation with respect to a fundamentals (Table 4.3). All values of the properties in Table 4.3 are represented as a value between one and four, with one representing the lowest and four the highest "mastery", motivation, etc. The competence level can be further divided with respect to specific mathematical competencies, such as "solve" and "model". The last two properties in Table 4.3 model situational factors, which are difficult to assess.[7] At the time being, they are provisionally supported in PAIGOS.

```
(:- (equivalent ?cl elementary)
    (call <= ?cl 1))

(:- (equivalent ?cl simple_conceptual)
    ((call > ?cl 1)
     (call <= ?cl 2)))

(:- (equivalent ?cl multi_step)
    ((call > ?cl 2)
     (call <= ?cl 3)))

(:- (equivalent ?cl complex)
    (call > ?cl 3))
```

Fig. 4.27. Translating terms from the learner model to metadata

A recurring problem for course generation is that information that is relevant for the generation process is stored in different components, using different terminologies. This problem motivated the development of the mediator for repository integration. A similar problem arises for learner properties, because often the metadata used to annotate the educational resources employs terms different from those used by the learner model. Ideally, the repository mediator (or a different one) is able to handle the translation. However, in the current implementation of PAIGOS, a set of axioms handles this necessary translation. They are shown in Figure 4.27. The axioms specify that the symbols `elementary`, `simple_conceptual`, `multi_step`, and `complex` (used in the metadata) correspond to numerical values v with $v \leq 1$, $1 < v \leq 2$, $2 < v \leq 3$, and $v > 3$, respectively. In the current version of PAIGOS, these are the only cases which require a translation

---

[7] The learner model of LEACTIVEMATH uses the user's performance in exercise solving to estimate his motivation and anxiety.

4.6.8 Processing Resources Depending on Learner Characteristics

The axioms and methods in this section infer information about resources and modify the world state depending on characteristics of the learner.

```
(:- (known ?f)
    (
     (learnerProperty hasCompetencyLevel ?f ?cl)
     (call >= ?cl 3)
    )
)
```

Fig. 4.28. known tests whether the learner "knows" a concept

In the PISA competency framework, a learner who has reached a competency level of three is able to perform extensive computations. The axiom shown in Figure 4.28 is satisfied if the learner has reached a competency level greater or equal to three with respect to the given fundamental. In other words, the axiom checks whether the concept is "known".

```
(:- (allKnownOrInserted (?head . ?tail))
    (
     (or (inserted ?head) (known ?head))
     (allKnownOrInserted ?tail)
    )
)

(:- (allKnownOrInserted nil)
    ())
```

Fig. 4.29. allKnownOrInserted tests whether all resources in a given list are either known or were inserted into the course

Figure 4.29 contains axioms that are used to test whether all resources in a given list are either known or were inserted into the course. The top axiom performs the test and, if successful, the recursion step; and the bottom axiom ends the recursion.

In most cases, an auxiliary r (e. g., an example, text, and exercise) should be inserted into a course only if the learner is prepared to understand it. In PAIGOS, such a test is encoded in the axiom illustrated in Figure 4.30. In short, the axiom checks whether all fundamentals that r is for are either known or were inserted into the course (in other words whether an opportunity is provided to the learner to understand the necessary fundamentals before

```
1    (:- (readyAux ?r ?f)
2        (
3        (learnerProperty hasEducationalLevel ?el)
4        (removeElement ?result ?f
5                      (call GetResources
6                            ((class Fundamental)
7                             (relation inverseIsFor ?r)
8                             (property hasLearningContext ?el))))
9        (allKnownOrInserted ?result)
10       (allInserted (call GetResources
11                          ((class Auxiliary)
12                           (relation isRequiredBy ?r)
13                           (property hasLearningContext ?el))))))
```

Fig. 4.30. The axiom `readyAux` tests whether the learner is ready to see an auxiliary

he reaches r). What makes the matter complicated is the fact that often a resource r is used relative to a specific fundamental f, e. g., when training f. In this case, f should be excluded from the list of concepts that need to be known. Otherwise, the contradiction might arise that an auxiliary r should be used for learning an unknown fundamental f, but r would never be presented since one of the fundamental it is for (namely f) is unknown.

In detail, the axiom in Figure 4.30 works as follows: first, it retrieves the educational level of the learner (line 3). Then, it collects all fundamentals that r is for, but removes from this list the fundamental f given as a parameter (lines 4–8). Then the axiom checks whether the remaining fundamentals are either known or were inserted into the course (line 9). In addition, r should only be presented if all other auxiliaries it requires where inserted before r (lines 10–13). If all conditions are fulfilled, then the auxiliary is classified as being "ready" for the learner.

The method displayed in Figure 4.31 uses the axiom `readyAux` to insert a given auxiliary if it wasn't already inserted and the learner is "ready" for it (relative to the given fundamental).

```
(:method (insertAuxOnceIfReady! ?r ?f)
         (
         (not (inserted ?r))
         (readyAux ?r ?f)
         )
         ((!insertResource ?r))
         )
```

Fig. 4.31. `insertAuxOnceIfReady!` inserts an auxiliary if the learner is ready to see it

```
(:method (insertAllAuxOnceIfReady (?head . ?tail) ?resource)
         ()
         (
          (insertAuxOnceIfReady ?head ?resource)
          (insertAllAuxOnceIfReady ?tail)
          )
         )

(:method (insertAllAuxOnceIfReady nil)
         ()
         ()
         )
```

Fig. 4.32. insertAllAuxOnceIfReady inserts all references in a list if the learner is ready

The methods shown in Figure 4.32 perform the same functionality, but on a list of references. Each reference is inserted into the course if the learner is "ready" for it and it was not yet inserted.

The axioms in Figure 4.33 remove all fundamentals from a given list of resources that are either known by the learner or inserted into the course, and it binds the result to the variable ?result. The helper axiom removeKnownFundamentalsH performs the main work. The first preconditions (lines 6–7) represent the base case and end the recursion if the list of left fundamentals is empty. The second preconditions (lines 11–14) check whether the current fundamental is either inserted or known. In this case, the current fundamental is discarded and the recursion continues with the rest of the fundamentals. Otherwise, the current fundamental is neither known nor inserted and hence is put into the result list (lines 18-21).

When resources are inserted into a course, often it is preferable to present new, previously unseen resources to the learner, and to show seen resources only if no new resources are available. This is achieved by the axiom shown in Figure 4.34. There, the axiom sortByAlreadySeen and a helper axiom partition the given list of resources into unseen and seen resources. Finally, these two lists are concatenated and returned as a single list in which unseen resources come first (lines 7–8). The preconditions in lines 12–15 use the learner property hasAlreadySeen to access the learner model for the required information. In case the resource was not yet seen, it is inserted into the first list. Otherwise it is inserted into the second list (lines 19–21).

4.6.9 Initializing and Manipulating Information about the Learning Goal

This section describes operators and methods that initialize a course generation problem and provide means to manipulate its learning goals.

```
1   (:- (removeKnownFundamentals ?result (?head . ?tail))
2       ((removeKnownFundamentalsH ?result nil ?head ?tail)))
3
4   (:- (removeKnownFundamentalsH ?result ?tempResult ?c ?tail)
5       (
6       (same ?c nil)
7       (assign ?result ?tempResult)
8       )
9
10      (
11      (or (inserted ?c) (known ?c))
12      (first ?next ?tail)
13      (rest ?newRest ?tail)
14      (removeKnownFundamentalsH ?result ?tempResult ?next ?newRest)
15      )
16
17      (
18      (first ?next ?tail)
19      (rest ?newRest ?tail)
20      (removeKnownFundamentalsH ?result (?c . ?tempResult)
21                              ?next ?newRest)
22      )
23      )
```

Fig. 4.33. removeKnownFundamentals removes from the given fundamentals those fundamentals the learner "knows"

The methods in Figure 4.35 add the information in the world state that the fundamentals in the list are the content learning goals of the current course. This is represented by the task atom (targetFundamental *fundamental*).

Figure 4.36 contains the method used to initialize the world state and start the course generation. Basically, it takes the goal task that was given in the definition of the planning problem (line 3) and breaks it up into its constituents, namely its pedagogical objective (represented in the world state using the atom scenario, line 7) and its fundamentals, which are inserted as target fundamentals using the methods of Figure 4.35 (line 8). The final subtask of the method performs some additional processing, explained in the next paragraph.

The method in Figure 4.37 analyzes the pedagogical objective of the course and starts the course generation. Technical issues with JSHOP2 require that the pedagogical objective is provided in string format, therefore the method maps the string to a task atom (e.g., lines 2–3 and 5–6). In addition, some pedagogical objectives are decomposed into a different objective and additional parameters. For instance, the tasks trainCompetencyThink and examSimulation30 are split into their main objective (trainCompetency and examSimulation)

```
1   (:- (sortByAlreadySeen ?result ?list)
2       (sortByAlreadySeenh ?result ?list nil nil)
3         )
4
5   (:- (sortByAlreadySeenh ?result ?list ?notSeen ?seen)
6       (
7        (same ?list nil)
8        (assign ?result (call Concat ?notSeen ?seen))
9         )
10
11      (
12       (first ?current ?list)
13       (learnerProperty hasAlreadySeen ?current nil)
14       (rest ?tail ?list)
15       (sortByAlreadySeenh ?result ?tail (?current . ?notSeen) ?seen)
16        )
17
18      (
19       (first ?current ?list)
20       (rest ?tail ?list)
21       (sortByAlreadySeenh ?result ?tail ?notSeen (?current . ?seen))
22        )
23  )
```

Fig. 4.34. sortByAlreadySeen partitions a list into unseen and seen resources

```
(:method (insertTargetFundamentals (?head . ?tail))
         ()
         (
          (!!addInWorldState (targetFundamental ?head))
          (insertTargetFundamentals ?tail)
          )
         )

(:method (insertTargetFundamentals nil)
         ()
         ()
         )
```

Fig. 4.35. insertTargetConcepts adds in the world state information about the content goals of a course

```
1    (:method (generateCourse)
2            (
3            (goalTask (?pedObjective ?resources))
4            (learnerProperty hasEducationalLevel ?el)
5            )
6            (
7            (!!addInWorldState (scenario ?pedObjective))
8            (insertTargetFundamentals ?resources)
9            (insertAndPlanGoal ?pedObjective ?resources)
10           )
11           )
```

Fig. 4.36. Initializing the world state

```
1    (:method (insertAndPlanGoal ?pedObjective ?resources)
2            ((same ?pedObjective "guidedTour"))
3            ((guidedTour ?resources))
4            . . .
5            ((same ?pedObjective "discover"))
6            ((discover ?resources))
7            . . .
8            ((same ?pedObjective "trainCompetencyThink"))
9            (
10           (!!changeScenario trainCompetency)
11           (trainCompetency think ?resources)
12           )
13           . . .
14           ((same ?pedObjective "examSimulation30"))
15           (
16           (!!changeScenario "examSimulation")
17           (examSimulation 30 ?resources)
18           )
19           . . .
20           )
```

Fig. 4.37. insertAndPlanGoal starts the course generation

and a parameter that indicates the specific competency to train or the time allocated for the exam simulation (lines 10 and 16). This requires changing the scenario (see the following operator).

Figure 4.37 only contains parts of the method: the actual method provides a set of preconditions and subtasks for each "public" pedagogical task, i.e., for each task that the course generator achieves as part of his service provision.

```
(:operator (!!changeScenario ?newScenario)
           (;; precondition
            (scenario ?oldScenario)
           )
           (;; delete list
            (scenario ?oldScenario)
           )
           (;; add list
            (scenario ?newScenario))
           )
```

Fig. 4.38. !!changeScenario changes the scenario of the current course

Changing the scenario is done using the operator !!changeScenario. It simply removes the logical atom denoting the scenario and inserts a new one (see Figure 4.38).

```
(:operator (!!setAchieved ?task)
           ()
           ()
           ((achieved ?task))
           )
```

Fig. 4.39. !!setAchieved marks a task as achieved

The operator shown in Figure 4.39 inserts a logical atom in the world state that marks the given task as achieved. After the application, the atom (achieved t) can be used for detecting whether a task t was already achieved.

Sometimes it is required to extract all fundamentals from a given list that are not the content goals of the course. This is done by the axioms shown in Figure 4.40. getNonTargetFundamentals uses a helper axiom to recurse onto a list and to remove all fundamentals that are content goals.

This completes the description of the axioms, operators and methods that serve as a general basis for the course generation domain. Chapter 5 describes how they are used in course generation scenarios. The remainder of the current chapter will focus on how to generate a course from a plan and novel features that become possible within PAIGOS.

4.7 Converting a Plan into a Course

After a plan is found, it is used to generate a course. This section describes the underlying process.

```
(:- (getNonTargetFundamentals ?result ?elements)
    (getNTCH ?result (call Reverse ?elements) nil))

(:- (getNTCH ?result ?elements ?temp)
    (
     (same ?elements nil)
     (assign ?result ?temp)
     )
    (
     (first ?el ?elements)
     (targetFundamental ?el)
     (rest ?tail ?elements)
     (getNTCH ?result ?tail ?temp))
    (
     (first ?el ?elements)
     (rest ?tail ?elements)
     (getNTCH ?result ?tail (?el . ?temp))
     )
    )
```

Fig. 4.40. getNonTargetFundamentals removes all content goals from a given list of fundamentals

PAIGOS represents courses using the element omgroup, which is an element from the OMDOC standard, a semantic knowledge representation for mathematical documents [84, 85, 107]. The purpose of the omgroup element is to represent collections of resources and is as such independent of the mathematical domain. It can also be easily mapped/transformed into other data structures with similar aims, such as IMS CP.

An omgroup element has a simple structure; it consist of metadata information (e. g., the author and title of the element), references to other OMDOC elements, other omgroup elements, and dynamic items that allow the dynamic inclusion of resources generated by services.

Example 4.19. Figure 4.41 contains an excerpt from a plan generated by PAIGOS, assembled for the task (discover (def_diff def_diff_f thm_diff-rule_sum)) (namespaces are omitted in the example; the complete plan is contained in the appendix). The first lines add the goal task information in the world state (lines 1–4). The following operators start several new sections: for the overall course (lines 5–6, note that the section includes the task for which the section was created), and then for the first section, which contains an explanation for the overall goals of the course (line 7–9). This section is closed, and new section begins, for the chapter on the first goal fundamental the "definition of the derivative, resp., differential quotient" (def_diff, line 10), and for the first page, the necessary prerequisites (line 11). The page starts with a dynamically created text that provides an explanation on the purpose of the

```
1   (!!addInWorldState (scenario discover))
2   (!!addInWorldState (targetFundamental def_diff))
3   (!!addInWorldState (targetFundamental def_diff_f))
4   (!!addInWorldState (targetFundamental thm_diffrule_sum))
5   (!startSection Discover (def_diff def_diff_f thm_diffrule_sum)
6                          (discover (def_diff def_diff_f thm_diffrule_sum)))
7   (!startSection Description (def_diff def_diff_f thm_diffrule_sum))
8   (!text discover.Description (def_diff def_diff_f thm_diffrule_sum))
9   (!endSection)
10  (!startSection Title (def_diff) (learnFundamentalDiscover (def_diff)))
11  (!startSection Prerequisites (def_diff) (learnPrerequisitesFundamentalsShortSection!
12          (def_diff)))
13  (!text discover.Prerequisites (def_diff))
14  (!insertResource def_diff_quot_FOS)
15  (!insertResource def_informal_limit)
16  (!endSection)
17  (!startSection Title (def_diff) (developFundamental (def_diff)))
18  (!text discover.Develop (def_diff))
19  (!insertResource def_diff)
20  (!insertResource note_diff)
21  (!dynamicTask illustrate! (def_diff))
22  (!endSection)
23  (!startSection Exercises (def_diff) (practiceSection! (def_diff)))
24  (!text discover.Practice (def_diff))
25  (!insertLearningService ExerciseSequencer TrainCompetencyLevel (def_diff))
26  (!dynamicTask train! (def_diff))
27  (!endSection)
28  (!startSection Connections (def_diff) (showConnectionsSection! (def_diff)))
29  (!text discover.Connect (def_diff))
30  (!insertLearningService CMap display (def_diff) (includeEdge1 isRequiredBy
31          includeEdge2 isA includeEdge3 inverseIsA includeCategory1 Definition
32          includeCategory2 Law computeNeighbourNodes 1.0))
33  (!endSection)
34  (!endSection)
35  (!startSection Title (def_diff_f) (learnFundamentalDiscover (def_diff_f)))
36  (!startSection Introduction (def_diff_f) (introduceWithSection! (def_diff_f)))
37  (!text discover.Introduction (def_diff_f))
38  (!insertResource cluso_diff_hiking)
39  (!endSection)
40  (!startSection Title (def_diff_f) (developFundamental (def_diff_f)))
41      ...
42  (!endSection)
43  (!startSection Title (thm_diffrule_sum) (learnFundamentalDiscover (thm_diffrule_sum)))
44      ...
45  (!startSection Title (thm_diffrule_sum) (developFundamental (thm_diffrule_sum)))
46  (!text discover.Develop (thm_diffrule_sum))
47  (!insertResource thm_diffrule_sum)
48  (!dynamicTask illustrate! (thm_diffrule_sum))
49  (!endSection)
50  (!startSection Proof (thm_diffrule_sum) (proveSection! (thm_diffrule_sum)))
51  (!text discover.Proof (thm_diffrule_sum))
52  (!insertResource prf_diffrule_diff_applet)
53  (!insertResource prf_diffrule_sum_applet)
54  (!insertResource prf_diffrule_sum)
55  (!endSection)
56      ...
57  (!endSection)
58  (!startSection Reflection (def_diff def_diff_f thm_diffrule_sum)
59                          (reflect (def_diff def_diff_f thm_diffrule_sum)))
60  (!insertLearningService OLM display (thm_diffrule_sum) (competencyId competency))
61  (!endSection)
62  (!endSection)
```

Fig. 4.41. Parts of a plan generated by the course generator

section (line 12), followed by a references to the prerequisites (lines 13–14). Dynamic tasks are inserted in line 20. When executed, the task will result in a sequence of examples for the definition in this section (see the next section). Another interesting case is line 24. There, a reference to a learning-support service is inserted: an exercise sequencer, a component specialized in training the learner. A different service, a concept mapping tool is shown in lines 29–31. The final lines insert a reference to another learning-support service, an Open Learner Model (OLM) (line 59). The precise meaning of the parameters of these learning-support service is not relevant for the purpose of this example, the important point is that they follow the general scheme of containing the service name, method name, resource references, and potentially additional parameters (as described in Section 4.6.3).

From a plan, a course represented as an `omgroup` is constructed in the following way:

- `!startSection` triggers the opening of an `omgroup` element. For the title generation, it uses the techniques described in section 4.9.4.
- `!endSection` inserts the closing tag of an `omgroup` element.
- `!insertResource` inserts the `ref` element that OMDoc uses for referencing to resources.
- `!insertLearningService` inserts the `dynamicItem` element that is used to create links to learning supporting services.
- `!text` inserts a `dynamicItem` element that serves as a symbolic representation for text generation (see Section 4.9.2).
- `!dynamicTask` inserts a `dynamicItem` element that is used for dynamic task expansion (see Section 4.6.5).
- Internal operators (marked with the prefix "!!") serve JSHOP2's internal bookkeeping purposes and hence are ignored.

The following lines contain parts of the `omgroup` that is generated from the plan shown in Figure 4.41. Due to XML's verbosity, I included only the first and last section, the complete course is contained in the appendix. The first metadata element (lines 4–18) contains the title of the section in several languages (lines 5–6), the task of this section (lines 7–13), and some administrative information (lines 14–17). Lines 24–28 contain the dynamic item from which at a later stage a text will be generated that explains the purpose and structure of this course. Then, the section is closed, and a new section containing the prerequisites is opened. Lines 53–54 contain the first references to educational resources in the proper sense of course generation: these two resources will be included on the page and shown to the learner. The OMDoc representation of a dynamic task is shown in the lines 71–73, and the dynamic item representing the exercise sequencer is contained in the lines 88–91.

```
1  <?xml version="1.0" encoding="UTF-8"?>
2  <omdoc xmlns:omd="http://www.mathweb.org/omdoc">
3    <omgroup id="4">
4      <metadata>
```

```
5      <Title xml:lang="de">Begriffe kennenlernen</Title>
6      <Title xml:lang="en">Discover</Title>
7      <extradata>
8        <pedtask pedobj="discover">
9          <ref xref="def_diff" />
10         <ref xref="def_diff_f" />
11         <ref xref="thm_diffrule_sum" />
12       </pedtask>
13     </extradata>
14     <Creator xml:lang="en" role="edt">Activemath</Creator>
15     <Creator xml:lang="en" role="aut">N/A</Creator>
16     <Contributor xml:lang="en" role="trl">N/A</Contributor>
17     <Date xml:action="updated" xml:who="Activemath">2007-03-09T17:19:48</Date>
18   </metadata>
19   <omgroup>
20     <metadata>
21       <Title xml:lang="de">Überblick</Title>
22       <Title xml:lang="en">Overview</Title>
23     </metadata>
24     <dynamic-item type="text" servicename="NLG" queryname="Item.Discover.Description">
25       <ref xref="def_diff" />
26       <ref xref="def_diff_f" />
27       <ref xref="thm_diffrule_sum" />
28     </dynamic-item>
29   </omgroup>
30   <omgroup>
31     <metadata>
32       <Title xml:lang="de">Definition der Ableitung bzw.
33                            des Differentialquotienten</Title>
34       <Title xml:lang="en">Definition of the derivative,
35                            resp., differential quotient</Title>
36       <extradata>
37         <pedtask pedobj="learnFundamentalDiscover">
38           <ref xref="def_diff" />
39         </pedtask>
40       </extradata>
41     </metadata>
42     <omgroup>
43       <metadata>
44         <Title xml:lang="de">Vorwissen</Title>
45         <Title xml:lang="en">Prerequisites</Title>
46         <extradata>
47           <pedtask pedobj="learnPrerequisitesFundamentalsShortSection!">
48             <ref xref="def_diff" />
49           </pedtask>
50         </extradata>
51       </metadata>
52       <dynamic-item type="text" servicename="NLG"
53                     queryname="Item.Discover.Prerequisites">
54         <ref xref="def_diff" />
55       </dynamic-item>
56       <ref xref="def_diff_quot_FOS" />
57       <ref xref="def_informal_limit" />
58     </omgroup>
59     <omgroup>
60       <metadata>
61         <Title xml:lang="de">Definition der Ableitung bzw.
62                              des Differentialquotienten</Title>
63         <Title xml:lang="en">Definition of the derivative,
64                              resp., differential quotient</Title>
65         <extradata>
66           <pedtask pedobj="developFundamental">
67             <ref xref="def_diff" />
68           </pedtask>
69         </extradata>
70       </metadata>
71       <dynamic-item type="text" servicename="NLG" queryname="Item.Discover.Develop">
```

```
72        <ref xref="def_diff" />
73      </dynamic-item>
74      <ref xref="def_diff" />
75      <ref xref="note_diff" />
76      <dynamic-item type="dynamicTask" servicename="tutorialControl"
77                    queryname="illustrate!">
78        <ref xref="def_diff" />
79      </dynamic-item>
80    </omgroup>
81    <omgroup>
82      <metadata>
83        <Title xml:lang="de">Übungen</Title>
84        <Title xml:lang="en">Exercises</Title>
85        <extradata>
86          <pedtask pedobj="practiceSection!">
87            <ref xref="def_diff" />
88          </pedtask>
89        </extradata>
90      </metadata>
91      <dynamic-item type="text" servicename="NLG" queryname="Item.Discover.Practice">
92        <ref xref="def_diff" />
93      </dynamic-item>
94      <dynamic-item type="learningService" servicename="ExerciseSequencer"
95                    queryname="TrainCompetencyLevel">
96        <ref xref="def_diff" />
97      </dynamic-item>
98      <dynamic-item type="dynamicTask" servicename="tutorialControl"
99                    queryname="train!">
100       <ref xref="def_diff" />
101     </dynamic-item>
102   </omgroup>
103   <omgroup>
104     <metadata>
105       <Title xml:lang="de">Zusammenhänge</Title>
106       <Title xml:lang="en">Connections</Title>
107       <extradata>
108         <pedtask pedobj="showConnectionsSection!">
109           <ref xref="def_diff" />
110         </pedtask>
111       </extradata>
112     </metadata>
113     <dynamic-item type="text" servicename="NLG" queryname="Item.Discover.Connect">
114       <ref xref="def_diff" />
115     </dynamic-item>
116     <dynamic-item type="learningService" servicename="CMap" queryname="display">
117       <ref xref="def_diff" />
118       <queryparam property="includeEdge1" value="isRequiredBy" />
119       <queryparam property="includeEdge2" value="isA" />
120       <queryparam property="includeEdge3" value="inverseIsA" />
121       <queryparam property="includeCategory1" value="Definition" />
122       <queryparam property="includeCategory2" value="Law" />
123       <queryparam property="computeNeighbourNodes" value="1.0" />
124     </dynamic-item>
125   </omgroup>
126 </omgroup>
127 ...
128 <omgroup>
129   <metadata>
130     <Title xml:lang="de">Rückblick</Title>
131     <Title xml:lang="en">Looking Back</Title>
132     <extradata>
133       <pedtask pedobj="reflect">
134         <ref xref="def_diff" />
135         <ref xref="def_diff_f" />
136         <ref xref="thm_diffrule_sum" />
137       </pedtask>
138     </extradata>
```

```
139    </metadata>
140    <dynamic-item type="learningService" servicename="OLM" queryname="display">
141      <ref xref="thm_diffrule_sum" />
142      <queryparam property="competencyId" value="competency" />
143    </dynamic-item>
144    </omgroup>
145  </omgroup>
146 </omdoc>
```

Therefore, the resulting OMDOC grouping consists of nested sections with the leaves being pointers to educational resources. As described in Section 2.3.1, there exist several e-learning standards that represent similar structures, the most prominent being IMS CP, IMS LD, and IMS SS.

IMS SS with its explicit control of the navigation process imposes a rather behavioristic pedagogical approach on the learning process, and thus might raise problems when employed in constructivist settings. On the other hand, IMS LD describes ordered activities in learning and the roles of the involved parties. It is a very broad approach, hard to implement, and not well suited for representing courses down to the level of educational resources. In contrast, the purpose of IMS CP is the exchange of content and organization of the content. Its **organization** element can be mapped directly to an OMDOC **omgroup** element and vice versa, and the IMS CP **item** element can represent references to content as well as to learning-supporting services. Therefore, IMS CP is a sensible output format of PAIGOS, and the Web service interface of PAIGOS (described in Section 6.3) exports this format. Since the resulting course does not include the "physical" resources themselves but only references, the output is not a complete content package, but only its manifest.

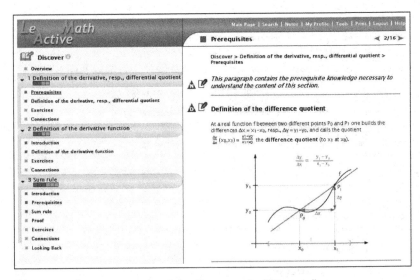

Fig. 4.42. A course generated for the scenario "Discover"

Figure 4.42 shows what the course of Figure 4.41 looks like in a learning environment, in this case ACTIVEMATH. The shown page is the second page of the course, which contains the prerequisites (only one of which is shown in the screenshot).

4.8 Generating Structure and Adaptivity: Dynamic Tasks

Course generation faces a dilemma: on the one hand it makes sense from a pedagogical point of view to generate a complete course immediately after receiving the learner's request, instead of selecting and presenting one resource after another, as it is done in dynamic content sequencing. The learner sees the complete sequence of content that leads him toward his learning goal, how the content is structured and can freely navigate, say, to have a look at the final fundamentals.

On the other hand, if a long time-span separates the generation and viewing of a page, assumptions about the learner made during course generation may have become invalid, resulting in an inadequate course. Hence, if possible, the course generating should be dynamic in the sense to use the most up-to-date information about the learner that is available.

In AI, execution monitoring and replanning offers a framework that can cope with situations in which assumptions made during planning can change while the plan is executed. An execution monitor constantly monitors the current world state and if it changes in a way that makes preconditions of an operator invalid, the execution monitor triggers replanning, i. e., tries to find a different sequence of operators that achieve the goal ([157], p. 441).

However, this framework cannot be applied to course generation as realized in PAIGOS. Here, the plan is completely applied before the course is presented, in fact, applying the plan produces the course. One alternative would be to keep the plan, to associate a planning step with the parts of the course it creates, and to use some mechanism to re-plan those parts affected by the changes in the world state. Some of these requirements are already provided by PAIGOS, for instance, sections contain information about the task context in which they were created. Yet, designing such a reactive planning algorithm would be a rather complex task, especially since JSHOP2 does not provide any facilities for it.

In this volume, I propose a different solution for this problem of dynamic course generation, based on dynamic subtask expansion. In this solution, planning may stop at the level of specially marked primitive tasks, called *dynamic tasks*. Each dynamic task encloses a pedagogical task t and is inserted into the course instead of t. Since a dynamic task is primitive, it counts as directly achieved by its operator and is not further expanded (see Section 4.6.5 for a description of the operators).

Later, at presentation time, when the learner first visits a page that contains a dynamic task, the task t it encloses is passed to the course generator. Then, the course generator assembles the sequence of resources that achieve t. The resulting identifiers of educational resources replace the task in the course structure with specific instances of educational resources (hence, when the page is revisited, the elements do not change, which avoids confusion of the learner reported in [30]). This means a course is partly static, partly dynamic, and thus the goal of presenting the complete course to the learner while still being able to adapt is realized.

An important aspect of dynamic tasks is that they can be used by human "course generators", i.e., authors that manually compose courses: an author can define a course where parts of the course are predefined and others dynamically computed, taking the learner model into account. In this way, an author can profit from the best of both worlds: she can compose parts of the course by hand and at the same time profit from the adaptive features of the course generator.

The following example shows that the above described realization of dynamic tasks is too simplistic:

Example 4.20. Let the current course contain references to the definition def_slope and the example exa_slope, which is for def_slope. Let d be a dynamic task that selects an example for the given definition, t=(illustrate (def_slope)). If the task is planned for without any further restrictions, it might happen that the selected example will be exa_slope, and hence will be contained in the course twice. This would not have happened if the course was generated in one shot since then the course generation methods would have ensured that the selected example did not occur previously in the course by testing against the word state.

As a consequence, dynamic task expansion needs to take the current course into account. The underlying algorithm uses a translation from a course, i.e., an omgroup element, to a world state: each reference to a resource r results in a logical atom (inserted r), which is inserted into the world state the course generator is started with.

Dynamic task expansion offers an additional benefit: since the course generation stops at a higher level and does not expand all subtasks, the planning process is much faster. The technical evaluations in Section 7 show an increase of performance up to a factor of ten.

4.9 Generation of Narrative Bridges and Structure

The courses generated by PAIGOS consist of structured sequences of references to educational resources. The same resource can be used in a multitude of courses and support the achievement of various learning goals. This re-use of educational resources imposes constraints on their content: in comparison to a standard textbook, absolute references to previous or latter content have to be avoided, because it is impossible to tell in advance whether the referenced educational resources will be presented at all and at which positions they will be presented. For the same reason, authoring introductions to a course or summaries is difficult: at authoring time, the educational resources contained in a particular course are unknown. But introductions, summaries and similar texts have pedagogical purposes that is relevant for a successful learning process, and which a simple sequence of educational resources lacks. Yet, during course generation information about the current learning goals and the used educational resources is available. In this section, I will show how to use that information in order to extend a sequence of educational resources with bridging texts that provide supportive information about a course to a learner.

The bridging texts we will discuss here serve the following purposes: firstly, they explain the purpose of a course or a section at a higher level of abstraction than the level of educational resources. Because they make the structure of a course explicit, they provide cues that the learners can use to structure their own learning process. Secondly, they serve to improve the coherence and the readability of a course. By providing texts that link different sections, they provide coherence that a mere sequence of educational resources might lack.

This section starts with empirical findings that provide evidence for the need of bridging texts. Then, the realization of bridging texts is described from the perspective of the course generation planner, which generates symbolic representations of bridging texts. These representations can be transformed into text in many ways, depending on the learning environment the course is used in (an example implementation is described in the chapter about integration, in Section 6.2.4). The final part of this section explains how additional structural information is provided through the generation of section titles.

4.9.1 Empirical Findings

Empirical studies suggest that learning of fundamentals can be improved by referencing other content and by providing explanations of the content to come on a higher level of abstraction. A well-known support technique for learning are advance organizers:

> *[Advance] organizers are introduced in advance of learning itself, and are also presented at a higher level of abstraction, generality, and inclusiveness; and since the substantive content of a given organizer or series of organizers is selected on the basis of its suitability for explaining, integrating, and interrelating the material they precede, this strategy simultaneously satisfies the substantive as well as the programming criteria for enhancing the organization strength of cognitive structure ([9], p. 81).*

Cognitive learning theories (as opposed to the behavioristic information transmission paradigm), provide additional support for the relevance of properly preparing the student's mind. According to Mayer [95], multimedia learning needs to consider the following:

1. selection of the important information in the lesson (for instance by providing overviews and summaries);
2. management of the limited capacity in working memory to allow the rehearsal needed for learning (for instance by providing structure such that chunks take up less space in working memory);
3. integration of auditory and visual sensory information in working memory with existing knowledge in long-term memory by way of rehearsal in working memory. This includes constructing a knowledge structure in the mind.
4. retrieval of knowledge and skills from long-term memory into working memory when needed later (which can be supported by providing a clear structure).
5. management of all these processes via meta-cognitive skills, which includes the skill of a learner of being able to structure the learning process on his own.

In PAIGOS, the goal of narrative bridges is to augment the dynamically generated courses with texts that set the student's mind (similar to an advanced organizer), support the students' understanding of the structure and of the learning goals, and make transitions between educational resources smoother.

The literature provides evidence that bridging texts should be concisely formulated. Summarizing research in user interface design, Nielsen [129] suggests that "[d]ialogues should not contain information which is irrelevant or rarely needed. Every extra unit of information in a dialogue competes with the relevant units of information and diminishes their relative visibility". Similarly, Shneiderman and Plaisant [166] argues to reduce short-term memory load: "[t]he limitation of human information processing in short-term memory requires that displays be kept simple, multiple page displays be consolidated ...". The importance of reducing the cognitive load also stressed by Kearlsey [77] in the domain of hypertext technology. Additional evidence for the importance of concise texts is provided by research on feedback: van der Linden [192] analyzed the usage of feedback texts during problem solving and reached the conclusion that "[f]eedback of more than three lines was hardly ever read to the end".

The results of these studies are taken into account for the generation of bridging texts in PAIGOS. The generation of bridging texts happens as follows.

1. During the course generation, specific methods trigger the application of operators. The instantiated operators encode sufficient information for a later text generation.

2. The resulting plan serves as the basis to generate a table of contents. The information contained in the operator applications of the previous stage is used to create *symbolic representations*. Stage 1 and 2 are described below.

3. The final stage uses the symbolic representation to generate text. This is "outside" the course generator and part of the learning environment the course is presented in. An exemplary realization in ACTIVEMATH is described in the chapter on integration in Section 6.2.4.

4.9.2 Operator and Methods for Text Generation

One goal of the narrative bridges is to convey to the learner the structure of a course and the purpose of the educational resources contained in a page. Therefore, the texts are inserted at the level of pages. However, course generation aims at avoiding duplication of educational knowledge as far as possible and to reuse existing knowledge, and thus different scenarios use partly the same, partly different methods and operators. Therefore, in different scenarios, the same methods may serve to achieve different goals. For instance, the example selection in the scenario discover is done by the same methods as in the scenario rehearse. Yet, the examples serve different purposes: in the former case, the examples are used to provide illustrative applications of a new fundamental; in the latter case, they are used to remind the learner how to apply the fundamental. As a consequence, the respective bridging texts should differ, depending on the scenario.

```
1   (:operator (!text ?type ?parameters)
2              ()
3              ()
4              ()
5              )
6
7   (:method (text ?type ?parameters)
8              ((scenario ?var))
9              ((!text (call Concat ?var "." ?type) ?parameters))
10             )
```

Fig. 4.43. !text and text generate symbolic text representations

The operator !text (the upper operator in Figure 4.43, it was briefly described earlier) encodes the information later used to create a symbolic representation of a bridging text. This operator has no preconditions, delete and add lists. Thus, it can always be applied and does not modify the planning world state. The variables in the head are used to specify the type of text (which consists of the current scenario and the specific type of bridging text) and ?parameters stands for a list of terms that can provide additional information. In the current implementation of PAIGOS, these are the identifiers of the fundamentals currently in focus.

```
(:method (descriptionScenarioSection ?parameters)
         MethodDescriptionScenarioSection
         ()
         ((!startSection Description ?parameters)
         (text Description ?parameters)
         (!endSection)
         )
         )
```

Fig. 4.44. descriptionScenarioSection inserts descriptions of scenarios

The method displayed in Figure 4.44 serves to generate descriptions of scenarios. In the current version of PAIGOS, these description are encapsulated in their own section and the method provides a convenient abbreviation to keep other methods less cluttered.

Example 4.21. The following operator instance triggers the generation of a symbolic representation of a text that is an introduction for a section about the "definition of the derivative quotient" in the scenario discover: (!text discover.introduction (def_diff)).

This operator requires to provide the scenario name in the variable ?type. However, because most of the time the scenario will not change during course generation (the exceptions will be explained in the next chapter), things can be simplified. The second method in Figure 4.43 wraps the call of the operator and automatically inserts the scenario name (line 8), thereby simplifying methods that use text generation.

Example 4.22. The following method illustrates the creation of a bridging text. The method adds a new section that introduces a fundamental. The section consists of an explanatory bridging text (highlighted), a motivation and potentially some introductory examples. The above method is applicable to the highlighted task.

```
(:method (introduceWithSection! ?c)
         ;; preconditions
         ()
         ;; subtasks
         (;; Start a new section for the motivation
          (!startSection Introduction (?c))
          (text introduction (?c))
         (motivate! ?c)
```

```
(introductionExamplify ?c)
(!endSection)
)
)
```

Example 4.23. The application of the method `MethodText` on the following task during the scenario `discover` results in the task shown in Example 4.21.

```
(introduceWithSection! (def_diff))
```

In some cases, a more precise control of the type of generated texts is needed. Methods can achieve this by using the operator `!!changeScenario` to modify the atom that represents the scenario. This gives methods the possibility to control the texts that will be generated. Take, e. g., the scenario `rehearse` in which two different sections present a sequence of examples. The first example section serves to remind the learner how to apply the fundamental. The second section, placed after an exercise section, provides additional examples. Consequently, even if both times the task is the same, namely (text illustrate *termlist*), the texts have to be different, which can be achieved by changing the scenario.

4.9.3 Symbolic Representations of Dynamic Text Items

After a plan was found, its operators are applied and generate a table of contents. The entries for bridging texts are realized by dynamic items. Figure 4.45 contains a schema of a dynamic item for texts. The actual application replaces *scenario*, *type* and *id_1*, ... , *id_n* with the terms that instantiate the variables of the head of the operator, which are ?scenario, type and ?parameters = *id_1*, ... , *id_n*, respectively. The dynamic items serve as the symbolic representation needed for text generation.

```
<dynamic-item
   type="text" servicename="NLGGenerator" queryname="scenario.type">
   <ref xref="id_1" />
   ...
   <ref xref="id_n" />
</dynamic-item>
```

Fig. 4.45. A schema of dynamic items for bridging texts

Example 4.24. The dynamic item created by the task of Example 4.21 looks as follows:

```
<dynamic-item
  type="text" servicename="NLGGenerator"
  queryname="discover.introduction">
  <ref xref="def_diff"/>
</dynamic-item>
```

In Section 6.2.4, I will describe how texts are be generated from these symbolic representations.

4.9.4 Generation of Structure Information

The course generator generates a hierarchically structured course that consists of nested sections. Each section requires a title that is used for referencing and displayed when the course is presented to the learner. Ideally, a title concisely indicates the content and purpose of the section it describes. This way, it can provide to the learner an overview on the structure of a course.

The generation of section titles follows the pattern of bridging texts generation: the methods that add tasks for creating new sections "know" the learning goals to be achieved within a section and include this information into the tasks.

```
(:operator (!startSection ?type)
           ()
           ()
           ()
           )

(:operator (!startSection ?type ?parameters)
           ()
           ()
           ()
           )

(:operator (!startSection ?type ?parameters ?task)
           ()
           ()
           ()
           )

(:operator (!endSection)
           ()
           ()
           ()
           )
```

Fig. 4.46. !startSection and !endSection create structure

The three upper operators in Figure 4.46 (repeated from Section 4.6.2) start a new section. Since they do not have preconditions, they can always be applied. The variables in the head specify the type of the title and additional parameters, such as the identifiers of the fundamentals presented in the section.

Example 4.25. The following tasks are generated while planning a course for the fundamental "definition of the average slope between two points":

```
(!startSection elementTitle (def_diff))
... some other tasks ...
(!startSection Introduction (def_diff))
... some other tasks ...
```

In contrast to bridging texts, titles need to be generated during the plan application, at the time the course is generated, rather than later by the learning environment that presents the course, since the standards used for the representation of table of contents, such as OMDOC or IMS CP require the titles to be static character strings.

PAIGOS possesses a selection of phrases, i. e., a set of keywords and corresponding texts (see Figure 4.47 for some examples). Each type of title corresponds to a phrase. At the time the table of content is generated from the plan, the corresponding texts are inserted as titles sections. If phrases are available in several languages, then a language specific title is generated for each language. The result is a multi-lingual educational resource. Which language is presented to the learner is determined by the learning management system at presentation time.

```
text.NLGGenerator.Title.Introduction=Introduction
text.NLGGenerator.Title.Exercises=Exercises
text.NLGGenerator.Title.Examples=Examples
text.NLGGenerator.Title.Connections=Connections
text.NLGGenerator.Title.Reflection=Looking Back
text.NLGGenerator.Title.Prerequisites=Prerequisites
```

Fig. 4.47. A selection of phrases for title generation

The only exception is the text type `elementTitle`, whose parameters have to consist of a list with only a single resource identifier. This text type uses the title of the referenced educational resource for the generated title. Typically, it is used to convey that the nested sections all refer to the same fundamental.

Example 4.26. The tasks in Example 4.25 results in the OMDOC table of contents in Figure 4.48. The title of the first section uses the title of the referenced educational resource as its own title (lines 5–6 in Figure 4.48). The

```
 1  <omgroup>
 2    <metadata>
 3      <Title xml:lang="de">Definition der Ableitung
 4                            bzw. des Differentialquotienten</Title>
 5      <Title xml:lang="en">Definition of the derivative,
 6                            resp., differential quotient</Title>
 7      ...
 8    </metadata>
 9    <omgroup>
10      <metadata>
11        <Title xml:lang="de">Vorwissen</Title>
12        <Title xml:lang="en">Prerequisites</Title>
13        ...
14      </metadata>
15      ...
16    </omgroup>
17    ...
18  </omgroup>
```

Fig. 4.48. Examples for generated section titles

title of the second section is taken from the phrases (line 12). Figure 4.49 shows a HTML rendering of a table of contents.

4.10 Summary

This chapter laid the foundations of PAIGOS and described the AI techniques used in this volume: ontological modeling to represent the types of educational resources the course generator reasons about, a mediator architecture and ontology mapping to access resources distributed in distinct repositories, and HTN axioms, operators and methods that provide a basic set of functionality to perform course generation. The following chapter describes how these axioms, operators and methods are used for formalizing several course generation scenarios.

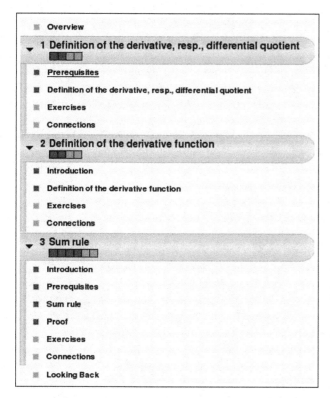

Fig. 4.49. A table of contents with generated section titles

5

Course Generation in Practice: Formalized Scenarios

This chapter puts the general techniques described in Chapter 4 to use. I describe several course generation scenarios: those in the first part of this chapter are based on a moderate constructivist competency-based approach and were developed in close collaboration with experts for mathematics education at the Mathematical Institute of Ludwig-Maximilians-University Munich. The scenario in the second part of this chapter is based on guidelines from instructional design.

To keep the following description in reasonable length, I will omit those methods and operators that are only slight variations of other, previously explained methods.

5.1 Moderate Constructivist Competency-Based Scenarios

The work presented in this chapter was performed as part of the EU FP6 project LeActiveMath, which developed an innovative, Web-based, intelligent, multi-lingual e-learning system for mathematics. One central component of LeActiveMath is the course generator described in this volume. The pedagogical knowledge formalized in the course generator was developed in cooperation with Marianne Moormann and Christian Groß, two members of the team of Prof. Reiss at the Mathematical Institute of Ludwig-Maximilians-University Munich. We identified six different learning scenarios that typically arise in a learning process. These scenarios were informally modeled using diagrams and natural language. As an example, a diagram compiled for the scenario "discover" is illustrated in Figure 5.1. The scenarios were modeled down to the level of selection of educational resources. In a final step, these descriptions were formalized using the HTN framework. The resulting formalization is described in this chapter. I will, however, start with a section discussing the underlying pedagogy and potential conflicts with course generation.

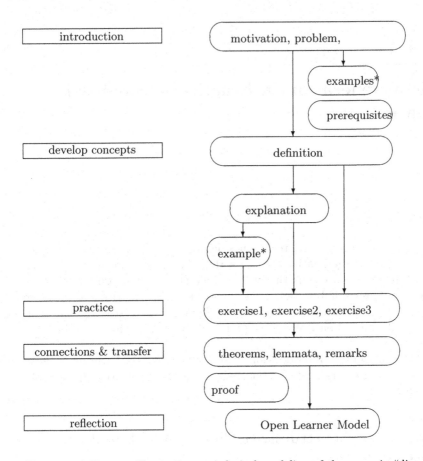

Fig. 5.1. A diagram illustrating an informal modeling of the scenario "discover"

5.1.1 Course Generation and Constructivism – a Contradiction?

The pedagogy underlying LEACTIVEMATH is based on moderate constructivism. Hence, learners have to play an active role and are to a large extent responsible for the outcome of their learning process. As a result, the course generation scenarios do not implement the knowledge "transmission" paradigm but aim at supporting the students in structuring their learning activities and developing strategic competence. Therefore, the main goals of the pedagogical scenarios developed in LEACTIVEMATH are that students are to become autonomous and self-regulated learners.

In addition, the scenarios implement a competency-based approach. Competency-based pedagogy claims that learning mathematics should not only aim at solving a problem but also at thinking mathematically and arguing about the correctness or incorrectness of the problem solving steps and involved methods, to perform simple and complex computations, etc.

In LEACTIVEMATH, we identified six major learning goals and used them as a basis to define the scenarios. They refer to typical learning phases, like *introduction* or *practice* as described, e. g., by Zech [215], p. 181ff. Each scenario determines the basic structure of a course, for instance, by prescribing that the presentation of an example should follow the presentation of a definition. The scenarios are adaptive, that is, different resources can be selected by taking information from the learner model into account, such as the learner's motivational state or his success in solving previous exercises.

Course generation selects, orders, and structures educational resources. Thus it performs a range of activities that a learner might have performed on her own. Does this contradict the constructivist paradigm that knowledge is and has to be constructed by the individual? We argue that it does not: constructivism does not imply to drop the learner in a labyrinth of educational resources and to let her find out a way on her own. Instead, providing structure and selection as done by PAIGOS is beneficial to learning:

Studies show that students rarely develop explicit learning strategies on their own: "[t]he majority of learners is (still) not prepared for this [learning with computer technology]. Therefore an efficient self-guided usage of the offered learning opportunities cannot take place" ([179], p. 110, translated by the author). He continues: "the first positive effects regarding the acquisition of knowledge are shown by learners with adequate learning requirements (e.g., possessing previous knowledge, a good spatial sense, appropriate learning strategies)". According to Tergan, disorientation and cognitive overload are the principal obstacles of self-regulated learning in technology-supported learning.

In a related study, Prenzel et al. [147] show that in particular low-achieving students may benefit from content organized according to pedagogical principles, a finding that is supported by other PISA studies [137].

These studies provide evidence that students must *learn* to self-regulate their learning process since most of them do not posses this skill. Consequently, providing structured content is an important requirement for course generation since then the generated courses provide examples of how to deal with the offered content. They show how the material can be structured or ordered depending on the educational objectives.

It is important to note that although the content is pre-structured, the generated courses do not impose any restrictions on the learner in contrast to standards as IMS SS. If the learning environment that presents the courses does not add limitations, then the learner is never constrained in his navigation. He can freely browse through a course and has full access to the complete content available via the search facility. Schulmeister [162], p. 151–162 showed in his comprehensive meta-review that placing the locus of control in the hands of the learner is one of the few measures in technology-supported learning that has repeatedly proven to increase motivation.

In the following, I describe the different scenarios formalized in LEACTIVEMATH. The first two sections cover the selection of the exercises and examples, which is shared across the different scenarios. Since all methods that select auxiliaries perform the selection with respect to a fundamental f, I will often omit this fact from the description of the methods.

5.1.2 Selecting Exercises

The methods presented in this section implement the pedagogical knowledge of selecting exercises that are "appropriate" for the learner. The exact meaning of "appropriate" differs depending on the individual learner. For instance, if he is highly motivated then a slightly more difficult exercise might be selected.

The most relevant factors are the educational level of the learner[1] and his current competency level. In general, the learning context of an educational resource (of all resources, not only exercises) should always correspond to the educational level of the learner. Otherwise, it may be inadequate, e. g., either too simple or too difficult (e. g., think of a second year university student being presented a definition for elementary school).

The competency level of a resource measures how far a specific competency has to be developed by the student in order to solve/understand the particular exercise/example with a certain probability. In most cases, resources presented to the learner should have a competency level that corresponds to the learner's since these are the resources he is able to master with a high probability. In some situations resources with a higher competency level need to be selected, e. g., when aiming at increasing the competency level.

Most of the following methods do not make use of the difficulty level of a resource. This is caused by the competency-based approach in LeActive-Math. There, the competency level takes precedence over the difficulty level, and the difficulty level allows differentiating between resources at the same competency level, which is only rarely required in the LeActiveMath scenarios.

5.1.2.1 Selecting Exercises for a Fundamental

The task that governs exercise selection is (trainWithSingleExercise! f), which triggers the insertion of an exercise for the fundamental f. All methods that formalize the knowledge of how to select an exercise follow a same basic scheme, which I will explain using the method in Figure 5.2. In short, the method specifies that if a learner is highly motivated, then it inserts a subtask that selects an exercise of the next higher competency level. This method is based on the strong positive correlation between motivation and performance [144]: with increasing motivation, performance increases, too (and vice versa).

---

[1] Recall that the learner has reached an "educational level", while an educational resource was written for a "learning context". The values of both properties correspond, i. e., for each educational level there exists the corresponding learning context.

```
1   (:method (trainWithSingleExercise! ?c)
2          (;; preconditions
3          (learnerProperty hasMotivation ?c ?m)
4          (call >= ?m 4)
5          (learnerProperty hasField ?field)
6          (learnerProperty hasEducationalLevel ?el)
7          (learnerProperty hasCompetencyLevel ?c ?cl)
8          (equivalent (call + 1 ?cl) ?ex_cl)
9          (assign ?unsortedExercises
10                 (call GetResources
11                  ((class Exercise)
12                   (relation isFor ?c)
13                   (property hasLearningContext ?el)
14                   (property hasCompetencyLevel ?ex_cl)
15                   (property hasField ?field))))
16         (sortByAlreadySeen ?exercises ?unsortedExercises)
17         (assignIterator ?exercise ?exercises)
18         )
19         (;; subtask
20         (insertWithVariantsIfReady! ?exercise ?c)
21         )
22         )
```

Fig. 5.2. Example of a method for `trainWithSingleExercise`

In the figure, lines 3–8 prepare the ground for selecting the exercise (all axioms and operators used in the method were explained in Chapter 4). The first two lines (lines 3–4) specify the condition under which the method can be applied, in this case, if the learner is highly motivated. The axiom `learnerProperty` binds the current motivation represented by a number between 1 and 4 to the variable ?m (line 3). The call expression in line 4 tests whether ?m is greater or equal to 4.[2] The following lines 5–8 collect information about the learner used to specify the metadata constraint, i. e., the field of interest of the learner (line 5), his educational level (line 6), and his competency level (lines 7–8). Since the competence level of a learner is given as a integer between 1 and 4, but the metadata of the resources use keywords, the keyword that corresponds to the integer has to be retrieved using an axiom (line 8). In addition, the integer value is increased by 1, since the exercise should be of a higher competence level.[3] The information collected up to now is used to instantiate a mediator request. The request includes the constraints

---

[2] In theory, it would be sufficient to test whether ?m is *equal* to 4, the highest possible value. However, due to technical reasons, it is necessary to test *greater or equal*.

[3] In case the learner has reached the highest competence level, increasing the value has no effect (as does decreasing the competency level below 1.)

that the resources have the type `exercise` (line 11) and that they are `for` f (line 12). In lines 10–15, the request is sent to the mediator. If there exist any educational resources that fulfill the constraint, then they are bound to the variable `?unsortedExercises` in line 9. Line 16 sorts the list and moves any not yet seen resources to the front of the list. The axiom `assignIterator` causes to iterate through the list of exercises (line 17), and the subtask of the method inserts the first exercise that the learner is ready to see (line 20). If there is such an exercise, it is inserted and all its variants are marked as inserted. Otherwise, if none of the exercises bound to `?exercises` can be inserted or no exercises was found at all, then the planning algorithm backtracks and applies the next possible operator or method.

```
(learnerProperty hasMotivation ?c ?m)
(call >= ?m 4)
(learnerProperty hasField ?field)
(learnerProperty hasEducationalLevel ?el)
(learnerProperty hasCompetencyLevel ?c ?cl)
(equivalent (call + 1 ?cl) ?ex_cl)
```

Fig. 5.3. Selecting an exercise, high motivation

In the following explanations of methods, I will often show only those parts of the methods that vary (besides the call to the mediator, which varies, too). As an example, the relevant lines of the method of Figure 5.2 (lines 3–8) are shown in Figure 5.3.

```
1   (learnerProperty hasMotivation ?c ?m)
2   (call <= ?m 1)
3   (learnerProperty hasField ?field)
4   (learnerProperty hasEducationalLevel ?el)
5   (learnerProperty hasCompetencyLevel ?c ?cl)
6   (equivalent (call - ?cl 1) ?ex_cl)
```

Fig. 5.4. Selecting an exercise, low motivation

The method in Figure 5.3 is the first method evaluated for the exercise selection triggered by the task `trainWithSingleExercise!`. The second method is illustrated in Figure 5.4. In case the learner exhibits a low motivation (lines 1–2), then an exercise of a lower competence level (lines 5–6) is presented if available.

Otherwise, the course generator tries to insert an exercise whose metadata corresponds directly to the learner's characteristics: if available, an exercise

```
(learnerProperty hasField ?field)
(learnerProperty hasEducationalLevel ?el)
(learnerProperty hasCompetencyLevel ?c ?cl)
(equivalent ?cl ?ex_cl)
```

Fig. 5.5. Selecting an exercise, adequate competence level

is selected that has the learner's field and corresponds to the learner's educational and competency level (Figure 5.5). The subsequent methods relax the preconditions, starting by omitting the constraint on the field value (see Figure 5.6).

```
(learnerProperty hasEducationalLevel ?el)
(learnerProperty hasCompetencyLevel ?c ?cl)
(equivalent ?cl ?ex_cl)
```

Fig. 5.6. Selecting an exercise, any field

```
(learnerProperty hasField ?field)
(learnerProperty hasEducationalLevel ?el)
(learnerProperty hasCompetencyLevel ?c ?cl)
(equivalent (call - ?cl 1) ?ex_cl)
```

Fig. 5.7. Selecting an exercise, lower competence level

```
(learnerProperty hasEducationalLevel ?el)
(learnerProperty hasCompetencyLevel ?c ?cl)
(equivalent (call - ?cl 1) ?ex_cl)
```

Fig. 5.8. Selecting an exercise, lower competence level, any field

If still no adequate exercise was found, the methods in Figure 5.7 and 5.8 search for exercises on the next lower competency level, first with and then without the field constraint. The rationale is that it is better to present a exercise with a too low competency level than one of a different learning context since resources from a different learning context might be harder to understand than "easier" resources.

```
1    (learnerProperty hasField ?field)
2    (learnerProperty hasMotivation ?c ?m)
3    (call >= ?m 4)
4    (learnerProperty hasCompetencyLevel ?c ?cl)
5    (equivalent (call + 1 ?cl) ?ex_cl)
6    (learnerProperty hasAllowedEducationalLevel ?aels)
7    (assignIterator ?el ?aels)
```

Fig. 5.9. Selecting an exercise, high motivation, lower educational level

The next set of methods repeats the approach described in the methods illustrated in Figures 5.3 to 5.8 but relax the constraint on the educational level. The learner property `hasAllowedEducationalLevel` returns a list of all educational levels that the current user is able to understand, besides his original one. For instance, resources for university first year student are "allowed" for second year university students. The precise meaning of this learner property is handled by the part of the learner model that stores the learner's preferences. Since these six methods are analogous to the above methods, only one is displayed (see Figure 5.9). The difference to the previous methods is that the lines 6–7 cause the method to iterate over all allowed educational levels: in case no suited exercise is found for the first allowed educational level, then backtracking causes to try the next one, until either an exercise could be inserted or backtracking leads to apply the next method. However, no further methods for exercise selection that use the task (`trainWithSingleExercise!` f) exist. Thus, if no exercise was found at this place, then the task cannot be achieved.

5.1.2.2 Selecting Exercises for a Fundamental with Additional Constraints

Sometimes it is necessary to search for exercises that are of a specific competency and difficulty level. Hence, a set of methods equivalent to those described in the previous section exists that adds constraints on difficulty and competency. A complete example is shown in Figure 5.10. The displayed method is analogous to the method show in Figure 5.2, but uses the values of difficulty and competency given as parameters to further restrict the mediator query (lines 16–17). To keep the volume within reasonable length, I omit the remaining methods from the description.

5.1.2.3 Least Constrained Exercise Selection

A method for least constrained exercise selection is shown in Figure 5.11. This method is applicable on the task atom `trainWithSingleExerciseRelaxed!`. This task serves as a fallback task in case none of the above methods could

```
1    (:method (trainWithSingleExercise! ?c ?difficulty ?competency)
2             (
3             (learnerProperty hasMotivation ?c ?m)
4             (call >= ?m 4)
5             (learnerProperty hasField ?field)
6             (learnerProperty hasEducationalLevel ?el)
7             (learnerProperty hasCompetencyLevel ?c ?cl)
8             (equivalent (call + 1 ?cl) ?ex_cl)
9             (assign ?unsortedExercises
10                       (call GetResources
11                         ((class Exercise)
12                          (relation isFor ?c)
13                          (property hasLearningContext ?el)
14                          (property hasCompetencyLevel ?ex_cl)
15                          (property hasField ?field)
16                          (property hasDifficulty ?difficulty)
17                          (property hasCompetency ?competency))))
18             (sortByAlreadySeen ?exercises ?unsortedExercises)
19             (assignIterator ?exercise ?exercises)
20             )
21             (
22             (insertWithVariantsIfReady! ?exercise ?c)
23             )
24             )
```

Fig. 5.10. Selecting an exercise, for specific difficulty and competency

be applied but presenting a potentially slightly inadequate exercise is preferred over presenting no exercise at all. This method omits the constraint on the competency level and traverses all potential educational levels. In addition, it does not check whether the learner is "ready" to understand the exercise but directly inserts it if it was not already inserted (using the task insertResourceOnce!).

5.1.2.4 Selecting a Sequence of Exercises That Covers All Competencies

Figure 5.12 contains parts of the method that selects a sequence of exercises. The exercises cover all competencies as far as there exist adequate exercises for the competencies. The rationale of this method was to implement what Reinmann-Rothmeier and Mandl [151] call "learning in multiple contexts": present new content in different application situations.

First, the method tests whether there exists a resource that will ensure that any of its subtasks are achievable, otherwise the method is not applicable. Although this test is not required technically speaking, it increases the

```
(:method (trainWithSingleExerciseRelaxed! ?competency ?c)
        (
        (learnerProperty hasAllowedEducationalLevel ?aels)
        (learnerProperty hasEducationalLevel ?edl)
        (assignIterator ?el (?edl . ?aels))
        (assign ?unsortedExercises
                (call GetResources
                  ((class Exercise)
                   (relation isFor ?c)
                   (property hasLearningContext ?el)
                   (property hasCompetency ?competency))))
        (sortByAlreadySeen ?exercises ?unsortedExercises)
        (assignIterator ?exercise ?exercises)
        )
        (
        (insertResourceOnce! ?exercise)
        )
        )
```

Fig. 5.11. Selecting an exercise, any competency level, applicable on `trainWith-SingleExerciseRelaxed!`

```
 1   (:method (train! ?c)
 2           MethodTrain!
 3           (
 4           (learnerProperty hasAllowedEducationalLevel ?aels)
 5           (learnerProperty hasEducationalLevel ?edl)
 6           (assignIterator ?el (?edl . ?aels))
 7           (call GetResources
 8                   ((class Exercise)
 9                    (relation isFor ?c)
10                    (property hasLearningContext ?el))))
11           (
12           (trainWithSingleExercise ?c very_easy think)
13           (trainWithSingleExercise ?c very_easy solve)
14           (trainWithSingleExercise ?c very_easy represent)
15           (trainWithSingleExercise ?c very_easy language)
16           (trainWithSingleExercise ?c very_easy model)
17           (trainWithSingleExercise ?c very_easy argue)
18           (trainWithSingleExercise ?c very_easy tools)
19           (trainWithSingleExercise ?c very_easy communicate)
20           ...
21           (trainWithSingleExerciseRelaxed ?c)
22           )
23           )
```

Fig. 5.12. Inserting a sequence of exercises

efficiency of the course generation process significantly. The planner will avoid attempting to expand the subtasks in case none of them is achievable. If the method is applicable, the method inserts subtasks that for each difficulty level and for each competency cause the insertion of an exercise if it exists. In the figure, the lines 12–19 show the first set of tasks. For each competency, the subtasks try to insert a very easy exercise. This pattern is repeated for each difficulty level (not shown in the figure). The preconditions of the method for the final subtask (`trainWithSingleExerciseRelaxed`) correspond to the preconditions of this method. In this manner, if the preconditions are fulfilled, then at least the final subtask of the method can be achieved.

A previous version of the method did not include the final relaxed subtask. However, it turned out that this imposed too hard constraints on the content. Often, no completely adequate resource would exist and thus no exercises were presented at all. Thus, we decided to add the relaxed subtask in this and similar methods, in order to present at least some resources. The formative and summative evaluation investigated whether this design decision had any negative impact on the learners' opinion regarding resource selection. This was not the case as the results discussed in Section 7 will show.

5.1.2.5 Selecting a Sequence of Exercises for a Specific Competency

The task (`practiceCompetency` *competency* f) triggers the insertion of exercises that train a specific competency *competency* for a given fundamental f. The method that achieves the task is shown in Figure 5.13. Its precondition serves to test whether there exists at least one exercise that fulfills one of the subtasks. If so, the method's task is decomposed into subtasks that try to insert exercises for the given competency with increasing difficulty. The final subtasks guarantees that at least one exercise is inserted.

5.1.3 Selecting Examples

The example selection formalized in PAIGOS is very similar to the exercise selection. The main difference is that the field of an example is considered as being more important than in exercise selection: examples illustrate aspects of a fundamental and should, if possible, use situations and provide context of the learner's field of interest.

5.1.3.1 Selecting Examples for a Fundamental

The task that governs example selection is (`illustrateWithSingleExample!` f). If achieved, it triggers the insertion of an example for the fundamental f. The method in Figure 5.14 is the first method that is applied when selecting an example and is applicable if there exists an example with a field that matches

```
(:method (practiceCompetency ?competency ?c)
        (
          (learnerProperty hasAllowedEducationalLevel ?aels)
          (learnerProperty hasEducationalLevel ?edl)
          (assignIterator ?el (?edl . ?aels))
          (call GetResources
            ((class Exercise)
             (relation isFor ?c)
             (property hasLearningContext ?el)
             (property hasCompetency ?competency)))
        )
        (
          (trainWithSingleExercise ?c very_easy ?competency)
          (trainWithSingleExercise ?c very_easy ?competency)
          (trainWithSingleExercise ?c easy ?competency)
          (trainWithSingleExercise ?c easy ?competency)
          (trainWithSingleExercise ?c medium ?competency)
          (trainWithSingleExercise ?c medium ?competency)
          (trainWithSingleExercise ?c difficult ?competency)
          (trainWithSingleExercise ?c difficult ?competency)
          (trainWithSingleExercise ?c very_difficult ?competency)
          (trainWithSingleExercise ?c very_difficult ?competency)
          (trainWithSingleExerciseRelaxed ?competency ?c)
        )
)
```

Fig. 5.13. Training a competency with increasing difficulty level

the field of the learner and a learning context and competency level that corresponds to the learner's educational level and competency level (lines 3–6). Similar to the exercise selection, examples that the learner has not yet seen are preferred (line 14). In the reminder of this section, I explain only those parts of the methods that vary. For the method in Figure 5.14, these are the lines 3–6, shown in Figure 5.15.

The second method, shown in Figure 5.16 omits the constraint on the competency level and tries to insert an example that has the field of the learner and corresponds to her educational level.

If still no example was found, then the next method omits the constraint on the field, but reintroduces the competency level (Figure 5.17).

The methods in Figures 5.18–5.20 perform the same functionality as the first three methods, but relax the constraint on the educational level by taking into account all allowed educational levels.

```
1   (:method (illustrateWithSingleExample! ?c)
2           (
3           (learnerProperty hasField ?field)
4           (learnerProperty hasEducationalLevel ?el)
5           (learnerProperty hasCompetencyLevel ?c ?cl)
6           (equivalent ?cl ?ex_cl)
7           (assign ?unsortedExamples
8                   (call GetResources
9                    ((class Example)
10                     (relation isFor ?c)
11                     (property hasLearningContext ?el)
12                     (property hasCompetencyLevel ?ex_cl)
13                     (property hasField ?field))))
14          (sortByAlreadySeen ?examples ?unsortedExamples)
15          (assignIterator ?example ?examples)
16          )
17          (
18          (insertWithVariantsIfReady! ?example ?c)
19          )
20          )
```

Fig. 5.14. Selecting an example for illustrateWithSingleExample!

```
(learnerProperty hasField ?field)
(learnerProperty hasEducationalLevel ?el)
(learnerProperty hasCompetencyLevel ?c ?cl)
(equivalent ?cl ?ex_cl)
```

Fig. 5.15. Selecting an example, adequate field and competency level

```
(learnerProperty hasField ?field)
(learnerProperty hasEducationalLevel ?el)
```

Fig. 5.16. Selecting an example, adequate field

```
(learnerProperty hasEducationalLevel ?el)
(learnerProperty hasCompetencyLevel ?c ?cl)
(equivalent ?cl ?ex_cl)
```

Fig. 5.17. Selecting an example, adequate competency level

```
(learnerProperty hasField ?field)
(learnerProperty hasCompetencyLevel ?c ?cl)
(equivalent ?cl ?ex_cl)
(learnerProperty hasAllowedEducationalLevel ?aels)
(assignIterator ?el ?aels)
```

Fig. 5.18. Selecting an example, adequate field and competency level, lower educational level

```
(learnerProperty hasField ?field)
(learnerProperty hasAllowedEducationalLevel ?aels)
(assignIterator ?el ?aels)
```

Fig. 5.19. Selecting an example, adequate field, lower educational level

```
(learnerProperty hasCompetencyLevel ?c ?cl)
(equivalent ?cl ?ex_cl)
(learnerProperty hasAllowedEducationalLevel ?aels)
(assignIterator ?el ?aels)
```

Fig. 5.20. Selecting an example, adequate competency level, lower educational level

5.1.3.2 Selecting Examples for a Fundamental with Additional Constraints

Analogous to the exercise selection, a second set of methods exists for the example selection that adds constraints on difficulty and competency. Figure 5.21 shows the first of these methods, which corresponds to the first method for general example selection shown in Figure 5.14, but extends the mediator query with values for difficulty and competency (lines 14–15). The five other methods are not shown in this volume.

5.1.3.3 Least Constrained Example Selection

Figure 5.22 contains the fallback method used in case an example needs to be presented, but none of the previous methods was successfully applied (task illustrateWithSingleExampleRelaxed!). In order to be selected by the method, an example needs to have an allowed learning context and must not yet been inserted in the course.

```
1   (:method (illustrateWithSingleExample! ?c ?difficulty ?competency)
2            (;; preconditions
3             (learnerProperty hasField ?field)
4             (learnerProperty hasEducationalLevel ?el)
5             (learnerProperty hasCompetencyLevel ?c ?cl)
6             (equivalent ?cl ?ex_cl)
7             (assign ?unsortedExamples
8                     (call GetResources
9                       ((class Example)
10                       (relation isFor ?c)
11                       (property hasLearningContext ?el)
12                       (property hasCompetencyLevel ?ex_cl)
13                       (property hasField ?field)
14                       (property hasDifficulty ?difficulty)
15                       (property hasCompetency ?competency))))
16            (sortByAlreadySeen ?examples ?unsortedExamples)
17            (assignIterator ?example ?examples)
18            )
19            (;; subtask
20             (insertWithVariantsIfReady! ?example ?c)
21            )
22            )
```

Fig. 5.21. Selecting an example, taking difficulty and competency into account

```
(:method (illustrateWithSingleExampleRelaxed! ?c)
         (
          (learnerProperty hasAllowedEducationalLevel ?aels)
          (learnerProperty hasEducationalLevel ?edl)
          (assignIterator ?el (?edl . ?aels))
          (assign ?unsortedExamples
                  (call GetResources
                    ((class Example)
                     (relation isFor ?c)
                     (property hasLearningContext ?el))))
          (sortByAlreadySeen ?examples ?unsortedExamples)
          (assignIterator ?example ?examples)
          )
         (
          (insertResourceOnce! ?example)
          )
         )
```

Fig. 5.22. Selecting an example, any competency level, applicable on illustrateWithSingleExampleRelaxed!

5.1.3.4 Selecting a Sequence of Examples That Covers All Competencies

The method shown in Figure 5.23 is applicable on the task illustrate! and inserts a sequence of examples. It has the same structure as the method for exercise selection shown in Figure 5.12: the preconditions test whether there exists at least one example that can be inserted by one of the subtasks. If so, the method inserts subtasks that for each difficulty level and for each competency try to insert an example (in the figure, the pattern is only shown for the easiest difficulty level). The final subtask ensures that at least a single example is inserted.

```
(:method (illustrate! ?c)
        (
        (learnerProperty hasAllowedEducationalLevel ?aels)
        (learnerProperty hasEducationalLevel ?edl)
        (assignIterator ?el (?edl . ?aels))
        (call GetResources
              ((class Example)
               (relation isFor ?c)
               (property hasLearningContext ?el))))
        (
        (illustrateWithSingleExample ?c very_easy think)
        (illustrateWithSingleExample ?c very_easy solve)
        (illustrateWithSingleExample ?c very_easy represent)
        (illustrateWithSingleExample ?c very_easy language)
        (illustrateWithSingleExample ?c very_easy model)
        (illustrateWithSingleExample ?c very_easy argue)
        (illustrateWithSingleExample ?c very_easy tools)
        (illustrateWithSingleExample ?c very_easy communicate)
        ...
        (illustrateWithSingleExampleRelaxed ?c)
        )
        )
```

Fig. 5.23. Inserting a sequence of examples

5.1.3.5 Selecting a Sequence of Examples for a Specific Competency

The task (illustrateCompetency! *competency f*) inserts a sequence of examples that illustrate the given competency *competency* of the given fundamental *f*. The method applicable on this task is shown in Figure 5.24. Its precondition serves to test whether there exists at least one example that can

```
(:method (illustrateCompetency! ?competency ?c)
         (
         (learnerProperty hasAllowedEducationalLevel ?aels)
         (learnerProperty hasEducationalLevel ?edl)
         (assignIterator ?el (?edl . ?aels))
         (call GetResources
          ((class Example)
           (relation isFor ?c)
           (property hasLearningContext ?el)
           (property hasCompetency ?competency)))
         )
         (
         (illustrateWithSingleExample ?c very_easy ?competency)
         (illustrateWithSingleExample ?c very_easy ?competency)
         (illustrateWithSingleExample ?c easy ?competency)
         (illustrateWithSingleExample ?c easy ?competency)
         (illustrateWithSingleExample ?c medium ?competency)
         (illustrateWithSingleExample ?c medium ?competency)
         (illustrateWithSingleExample ?c difficult ?competency)
         (illustrateWithSingleExample ?c difficult ?competency)
         (illustrateWithSingleExample ?c very_difficult ?competency)
         (illustrateWithSingleExample ?c very_difficult ?competency)
         (illustrateWithSingleExampleRelaxed ?competency ?c)
         )
         )
```

Fig. 5.24. Illustrating a competency with increasing difficulty level

fulfill one of the subtasks. If so, the task is decomposed into subtasks that try to insert examples for the given competency with increasing difficulty. The final subtask guarantees that at least one example is inserted.

In the following sections, I describe the formalization of the six scenarios developed in LEACTIVEMATH. Each scenario is explained in a top-down manner, starting with the goal task of the scenario and then gradually diving into the hierarchy of tasks and subtasks.

5.1.4 Scenario "Discover"

The scenario "discover" generates courses that contain those educational resources that support the learner in reaching an in-depth understanding of the fundamentals given in the goal task. The course includes the prerequisites fundamentals that are unknown to the learner. It also provides the learner with several opportunities to use learning-supporting services.

The basic structure of the scenario follows the course of action in a classroom as described by Zech [215], which consists of several stages that typically occur when learning a new fundamental. For each stage, the course contains a corresponding section. The following sections are created:

Description. The course starts with a description of its aim and structure. Then, for each fundamental given in the goal task, the following sections are created.

Introduction. This section motivates the usefulness of the fundamental using adequate auxiliaries (for all stages, the precise meaning of an "adequate" educational resources is explained in the formalized methods below). It also contains the unknown prerequisites.

Develop. This section presents the fundamental and illustrates how it can be applied.

Proof. For some fundamentals (theorems), proofs, or more general evidence supporting the fundamentals is presented.

Practice. This section provides opportunities to train the fundamental.

Connect. This section illustrates the connections between the current fundamental and related fundamentals.

Reflection. Each course closes with a reflection section, which provides the learner with opportunity to reflect on what he has learned in the course.

5.1.4.1 Top-Level Decomposition of "Discover"

The two methods illustrated in Figure 5.25 start the generation of a course for the scenario "discover". The upper method decomposes the task (discover f) into five subtasks. First, a new section is started, in this case the course itself (line 4). Then, a description about the course's aims and structure is inserted (line 5). The third subtask triggers a method that recursively inserts the task (learnFundamentalDiscover g) for each identifier g in the list of identifiers bound to ?fundamentals. The last two subtasks insert the reflection section and close the course.

The methods that insert the tasks (learnFundamentalDiscover g) for each fundamental g are not shown in the figure since they follow the schema illustrated previously in other methods: one method recursively inserts the task for each element in the list, and a second method ends the recursion if the list becomes empty (the base case).

For each fundamental g, a task (learnFundamentalDiscover g) is created. The bottom method in Figure 5.25 decomposes the task into subtasks which closely resemble the structure of the scenario as described in the previous section. They will be discussed in the following.

5.1.4.2 Section "Introduction"

An introduction of a fundamental f in the scenario "discover" consists of a section that contains one or several educational resources that introduce f and of a section that contains the prerequisite fundamentals that the learner

```
1    (:method (discover ?fundamentals)
2            ()
3            (
4            (!startSection Discover ?fundamentals
5                          (discover ?fundamentals))
6            (descriptionScenarioSection ?fundamentals)
7            (learnFundamentalsDiscover ?fundamentals)
8            (reflect ?fundamentals)
9            (!endSection)
10           )
11           )
12
13   (:method (learnFundamentalDiscover ?c)
14           ()
15           (
16           (!startSection Title (?c
17                          (learnFundamentalDiscover (?c)))
18           (introduceWithPrereqSection ?c)
19           (developFundamental ?c)
20           (proveSection ?c)
21           (practiceSection ?c)
22           (showConnectionsSection ?c)
23           (!endSection)
24           )
25           )
```

Fig. 5.25. Top-level decomposition in the scenario "discover"

```
(:method (introduceWithPrereqSection! ?c)
        ()
        ((introduceWithSection! ?c)
         (learnPrerequisitesFundamentalsShortSection! ?c)))
```

Fig. 5.26. introduceWithPrereqSection generates an introduction that includes prerequisites

needs to see. The method in Figure 5.26 displays the method for the critical task. As explained earlier, for each critical task there exists an optional task and the corresponding methods. Due to space reasons, they are not shown here.

The resources that introduce a fundamental f are determined by the method in Figure 5.27. The method starts a new section and inserts a text that explains the purpose of the section. The following three tasks try to insert several resources: a resource that motivates the fundamental f, a resource that

```
(:method (introduceWithSection! ?c)
         ()
         (
         (!startSection Introduction (?c)
                 (introduceWithSection! (?c)))
         (text Introduction (?c))
         (motivate! ?c)
         (problem! ?c)
         (insertIntroductionExample! ?c)
         (!endSection)
         )
         )
```

Fig. 5.27. introduceWithSection! generates an introduction

```
1    (:method (problem! ?c)
2            (
3            (learnerProperty hasEducationalLevel ?el)
4            (assignIterator ?r
5                    (call GetResources
6                        ((class RealWorldProblem)
7                        (relation isFor ?c)
8                        (property hasLearningContext ?el)))))
9            (
10           (insertResourceOnce! ?r)
11           )
12           )
```

Fig. 5.28. problem! selects a real-world-problem

contains a real-world-problem involving f, and an example that illustrates the application of f.

Figure 5.28 contains the method responsible for the selection of a real-world-problem. (task (problem! f)). It retrieves all resources that are of type RealWorldProblem (lines 4–7) and inserts the first one not already inserted (line 9). An analogous method exists that takes all allowed educational levels into account.

5.1.4.3 Motivating a Fundamental

Several methods encode the knowledge how to catch the learner's interest regarding a fundamental. If the learner exhibits no fear of mathematics, then the method in Figure 5.29 tries to insert into the course a very easy exercise that is also an introduction (an equivalent method exists for an easy exercise).

```
(:method (motivate! ?c)
        (
        (learnerProperty hasAnxiety ?c ?an)
        (call <= ?an 2)
        (learnerProperty hasEducationalLevel ?el)
        (assignIterator ?r
                        (call GetResources
                         ((class Exercise)
                          (class Introduction)
                          (relation isFor ?c)
                          (property hasLearningContext ?el)
                          (property hasDifficulty very_easy)))))
        (
        (insertAuxOnceIfReady! ?r ?c)
        )
        )
```

Fig. 5.29. Motivating a fundamental, no anxiety

```
(:method (motivate! ?c)
        ()
        ((insertIntroductionExample! ?c)))
```

Fig. 5.30. Motivating a fundamental using an example

The rationale is to provide a challenging but achievable exercise to the learner, which according to [91] fosters motivation.

Otherwise or if no such exercises exist, the method in Figure 5.30 uses the task (insertIntroductionExample! *f*) to insert an example as introduction. A specific set of methods explained in the following section implements this functionality since it is also required in other scenarios, in contrast to the introductory exercise selection explained above.

The method shown in Figure 5.31 searches for an educational resource that is an introduction and inserts it if available. An equivalent method extends the educational level to the allowed educational levels.

5.1.4.4 Using an Example as Introduction

The task of inserting an example as an introduction is performed by the method in Figure 5.32. It inserts a very easy example which is also an introduction if available. Two additional methods for the same task search for an easy and medium difficult example (not shown).

```
(:method (motivate! ?c)
        (
         (learnerProperty hasEducationalLevel ?el)
         (assignIterator ?r
                         (call GetResources
                          ((class Introduction)
                           (relation isFor ?c)
                           (property hasLearningContext ?el)))))
        (
         (insertAuxOnceIfReady! ?r ?c)
         )
        )
```

Fig. 5.31. Motivating a fundamental using an introduction

```
(:method (insertIntroductionExample! ?c)
        (
         (learnerProperty hasEducationalLevel ?el)
         (assignIterator ?r
                         (call GetResources
                          ((class Example)
                           (class Introduction)
                           (relation isFor ?c)
                           (property hasLearningContext ?el)
                           (property hasDifficulty very_easy))))
         )
        (
         (insertAuxOnceIfReady! ?r ?c)
         )
        )
```

Fig. 5.32. Introducing a fundamental using an example

5.1.4.5 Inserting Prerequisites

In the scenario "discover", all prerequisite fundamentals that are unknown to
the learner are presented on a single page. Thus the students easily distinguish
between the target fundamentals and the prerequisites.

The axiom shown in Figure 5.33 is used to retrieve the prerequisite fundamentals. In a first step, all fundamentals that are required by the fundamental
bound to ?c and whose learning context corresponds to the educational level
of the learner are collected using the call term GetRelated (lines 4–7). In case
some were found (line 8), they are sorted with respect to the prerequisite relationship requires (lines 9–12). Finally, those fundamentals that are known

```
1   (:- (collectUnknownPrereq ?c ?result)
2       (
3       (learnerProperty hasEducationalLevel ?el)
4       (assign ?resources (call GetRelated (?c) -1
5                           (((class Fundamental)
6                             (relation isRequiredBy ?c)
7                             (property hasLearningContext ?el)))))
8       (not (same ?resources nil))
9       (assign ?sorted (call Sort ?resources
10                          (((class Fundamental)
11                            (relation isRequiredBy ?c)
12                            (property hasLearningContext ?el)))))
13      (removeKnownFundamentals ?reversedUnknown ?sorted)
14      (assign ?result (call Reverse ?reversedUnknown))
15      )
16      )
```

Fig. 5.33. collectUnknowPrerq collects all unknown prerequisites

```
1   (:method (learnPrerequisitesFundamentalsShort! ?c)
2       (
3       (collectUnknownPrereq ?c ?result)
4       (not (same ?result nil))
5       )
6       ((insertAllResources ?result)))
```

Fig. 5.34. Inserting all unknown prerequisites

to the learner are removed using the axiom removeKnownFundamentals and
the result is bound to the variable ?result.

The axiom is used by the method shown in Figure 5.34. It first collects all
unknown fundamentals (in the precondition in line 3) and, if there are any,
adds a task that inserts them (line 6).

5.1.4.6 Section "Develop"

The section "develop" presents the fundamental, together with auxiliaries
that help the learner to understand it. Figure 5.35 shows the corresponding
method. Both precondition-subtask pairs start a new section, include a text
that explains the purpose of the section and insert the fundamental the section
is about. In case the learner exhibits a high competency level (tested in the
first precondition), a single example illustrates the fundamental. Otherwise,
the learner does not exhibit a high competency level, and first a text explaining the fundamental is inserted, followed by several examples that aim at

providing the learner with a first understanding of the fundamental. The example insertion uses the dynamic task (!dynamicTask illustrate! (?c)): the planning process does not expand this subtask, hence the specific examples are selected at a later time. The final subtask closes the section.

```
(:method (developFundamental ?c)
         ((learnerProperty hasCompetencyLevel ?c ?cl)
          (call >= ?cl 3))
         (
         (!startSection Title (?c) (developFundamental (?c)))
         (text Develop (?c))
         (!insertResource ?c)
         (illustrateWithSingleExample ?c)
         (!endSection)
         )

         ()
         (
         (!startSection Title (?c) (developFundamental (?c)))
         (text Develop (?c))
         (!insertResource ?c)
         (explain ?c)
         (!dynamicTask illustrate! (?c))
         (!endSection)
         )
         )
```

Fig. 5.35. Developing a fundamental

```
(:method (explain! ?c)
         (
         (learnerProperty hasEducationalLevel ?el)
         (assignIterator ?r (call GetResources
                            ((class Remark)
                             (relation isFor ?c)
                             (property hasLearningContext ?el)))))
         (
         (insertAuxOnceIfReady! ?r ?c)
         )
         )
```

Fig. 5.36. Explaining a fundamental

```
1   (:method (prove! ?c)
2          (
3          (learnerProperty hasCompetencyArgue ?c ?argue)
4          (call >= ?argue 3)
5          (learnerProperty hasEducationalLevel ?el)
6          (assignIterator ?exercise
7                          (call GetResources
8                                  ((class Exercise)
9                                  (relation isFor ?c)
10                                 (property hasLearningContext ?el)
11                                 (property hasCompetency argue))))
12         )
13         (
14         (insertAuxOnceIfReady! ?exercise ?c)
15         )
16         )
```

Fig. 5.37. Presenting a proof exercise

The method shown in Figure 5.36 provides information about a fundamental by inserting an educational resource of the type **Remark**. The fallback method that relaxes the constraint on the educational level by considering all allowed educational levels is not shown.

5.1.4.7 Section "Prove"

Proofs play an important role in mathematics and being able to prove is one aspect of the competency "argue". The methods in this section govern the insertion of proofs and proof exercises. However, instead of inserting educational resources of type **Proof**, the methods implement a more abstract approach and insert resources of type **Evidence**, the superclass of **Proof**. This way, the pedagogical approach implemented in the methods is also applicable to other areas than mathematics, e. g., physics, where demonstrations and experiments play an important role.

Resources of the type **Evidence** are for resources of the type **Law**, including its subclasses **Theorem** and **LawOfNature**. In case the methods explained in this section are applied on different subclasses of **Fundamental** than **Law**, they will fail, since the required resources will not exist (e. g., a proof for a definition). But still, the overall course will be generated, since the task (**prove!** f) is embedded in an optional task.

In case the learner has a high competency "argue", then she is able to find proofs or establish evidence on her own. Thus, the method shown in Figure 5.37 does not insert an evidence but an exercise for the competency "argue". The preconditions of the method check whether the learner has reached a high competency level for the competency argue (lines 3–4). In that case, a proof exercise is selected, i. e., an exercise for the competency "argue".

If the learner has not reached a high competency "argue", then resources of the type Evidence are inserted. In case more than a single evidence exists, the evidences are inserted ordered by increasing abstractness using the representational type: visually oriented evidence is presented first, followed by verbal, numeric, and symbolic evidence, and finally evidence that is not annotated with a representational type (since one cannot assume that all resources are annotated with this metadata). The evidences are followed by exercises that train the competency "argue".

Figure 5.38 shows parts of the method. Lines 5–10 retrieve evidences with a visual representation type. In case there exist several evidences, there is often a preferred order in which to show them to the learner. This order does not have to be induced by the domain, but can be based on purely pedagogical considerations. Since PAIGOS does not distinguish between pedagogical and domain dependencies (it was not necessary for the formalized scenarios), both types of dependencies are represented using the relation requires, which is used by PAIGOS to sort the evidences (lines 11–17). The preconditions in lines 5–17 are repeated for each representational type (not included in the figure). Then, lines 19–32 collect and sort all existing evidences, thereby including evidence without a representation value. Lines 33–34 remove the previously collected evidences, thus keeping only evidences without a representation value. These five collected lists of evidences ("visual", "verbal", "numeric", "symbolic", and no representation value) are concatenated (line 35–38). The subtasks of the method insert the resulting list (line 42) and proof exercises (line 43, the subtask will be explained in detail later).

5.1.4.8 Section "Practice"

The methods in the section "practice" insert a list of exercises that provide the learner with opportunities to develop her own understanding of the fundamental, from a variety of perspectives.

The method illustrated in Figure 5.39 creates a corresponding section. Note that the result of the call term GetResource (lines 6–10) is not bound to a variable. Its only purpose is to test whether there exists an exercise that can be inserted at a later time, when the dynamic task is expanded. This test is performed for each allowed educational level until matching resources are found. In case no resource was found for any educational level, the method is not applicable and backtracking takes place. If this test would not be performed, then it might happen that a dynamic task is inserted even if there are no exercises that can fulfill it.

The subtasks of the method start the section and insert a text that explains the purpose of the section (lines 13–14). Line 15 inserts a reference to a learning-supporting service called *exercise sequencer*. An exercise sequencer

```
1   (:method (prove! ?c)
2           MethodProveByProve!
3           (
4           (learnerProperty hasEducationalLevel ?edl)
5           (assign ?visualProofsUnsorted
6                   (call GetResources
7                           ((class Evidence)
8                            (relation isFor ?c)
9                            (property hasLearningContext ?edl)
10                           (property hasRepresentationType visual))))
11          (assign ?visualProofs
12                  (call Sort ?visualProofsUnsorted
13                          (((class Evidence)
14                            (relation isFor ?c)
15                            (relation isRequiredBy ?visualProofs)
16                            (property hasLearningContext ?edl)
17                            (property hasRepresentationType visual)))))
18          ...
19          (assign ?allWithRep
20                  (call Concat ?visualProofs ?verbalProofs
21                               ?numericProofs ?symbolicProofs))
22          (assign ?allProofsUnsorted
23                   (call GetResources
24                          ((class Evidence)
25                           (relation isFor ?c)
26                           (property hasLearningContext ?edl))))
27          (assign ?allProofs
28                  (call Sort ?allProofsUnsorted
29                          (((class Evidence)
30                            (relation isFor ?c)
31                            (relation isRequiredBy ?allProofsUnsorted)
32                            (property hasLearningContext ?edl)))))
33          (assign ?allProofsWithoutRep
34                  (call Restrict ?allProofs ?allWithRep))
35          (assign ?all
36                  (call Concat ?visualProofs ?verbalProofs
37                               ?numericProofs ?symbolicProofs
38                               ?allProofsWithoutRep))
39          (not (same nil ?all))
40          )
41          (
42          (insertAllResources ?all)
43          (practiceCompetencyForAllFundamentals argue ?all)
44          )
45          )
```

Fig. 5.38. Presenting proofs

```
1   (:method (practiceSection! ?c)
2            MethodPracticeSection!
3            (
4             (learnerProperty hasAllowedEducationalLevel ?aels)
5             (learnerProperty hasEducationalLevel ?edl)
6             (assignIterator ?el (?edl . ?aels))
7             (call
8              GetResources
9              ((class Exercise)
10              (relation isFor ?c)
11              (property hasLearningContext ?el)))
12            )
13            (
14             (!startSection Exercises (?c) (practiceSection! (?c)))
15             (text Practice (?c))
16             (!insertLearningService
17                    ExerciseSequencer TrainCompetencyLevel (?c))
18             (!dynamicTask train! (?c))
19             (!endSection)
20            )
21           )
```

Fig. 5.39. Training a fundamental

leads the learner interactively through a sequence of exercises until a terminating condition is reached, given by the second parameter. In this case, the parameter TrainCompetencyLevel specifies that the learner should reach the next higher competency level. Since some learners prefer not to use the exercise sequencer, the following subtask, a dynamic task, triggers the insertion of exercises (line 16, the task train! was explained in Section 5.1.2). Due to the preconditions, it is certain that this subtask can be fulfilled. The final subtask closes the section.

5.1.4.9 Section "Connect"

The section "connect" illustrates the connections between the current fundamental and related fundamentals of type law (including theorems). Figure 5.40 contains the corresponding method. If a concept mapping tool is available (tested in the precondition in line 2), it is used for displaying the connections (the subtask in line 3). Otherwise, the resources of the type law are inserted in the course.

The method in Figure 5.41 inserts the reference to a learning-support service of type CMap, i.e., a concept mapping tool (lines 10–13). The tool displays a given fundamental f and all fundamentals of the given type that

```
1   (:method (showConnections! ?c)
2            ((learningServiceAvailable CMap))
3            ((showConnectionsByCMap! ?c))
4
5            ()
6            ((showConnectionsByTheoremWithProof! ?c))
7            )
```

Fig. 5.40. Illustrating the connections of a fundamental to other fundamentals

```
1    (:method (showConnectionsByCMap! ?c)
2             (
3             (learnerProperty hasEducationalLevel ?el)
4             (call GetResources ((class Law)
5                                 (relation requires ?c)
6                                 (property hasLearningContext ?el)))
7             )
8             (
9             (text Connect (?c))
10            (!insertLearningService CMap display (?c)
11               (includeEdge1 isRequiredBy includeEdge2 isA
12                 includeEdge3 inverseIsA includeCategory1 Definition
13                 includeCategory2 Law computeNeighbourNodes 1))
14            )
15            )
```

Fig. 5.41. Illustrating connections using a concept mapping tool

are connected to f by the given relations. The method is applicable only if there exist resources that can be displayed (tested in lines 4–6).

In case a concept mapping tool is not available, the connections are made visible in the course by inserting all laws that require the current fundamental (the upper method in Figure 5.42, lines 4–7). The variables contain the word "Theorem" for historical reasons, but of course include resources of the type law. Those laws that are target fundamentals (line 8) and those that were already inserted (line 9) are excluded. The sorted laws are then inserted in the course, together with explanations and evidence (the lower method in Figure 5.42).

A similar method exists that is applicable on the task (showConnections-Theorem f). This method does not insert the subtask (prove ?theorem).

5.1.4.10 Section "Reflect"

Each course generated for the scenario "discover" closes with a reflection step, which provides the learner with opportunity to reflect on what he has

```
1    (:method (showConnectionsByTheoremWithProof! ?c)
2            (
3            (learnerProperty hasEducationalLevel ?el)
4            (assign ?allTheoremsH
5                    (call GetResources
6                        ((class Law)
7                        (relation requires ?c)
8                        (property hasLearningContext ?el))))
9            (getNonTargetFundamentals ?allTheoremsHH ?allTheoremsH)
10           (getNonInserted ?allTheorems ?allTheoremsHH)
11           (assign ?sortedTheorems
12                   (call Sort ?allTheorems
13                       (((class Law)
14                        (relation isRequiredBy allTheorems)
15                        (property hasLearningContext ?el)))))
16           (not (same ?sortedTheorems nil))
17           )
18           (
19           (text Connect (?c))
20           (showConnectionsTheoremsWithProof ?sortedTheorems)
21           )
22           )
23
24   (:method (showConnectionsTheoremWithProof ?theorem)
25           ()
26           ((insertResourceOnce! ?theorem)
27           (explain ?theorem)
28           (prove ?theorem)))
```

Fig. 5.42. Illustrating connections using theorems

learned in the course. Preferably, this is done using an Open Learner Model (OLM, [35]). The OLM in LEACTIVEMATH shows the learner its current beliefs about his competencies. The first precondition-subtask pair is applicable if an OLM is available. In that case, the method inserts a reference to the learning-support service whose parameters encode the fundamentals and the competency to display. The keyword competency denotes the aggregated competency.

In case, an OLM is not available, a text is inserted that prompts the learner to perform this reflection manually, e. g., "Please think about your learning process: How did you proceed? Did you understand everything? If not, try to look up the necessary content using the system".

```
1  (:method (reflect ?fundamentals)
2           ((learningServiceAvailable OLM))
3           (
4            (!startSection Reflection
5                          ?fundamentals (reflect ?fundamentals))
6            (!insertLearningService OLM display ?fundamentals
7                                 (competencyId competency))
8            (!endSection)
9            )
10
11           ()
12           ((!startSection Reflection
13                          ?fundamentals (reflect ?fundamentals))
14           (text Reflect ?fundamentals)
15           (!endSection)))
```

Fig. 5.43. Reflecting over the learned fundamentals

5.1.4.11 Example

Figure 5.44 contains a screenshot of a course generated for the scenario "discover" and the goal fundamentals "the definition of the derivative, resp., the differential quotient", "the definition of the derivative function" and the theorem "sum rule". The page displayed on the right hand side of the figure is the second page of the course. It contains the first items of the prerequisites page:

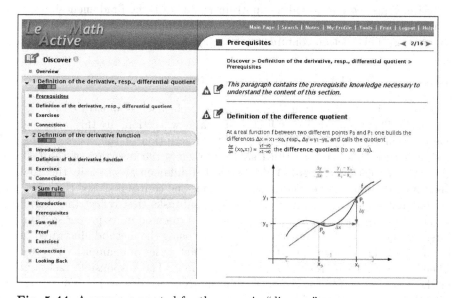

Fig. 5.44. A course generated for the scenario "discover"

the generated text that describes the purpose of the section and the first of the prerequisite fundamentals. The sections displayed in the table of contents vary in the pages they contain. For instance, the first section does not contain an introduction page. The reason is that no elements could be found to be displayed in this section and therefore, the section was skipped.

In the following, after each scenario description I present a screenshot of a course generated for the corresponding scenario, always for the same goal fundamentals. These examples illustrate the different kinds of course PAIGOS can generate.

5.1.5 Scenario "Rehearse"

Courses of the type "rehearse" are designed for learners who are already acquainted with the target fundamentals but do not yet master them completely. Such a course provides several opportunities to examine and practice applications of the fundamentals and illustrates the connections between fundamentals. The structure is as follows:

Description. The course starts with a description of its aim and structure. Then, for each fundamental given in the goal task, the following sections are created.

Rehearsing the Fundamental. This section presents the fundamental of the section.

Illustrate. This section presents example applications of the fundamental.

Connect. This section illustrate the connections between the current fundamental and related fundamentals.

Practice. This section provides opportunities to train the fundamental.

Illustrate–2. This section contains additional examples.

Practice–2. This section contains additional exercises.

5.1.5.1 Top-Level Decomposition of "Rehearse"

The top-level decomposition in the scenario "rehearse" is illustrated in Figure 5.45. The upper method first starts a new section, in this case the course itself (line 4), and then inserts the description of the course's aims and structure (line 5). The third subtask triggers the insertion of the task (rehearseSingleFundamental f) for each fundamental given in the goal task (line 6). Finally, the section that contains the course is closed (line 7).

The lower method in Figure 5.45 inserts subtasks that reflect the overall structure of the scenario. Each fundamental is presented in its proper section. First, in line 15, the fundamental is presented, using the method illustrated in Figure 5.46. The following subtask inserts a first series of examples (line 16). Then, connections to related laws are presented. The responsible task and methods correspond to those described in the scenario "discover", Figure 5.42, with the difference that evidences are not presented. The rationale behind this

```
1    (:method (rehearse ?fundamentals)
2            ()
3            (
4            (!startSection Rehearse
5                           ?fundamentals (rehearse ?fundamentals))
6            (descriptionScenarioSection ?fundamentals)
7            (rehearseFundamentals ?fundamentals)
8            (!endSection)
9            )
10           )
11
12   (:method (rehearseSingleFundamental ?c)
13           ()
14           (
15           (!startSection Title (?c)
16                                (rehearseSingleFundamental (?c)))
17           (insertFundamentalSectionWithText ?c)
18           (illustrateSection ?c)
19           (showConnectionsTheoremSection ?c)
20           (practiceSection ?c)
21           (!!changeScenario RehearseDeeper)
22           (illustrateSection ?c)
23           (practiceSection ?c)
24           (!!changeScenario Rehearse)
25           (!endSection)
26           )
27           )
```

Fig. 5.45. Top-level Decomposition in the scenario "rehearse"

```
(:method (insertFundamentalSectionWithText ?c)
        ()
        (
        (!startSection Title (?c)
                       (insertFundamentalSectionWithText (?c)))
        (text Develop (?c))
        (!insertResource ?c)
        (!endSection)
        )
        )
```

Fig. 5.46. Presenting a fundamental in a section

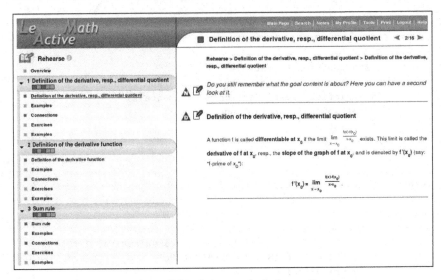

Fig. 5.47. A course generated for the scenario "rehearse"

decision is that while learning of a fundamental benefits from presenting it in context, in this scenario the focus does not lie on working with evidences, e. g., proofs. Since the methods differ only in that the task (prove c) is not inserted, they are not shown here.

The task in line 18 triggers the insertion of a number of exercises. After having worked on this section, the learner should have solved a number of exercises and her competency level should have changed accordingly. In order to deepen the learner's competencies, the lines 20–21 insert additional examples and exercises. The selected resources correspond to the learner's current level, since the selection is performed using dynamic tasks (see the subtasks of illustrate and train explained in Section 5.1.2 and 5.1.3). However, although the methods are reused, the texts explaining the purposes of the sections "illustrate" and "train" should differ from the texts introduced in the previous sections (in the lines 16 and 18). This is achieved by changing the scenario name (line 19). Since the operators used for text insertion use the scenario name as a context for text generation, changing the context will result in different titles. The last two lines revert to the old scenario name (line 22) and close the section (line 23).

5.1.5.2 Example

Figure 5.47 contains a screenshot of a course generated for the scenario "rehearse" and the same goal fundamentals as in the previous example: "the definition of the derivative, resp., the differential quotient", "the definition of the derivative function" and the theorem "sum rule". The page displayed on the right hand side of the figure is the second page of the course, which contains the definition rehearsed in the first section of the course.

5.1.6 Scenario "Connect"

The scenario "connect" helps the learner to discover connections among the fundamentals given in the goal task and other fundamentals and to provide opportunities to train the fundamentals. The rationale of this scenario is that laws connect definitions by describing some relationship between the definition, for instance, laws in physics put physical concepts in relation to each other, and that becoming aware of these connections is beneficial to the user's learning [133].

At first glance, the structure of the scenario seems complicated, therefore I will use the graph shown in Figure 5.48 as an example. In the graph, A, B, C and D denote definitions, and T_1 and T_2 denote theorems or other laws. The edges between the nodes denote the **requires** relationship, e. g., T_1 requires A. A course generated using the scenario "connect" is structured as follows:

Description. The course starts with a section that describes its aim and structure. Then, for each fundamental given in the goal task, say, A, the following sections are inserted.

Present Fundamental. The fundamental is inserted, together with a concept map that shows its connections to laws and definitions.

Connect. For this section, all definitions (excluding A) are retrieved that are required by those theorems that require A. In the figure, these are the definitions B, C and D since T_1 and T_2 both require A and require B, C and D. These are the definitions that are connected to A by theorems. Then, for each retrieved definition, say B, the following sections are created:

Illustrate. This section presents example applications of the definition.

Train. This section provide opportunities to train the definition.

Develop. This section develops the definition in the following way:

Present. The definition is presented.

Connect-2. This section presents all theorems that connect the original fundamental A with the definition B (T_1 in the example) and all previously processed definitions.

Train-Connection. The course ends with a section that contains a concept map exercise.

The scenario was developed in the context of mathematics, therefore, the following methods often use the term "theorem". However, the scenario applies to all educational resources of the type **law**.

5.1.6.1 Top-Level Decomposition of "Connect"

The top-level decomposition of the scenario "connect" (illustrated in Figure 5.49) is analogous to the other scenarios: a description is inserted, followed

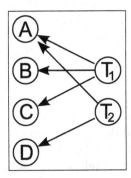

Fig. 5.48. An example illustrating the scenario "connect"

```
(:method (connect ?fundamentals)
         ()
         (
          (!startSection Connections
                         ?fundamentals (connect ?fundamentals))
          (descriptionScenarioSection ?fundamentals)
          (connectFundamentals ?fundamentals)
          (!endSection)
          ))
```

Fig. 5.49. Top-level decomposition of the scenario "connect"

by a subtask that triggers the insertion of tasks for all fundamentals of the goal task (`connectSingleFundamental`).

Figure 5.50 contains the principal method of the scenario "connect". It first retrieves all laws that require the current fundamental (lines 4–7). In the example, for the fundamental A the laws T_1 and T_2 are retrieved. In case no theorems were found, and thus no connections could be illustrated, the method is not applicable (line 8). Otherwise, in the lines 9–13 all definitions are collected that are required by the theorems (A, B and C in the example). The current resource is removed from the result (line 14) and the remaining resources are sorted (lines 15–19).

Then, a new section is started that first inserts the current fundamental (line 25) and a concept map (line 26). The concept map visualizes the connections to come. In line 29 a subtask is inserted that adds a new section for each collected definition. Its parameters contain the definitions for which a section still needs to be created and the already processed definitions, initialized with the current fundamental. The corresponding method is described below (Section 5.1.6.3). Finally, a concept map exercise is inserted into the course. In this exercise, the learner has to construct the previously shown relationships on his own.

```
1  (:method (connectSingleFundamental ?c)
2          (
3          (learnerProperty hasEducationalLevel ?el)
4          (assign ?theorems
5                  (call GetResources
6                          ((class Law)
7                           (relation requires ?c)
8                           (property hasLearningContext ?el))))
9          (not (same ?theorems nil))
10         (assign ?definitionsH
11                 (call GetRelated ?theorems 1
12                         (((class Definition)
13                           (relation isRequiredBy ?theorems)
14                           (property hasLearningContext ?el)))))
15         (removeElement ?definitions ?c ?definitionsH)
16         (assign ?sortedDefinitions
17                 (call Sort ?definitions
18                         (((class Definition)
19                           (relation isRequiredBy ?definitions)
20                           (property hasLearningContext ?el)))))
21         )
22         (
23         (!startSection Connections (?c)
24                         (connectSingleFundamental ?c))
25         (!startSection Title (?c))
26         (text Introduction (?c))
27         (!insertResource ?c)
28         (CMapConnect (call Concat (?c) ?theorems
29                                   ?sortedDefinitions))
30         (!endSection)
31         (!startSection ConnectionsOverview ?sortedDefinitions)
32         (developConnections ?sortedDefinitions (?c))
33         (!endSection)
34         (CMapConnectExerciseSection
35              (call Concat (?c) ?theorems ?sortedDefinitions))
36         (!endSection)
37         )
38         )
```

Fig. 5.50. Connecting a fundamental in the scenario "connect"

5.1.6.2 Displaying Concept Maps in the Scenario "Connect"

Figure 5.51 illustrates the method that inserts the concept map. The first pre-condition tests whether a concept map service is available. If so, then a reference to the service is inserted. Its parameters specify that the given resources should displayed, including all definitions and laws that are connected to the resources by the relation `requires` and `isRequiredBy`. If no concept map service is available then no subtask is inserted (the second precondition-subtask pair). An analogous method applicable on the task (`CMapConnectExercise resources`) inserts a link to a concept map exercise. In this exercise, the learner has to compose the concept map on his own.

```
(:method (CMapConnect ?resources)
         ((learningServiceAvailable CMap))
         (
          (!insertLearningService CMap display ?resources
             (includeEdge1 isRequiredBy includeEdge2 requires
              includeCategory1 Definition includeCategory2 Law))
         )

         ()
         ()
         )
```

Fig. 5.51. The concept mapping tool displays relationships

5.1.6.3 The Section "Connect"

The method in Figure 5.52 presents the definitions which were retrieved for the current fundamental from the goal task. Its first parameter contains the definitions that still need to be inserted in the course; its second parameter is instantiated with the already processed resources. They were initialized with all definitions collected previously and the current fundamental from the goal task (see the method illustrated in Figure 5.50). Each definition is illustrated and trained (lines 5–6). The subtask in line 7 presents the connections of the definition (described below). The final subtask serves to iterate through all collected definitions and adds the currently processed fundamental to the already processed fundamentals (the second parameter). The method applicable for the base case is not shown.

The method illustrated in Figure 5.53 inserts the laws that connect the already processed and the current definition (collected using the axiom in line 3, see below). The sorted laws are then inserted together with evidences (e. g., proofs). Each law is inserted only once, at the first occurrence.

```
1   (:method (developConnections (?c . ?rest) ?connected)
2              ()
3              (
4              (!startSection Title (?c) (developConnections (?c . ?rest)))
5              (illustrateSection ?c)
6              (practiceSection ?c)
7              (developConnectionSingleFundamental ?c ?connected)
8              (!endSection)
9              (developConnections ?rest (?c . ?connected))
10             )
11             )
```

Fig. 5.52. Developing a connected definition

```
1   :method (developConnectionSingleFundamental ?c ?fundamentals)
2              (
3              (collectConnectedTheorems ?theorems ?c ?fundamentals)
4              (learnerProperty hasEducationalLevel ?el)
5              (assign ?sortedTheorems
6                     (call Sort ?theorems
7                            (((class Law)
8                              (relation isRequiredBy placeholder)
9                              (property hasLearningContext ?el)
10                             )))))
11             (
12             (!startSection ConnectionsDetail (?c)
13                   (developConnectionSingleFundamental (?c)))
14             (text Connect (?c))
15             (!insertResource ?c)
16             (showConnectionsTheoremsWithProof ?sortedTheorems)
17             (!endSection)
18             )
19             )
```

Fig. 5.53. Inserting connecting laws

The axiom shown in Figure 5.54 retrieves all laws that connect the fundamental f that instantiates the parameter ?c with the fundamentals fs that instantiate ?fundamentals. It first collects all laws that require f (lines 4–7). Then, it retrieves the laws that require the fundamentals fs (lines 8–12). Line 13 removes those laws from the first list of laws that are not contained in the second list, i. e., it retains all laws that are required by f as well as by any fundamental contained in fs.

The remaining tasks and methods used in this scenario were described in the previous sections.

```
1    (:- (collectConnectedTheorems ?theorems ?c ?fundamentals)
2        (
3        (learnerProperty hasEducationalLevel ?el)
4        (assign ?theoremsA
5              (call GetResources ((class Law)
6                                  (relation requires ?c)
7                                  (property hasLearningContext ?el))))
8        (assign ?theoremsB
9              (call GetRelated ?fundamentals 1
10                   (((class Law)
11                     (relation requires placeholder)
12                     (property hasLearningContext ?el)))))
13        (assign ?theorems (call Retain ?theoremsA ?theoremsB))
14        )
15        )
```

Fig. 5.54. Collecting theorems for the connect step

5.1.6.4 Example

Figure 5.55 contains a screenshot of a course generated for the scenario "connect" and the goal fundamentals: "the definition of the derivative, resp., the differential quotient", "the definition of the derivative function" and the theorem "sum rule". The page displayed on the right hand side of the figure is the second page of the course, which contains the definition rehearsed in the first section and a concept map exercise that displays the connection between the fundamentals.

5.1.7 Scenario "Train Intensively"

A course generated for the scenario "train intensively" generates a workbook that aims at increasing the competency level of the learning by presenting a large selection of exercises. The exercises cover all competencies and are presented with increasing difficulty level.

5.1.7.1 Top-Level Decomposition of "Train Intensively"

Similar to the previous scenarios, for each fundamental in the goal task, a section is introduced that trains the single fundamental using the task (train-IntenseSingleFundamental ?c). Since the methods responsible for the decomposition are very similar to those described previously, I will omit them.

A fundamental is trained intensely by presenting numerous exercises, first at the learner's current competency level, then at the next higher competency level. The responsible method is shown in figure 5.56. The first precondition-subtask pair is applicable if the learner has reached the highest competency

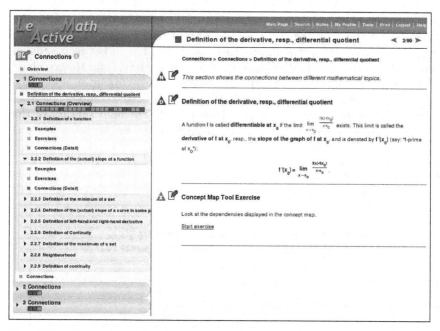

Fig. 5.55. A course generated for the scenario "connect"

```
1   (:method (trainIntenseSingleFundamental ?c)
2            (
3            (learnerProperty hasCompetencyLevel ?c ?v)
4            (call >= ?v 4.0)
5            )
6            (
7            (practiceAllCompetenciesSection ?c)
8            )
9
10           (
11           (learnerProperty hasCompetencyLevel ?c ?cl)
12           (assign ?newCl (call + ?cl 1.0))
13           )
14           (
15           (practiceAllCompetenciesSection ?c)
16           (!!setCompetencyLevel ?c ?newCl)
17           (practiceAllCompetenciesSection ?c)
18           (!!deleteSetCompetencyLevel ?c ?newCl)
19           )
20           )
```

Fig. 5.56. Intense training of a fundamental

level. In this case, only a single section of exercises is inserted into the course (using the task (practiceAllCompetenciesSection ?c)). The second precondition-action pair inserts this task twice, but in between adds an atom in the world state that changes the competency level (line 16, explained below). Since the methods for exercise selection use information about the competency level to perform their selection, increasing the competency level results in a selection of exercises of a higher level. The final subtask of the method removes the previously inserted atom from the world state.

```
1    (:operator (!!setCompetencyLevel ?c ?cl)
2                ()
3                ()
4                (
5                  (learnerProperty hasCompetencyLevel ?c ?cl)
6                  (set (learnerProperty hasCompetencyLevel ?c))
7                )
8                )
9
10   (:operator (!!deleteSetCompetencyLevel ?c ?cl)
11                (
12                  (learnerProperty hasCompetencyLevel ?c ?cl)
13                )
14                (
15                  (learnerProperty hasCompetencyLevel ?c ?cl)
16                  (set (learnerProperty hasCompetencyLevel ?c))
17                )
18                ()
19                )
20
21   (:- (learnerProperty ?property ?r ?value)
22        ((not (set (learnerProperty ?property ?r)))
23        (user ?userId)
24        (assign ?value (call LearnerProperty ?userId ?property ?r))))
```

Fig. 5.57. Manually setting the competency level

Figure 5.57 contains the operators used for changing the competency level. The first operator has no preconditions and an empty delete list, and adds in the world state an atom representing the new competency level (line 5) and an atom that indicates the fact that the competency was "manipulated". The second operator removes both facts previously inserted. An additional change is required to the axiom learnerProperty that accesses the learner model. The axiom now first checks whether a learner property was manually inserted in the world state (line 22). If so, the axiom is not applicable since the requested information about the learner is to be taken from the world state and not from the learner model.

5.1.7.2 Training all Competencies in the Scenario "Train Intensively"

The method illustrated in Figure 5.58 decomposes a task (practiceCompetency f) into subtasks (practiceCompetency f) that trigger the insertion of exercises for each competency. These subtasks were explained in Section 5.1.2.5.

```
(:method (practiceAllCompetencies ?c)
         ()
         (
           (practiceCompetency think ?c)
           (practiceCompetency solve ?c)
           (practiceCompetency represent ?c)
           (practiceCompetency language ?c)
           (practiceCompetency model ?c)
           (practiceCompetency argue ?c)
           (practiceCompetency tools ?c)
           (practiceCompetency communicate ?c)
         )
         )
```

Fig. 5.58. Training all competencies

5.1.7.3 Example

A example course generated for the scenario "train intensively" is illustrated in Figure 5.59. The goal fundamentals were "the definition of the derivative, resp., the differential quotient", "the definition of the derivative function" and the theorem "sum rule". For each fundamental, two pages were created that contain the exercises.

5.1.8 Scenario "Train Competencies"

A course generated for the scenario "train competency" trains a specific competency by presenting sequences of examples and exercises with increasing difficulty and competency level. The courses are structured as follows:

Description. This section provides a description of the scenario. Then, for each fundamental given in the goal task, the following sections are created:

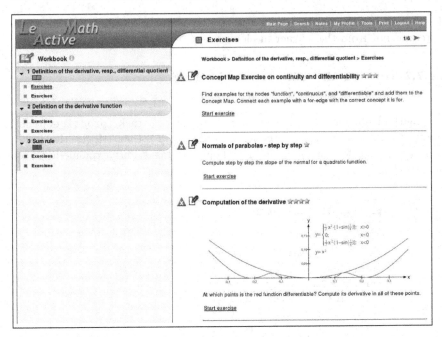

Fig. 5.59. A course generated for the scenario "train intensively"

Rehearse. This section presents the current fundamental.

Illustrate and Practice. The following two sections are repeated for each competency level starting with the competency level one below the learner's current level:

Illustrate. This section contains a sequence of examples of the competency level of the learner and of increasing difficulty level.

Practice. This section contains a sequence of exercises of the competency level of the learner and of increasing difficulty level.

5.1.8.1 Top-Level Decomposition of "Train Competencies"

Analogous to the other scenarios, several methods exist that perform the principal decomposition and introduce a subtask for each fundamental. These methods are not included here, since they are very similar to the previously described ones.

For each fundamental, the task (`trainCompetencySingleFundamental` f) is created. The method shown in Figure 5.60 decomposes the task into subtasks that first insert the fundamental. The last subtask triggers the insertion of examples and exercises, starting at a competency level one below the current one of the learner. A similar method exists that caters for the case in which the competency level equals 1.

```
(:method (trainCompetencySingleFundamental! ?competency ?c)
        (
        (learnerProperty hasCompetencyLevel ?c ?cl)
        (call > ?cl 1.0)
        (learnerProperty hasAllowedEducationalLevel ?aels)
        (learnerProperty hasEducationalLevel ?edl)
        (assignIterator ?el (?edl . ?aels))
        (call GetResources
                ((class Exercise)
                 (relation isFor ?c)
                 (property hasLearningContext ?el)
                 (property hasCompetency ?competency)
                ))
        (assign ?newCl (call - ?cl 1.0))
        )
        (
        (!startSection Rehearse (?c))
        (!insertResource ?c)
        (!endSection)
        (trainCompetencyExamplesExercises ?competency ?c ?newCl)
        )
        )
```

Fig. 5.60. Top-level decomposition in the scenario "train competencies"

5.1.8.2 Sections "Illustrate" and "Train"

The first subtask of the method illustrated in Figure 5.61 sets the competency level that is used by the examples and exercises selection. The subsequent selection uses the tasks illustrateCompetencySection and practiceCompetencySection described earlier. Afterwards, the set competency level is removed from the world state. The final subtask starts the method again, this time with an incremented competency level. A different method, not included here, stops the recursion when the highest competency level is reached.

5.1.8.3 Example

The figure 5.62 contains a course generated for the scenario "trainCompetencySolve" and the goal fundamentals "the definition of the derivative, resp., the differential quotient", "the definition of the derivative function" and the theorem "sum rule".

5.1.9 Scenario "Exam Simulation"

The scenario "exam simulation" contains exercises that can be solved within a specified timeframe. In contrast to the previous scenarios, the exercises are

```
(:method (trainCompetencyExamplesExercises ?competency ?c ?cl)
         (
          (call < ?cl 4.0)
         )
         (
          (!!setCompetencyLevel ?c ?cl)
          (illustrateCompetencySection ?competency ?c)
          (practiceCompetencySection ?competency ?c)
          (!!deleteSetCompetencyLevel ?c ?cl)
          (trainCompetencyExamplesExercises ?competency ?c
                                        (call + 1.0 ?cl))
         )
```

Fig. 5.61. Sections "illustrate" and "train" in the scenario "train competency"

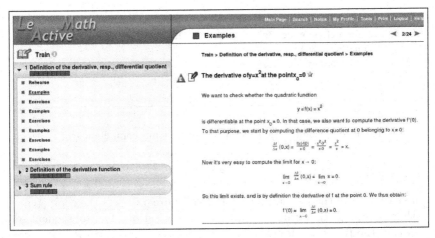

Fig. 5.62. A course generated for the scenario "train competency"

not selected with respect to learner properties since this is not the case in a real exam either. The generated courses consists of a number of pages, with each page consisting of exercises for the fundamentals given in the goal task. The final page of the course contains an estimation of the amount of minutes it takes a average learner to solve all exercises.

5.1.9.1 Top-Level Decomposition of "Exam Simulation"

Time plays an important role in this scenario since the selected exercises should be solvable within the specified timeframe. Therefore, the methods that implement the scenario need to know about the time typically required to solve an exercise. This information is represented in the resource metadata typicalLearningTime, which specifies the average time it takes a learner of the target group (specified by the educational level) to read/process a resource.

In addition, methods need to reason about the time that is taken up by the inserted exercises and the time left for the simulated exam. In the scenario, the atom (remainingTime *time*) is used to keep track of the time that is still left for additional exercises. It is initialized with the time originally assigned to the scenario by the learner.

The following methods perform several estimations about the time available for exercises for a fundamental. These estimations are necessary to ensure that exercises can be selected for *all* fundamentals given in the goal task. If the methods did not restrict the time available for the exercises, then the first fundamental will use up the available time and no exercises will be inserted for later fundamentals.

Figure 5.63 contains the central methods of this scenario. The upper method takes the current fundamental (the term that instantiates ?first) and estimates the amount of time that can be assigned to the section that inserts exercises for this fundamental. The estimation takes place in the lines 5–11. If r denotes the remaining time and l the amount of fundamentals still necessary to process, then the time t that can be spend on exercises for the current fundamental is defined as $t = max\{8, \frac{r}{l+1}\}$. That is, the remaining time is approximately the ratio of time left and fundamentals left. If t is too small, then a minimum value is assigned to it. The values were determined from technical experiments: if t becomes too small, then no exercises can be inserted.

The lower method in Figure 5.63 is applicable if all fundamentals were processed, i. e., exercises for all fundamentals were inserted. If there is still time left (lines 23–24), the exercise selection restarts and tries to insert additional exercises to fill up the time of the simulated exam. Additionally, the preconditions test whether an exercise was inserted during the last exercise selection by comparing the currently remaining time (remainingTime *t*) with the time remaining before the last exercise selection was performed (lastRemaining-Time *t*). If both times are equal, then no exercise was inserted in the last run, and hence it does not make sense to apply the method again (line 26). Otherwise, the exercise selection process restarts (line 31).

The previous methods have estimated the approximate time that can be allocated to the exercise selection for the current fundamental. The method in Figure 5.64 further specifies the exercises that should be selected. If there is still time left, then for each competency level, a task is inserted that selects exercises solvable in the given timeframe. The time is not divided by 4 (for the four competency levels), but by 2. This value was also determined by running several test-runs and evaluating the resulting courses by pedagogical experts.

```
1    (:method (examSimulationH (?first . ?rest) ?allIds)
2             (
3               (remainingTime ?remainingTime)
4               (call > ?remainingTime 0)
5               (assign ?estimatedTimePerFundamental
6                       (call / ?remainingTime
7                               (call + 1 (call Length ?rest))))
8               (imply (call > ?estimatedTimePerFundamental 8)
9                      (assign ?remainingTimePerFundamental
10                             ?estimatedTimePerFundamental))
11              (imply (call <= ?estimatedTimePerFundamental 8)
12                     (assign ?remainingTimePerFundamental 8))
13            )
14            (
15              (!startSection Exercises (?first))
16              (examSimulationSingleFundamental
17                      ?remainingTimePerFundamental ?first)
18              (!endSection)
19              (examSimulationH ?rest ?allIds)
20            )
21            )
22
23   (:method (examSimulationH nil ?allIds)
24            (
25              (remainingTime ?remainingTime)
26              (call > ?remainingTime 8)
27              (lastRemainingTime ?lastRemainingTime)
28              (not (call = ?remainingTime ?lastRemainingTime))
29            )
30            (
31              (!!removeFromWorldState
32                      (lastRemainingTime ?lastRemainingTime))
33              (!!addInWorldState (lastRemainingTime ?remainingTime))
34              (examSimulationH ?allIds ?allIds)
35            )
36
37            ()
38            ()
39            )
```

Fig. 5.63. Top-level methods for the scenario "exam simulation"

```
(:method (examSimulationSingleFundamental
              ?remainingTimePerFundamental ?first)
         (
         (remainingTime ?remainingTime)
         (call > ?remainingTime 0)
         (assign ?timePerCL (call / ?remainingTimePerFundamental 2))
         )
         (
         (getExercises ?timePerCL elementary ?first)
         (getExercises ?timePerCL simple_conceptual ?first)
         (getExercises ?timePerCL multi_step ?first)
         (getExercises ?timePerCL complex ?first)
         )
         )
```

Fig. 5.64. Start of the exercise selection for a fundamental in the scenario "exam simulation"

5.1.9.2 Exercise Selection in the Scenario "Exam Simulation"

The exercise selection in the scenario "exam simulation" is illustrated in Figure 5.65. Several preconditions of the method in the figure are replaced by text to improve the readability. In brief, the method retrieves easy, medium and difficult exercises that the learner has not yet seen and tries to find a combination of an easy, medium and difficult exercise that fits in the time assigned to the method.

The method first checks whether there is still time left (lines 3–4). Then it retrieves all very easy and easy exercises and removes the open exercises. (lines 6–7). Open exercises cannot be evaluated automatically and hence should not be used in this scenario. This is repeated for medium and for difficult and very difficult exercises (lines 9–10). If no exercises were found, the method is not applicable (line 12). Otherwise, the axiom assignIterator is used to find the first unseen easy exercise (lines 14–17). This is repeated for the medium and difficult exercises (lines 19–20). If there exists a set of exercises that fulfills these criteria, then their typical learning time is retrieved (lines 24–26). If they are not solvable in the timespan assigned to the method (lines 28–30), then backtracking causes the selection of a different set of exercises (if any). Otherwise they are inserted (lines 33–35) and the remaining time is updated (lines 36–37). A similar method exists that does not require the elements to be new to the learner.

5.1.9.3 Example

An example of a course generated for the scenario "exam simulation" is shown in Figure 5.66. It was generated on the same fundamentals as before ("the def-

```
1    (:method (getExercises! ?time ?cl ?c)
2             (
3              (remainingTime ?remainingTime)
4              (call > ?remainingTime 0)
5
6              retrieve very_easy and easy exercises
7              remove the open exercises
8
9              repeat for medium exercises
10             repeat for difficult and very difficult exercises
11
12             fail if no exercises were retrieved
13
14             (assignIterator ?easyExc ?allEasyExcsNotOpen)
15             (not (inserted ?easyExc))
16             (learnerProperty hasAlreadySeen ?easyExc ?seenEx1)
17             (same ?seenEx1 nil)
18
19             repeat for medium exercises
20             repeat for difficult and very difficult exercises
21
22             make sure that at least one exercise has been found
23
24             (typicalLearningTime ?easyExc ?time1)
25             (typicalLearningTime ?mediumExc ?time2)
26             (typicalLearningTime ?difficultExc ?time3)
27
28             (assign ?totalTime (call + ?time1 ?time2 ?time3))
29             (call >= ?time ?totalTime)
30             (assign ?remainingTimeNow
31                     (call - ?remainingTime ?totalTime))
32             )
33             (
34              (insertResourceOnce! ?easyExc)
35              (insertResourceOnce! ?mediumExc)
36              (insertResourceOnce! ?difficultExc)
37              (!!removeFromWorldState (remainingTime ?remainingTime))
38              (!!addInWorldState (remainingTime ?remainingTimeNow))
39              )
40             )
```

Fig. 5.65. Selecting exercises in the scenario "exam simulation"

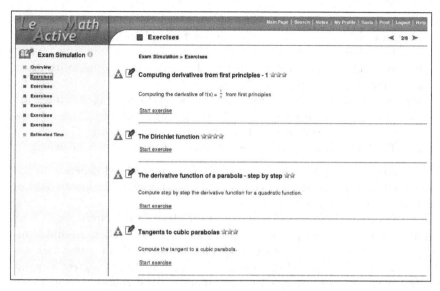

Fig. 5.66. A course generated for the scenario "exam simulation"

inition of the derivative, resp., the differential quotient", "the definition of the derivative function" and the theorem "sum rule") and for a time of 90 minutes.

This concludes the formalization of the scenarios based on moderate constructivist and competency-based pedagogy. The next section describes a scenario based on principles of instructional design.

5.2 Course Generation Based on Instructional Design Principles

According to Reigeluth [150], instructional design describes how to design educational resources that are "effective", "efficient", and "appealing". In the following, I will describe Merrill's "First Principles of Instruction", a set of guidelines that integrates results from several instructional design theories.

5.2.1 Merrill's "First Principles of Instruction"

Merrill [115] surveys research done in instructional design [97, 6, 114, 45, 68, 128, 160, 164] and describes the common underlying principles. He identifies five stages that he argues need to be present during the learning process in order for successful learning to take place:

Problem. "Learning is facilitated when learners are engaged in solving real-world problems."

Activation. "Learning is facilitated when relevant previous experience is activated."

Demonstration. "Learning is facilitated when the instruction demonstrates what is to be learned rather than merely telling information about what is to be learned."

Application. "Learning is facilitated when learners are required to use their new knowledge or skill to solve problems."

Integration. "Learning is facilitated when learners are encouraged to integrate (transfer) the new knowledge or skill into their everyday life." This integration happens foremost in collaboration with other learners. They should have the possibility to reflect, discuss, and defend their new knowledge.

The extent to which each of these stages can be realized depends on the learning environment. For instance, not all systems provide the functionalities required for collaborative learning.

The following scenario is partly based on Merrill's principles. One of its design goals was to formalize a scenario that poses the smallest possible constraints on metadata. Sophisticated scenarios as described in the previous section require the educational resources to be annotated with a great amount of metadata, e. g., competency level, competency, and representation value. Some of these metadata are not wide-spread, especially the ones related to competencies. The scenario formalized in this section uses "standard", established metadata, such as difficulty level.

5.2.2 Scenario "Guided Tour"

A course generated for the scenario "guided tour" provides the learner with the necessary resources to help him understand the target fundamentals in depth. In contrast to the scenario "discover", the prerequisites are included in detail and the exercise and example selection primarily uses the difficulty level. The sections in the course respect Merrill's "First Principles", as far as possible. For each fundamental given in the goal task, and for each unknown prerequisite fundamental, the following sections are created:

Introduction. This section arises a learner's interest by presenting educational resources of the type introduction.

Problem. This section inserts a real world problem for the fundamental.

Fundamental. This section presents the fundamental.

Explanation. This section contains educational resources that provide explaining and deepening information about the fundamental.

Illustration. This section provides opportunities for the learner to examine demonstrations of applications of the fundamentals.

Practice. This section enables a student to actively apply what he has learned about the fundamental.

Conclusion. This section presents educational resources that contain concluding information about the fundamental.

Reflection. This section provides the learner with an opportunity to reflect and discuss his new knowledge.

```
1    (:method (guidedTour ?fundamentals)
2            ()
3            (
4             (!startSection GuidedTour ?fundamentals
5                           (guidedTour ?fundamentals))
6             (learnFundamentalsGuidedTour ?fundamentals)
7             (reflect ?fundamentals)
8             (!endSection)
9             )
10           )
11
12   (:method (learnFundamentalsGuidedTour (?c . ?rest))
13           ()
14           (
15            (learnPrerequisitesFundamentalsGT ?c)
16            (learnSingleFundamentalGT ?c)
17            (learnFundamentalsGuidedTour ?rest)
18            )
19           )
```

Fig. 5.67. Methods used for the top-level decomposition of the scenario "guided tour"

5.2.2.1 Top-Level Decomposition of "Guided Tour"

The two methods displayed in Figure 5.67 perform the top-level decomposition: for each target fundamental f, first a task (learnPrerquisites-FundmentalsGT f) is created that inserts sections for all prerequisites of f that are unknown to the learner. Previously presented prerequisites are automatically detected and hence duplications are avoided. Then, the task (learnSingleFudamentalGT f) causes the creation of a section for the fundamental f. The final task causes the method to call itself recursively. The method for the base case (when all fundamentals were processed) is not shown.

The task (learnSingleFudamentalGT f) is processed by the method illustrated in Figure 5.68. First, it tests whether the section for the current fundamental was already created. In this case, the second precondition-subtask is applied. Since it has no subtasks, the task is achieved. This way, duplication of sections which might happen due to the handling of prerequisites in this scenario are avoided. In case the section was not yet created, the subtasks of the method create the structure described above. The final subtask adds an atom in the world state that represents that the current task was achieved.

5.2.2.2 Sections "Introduce", "Explanation" and "Conclusion"

The methods in Figure 5.69 handle the insertion of educational resources in the sections "introduction", "explanation" and "conclusion". They follow the

```
1    (:method (learnSingleFundamentalGT ?c)
2             (
3               (not (achieved (learnSingleFundamentalGT ?c)))
4             )
5             (
6               (!startSection Title (?c)
7                             (learnSingleFundamentalGT (?c)))
8               (introduceByIntroductionSection ?c)
9               (problemSection ?c)
10              (insertFundamentalSection ?c)
11              (explainSection ?c)
12              (illustrateWithIncreasedDiffSection ?c)
13              (trainWithIncreasingDiffSection ?c)
14              (concludeSection ?c)
15              (!endSection)
16              (!!addInWorldState
17                     (achieved (learnSingleFundamentalGT ?c)))
18            )
19
20            ((achieved (learnSingleFundamentalGT ?c)))
21            ()
22            )
```

Fig. 5.68. Creating a section for a fundamental in the scenario "guided tour"

same schema: a resource for the given fundamental and of a learning context that corresponds to the learner' educational level is inserted. If these methods cannot be applied, then an analogous set of methods relaxes the constraint on the educational level and searches for resources for all allowed educational levels.

5.2.2.3 Sections "Illustration" and "Practice"

The method in Figure 5.71 handles the insertion of examples. Depending on the learner's current competency level, a set of examples is selected. For instance, if the learner has a low competency level (≤ 2), then five very easy, five easy, three medium examples and one difficult and one very difficult example are inserted. The general rule implemented in the example selection is that most of the examples should correspond to the learner's current competency level. He should neither be demotivated nor bored. In addition, a sufficiently large amount of examples is presented. The given number is the maximum number if only a smaller amount of these resources exists, then the remaining ones are skipped. The methods for the subtask insertResourcesOfType first try to find sufficient resources that correspond to the learner's educational level, but relax the constraint if necessary. The methods are not shown in this volume. An analogous method exists that handle the exercise selection.

```
(:method (introduceShort! ?c)
         (
          (learnerProperty hasEducationalLevel ?el)
          (assign ?resources
                  (call GetResources
                        ((class Introduction)
                         (relation isFor ?c)
                         (property hasLearningContext ?el))))
          (assignIterator ?r ?resources)
          )
         (
          (insertAuxOnceIfReady! ?r ?c)
          )
         )

(:method (explain! ?c)
         (
          (learnerProperty hasEducationalLevel ?el)
          (assignIterator ?r
                          (call GetResources
                                ((class Remark)
                                 (relation isFor ?c)
                                 (property hasLearningContext ?el))))
          )
         (
          (insertAuxOnceIfReady! ?r ?c)
          )
         )

(:method (conclude! ?c)
         MethodConclude!Ideal
         (
          (learnerProperty hasEducationalLevel ?el)
          (assignIterator ?r
                          (call GetResources
                                ((class Conclusion)
                                 (relation isFor ?c)
                                 (property hasLearningContext ?el))))
          )
         (
          (insertAuxOnceIfReady! ?r ?c)
          )
         )
```

Fig. 5.69. Inserting texts in the scenario "guided tour"

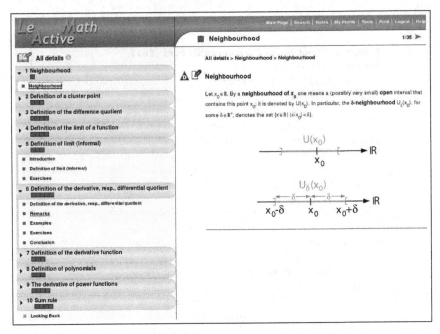

Fig. 5.70. A course generated for the scenario "guided tour"

5.2.2.4 Example

Figure 5.70 contains a screenshot of a course generated for the scenario "guided tour" and the goal fundamentals "the definition of the derivative, resp., the differential quotient", "the definition of the derivative function" and the theorem "sum rule". The difference to the course generated for the scenario "discover" is clearly visible: here, all prerequisites are included in their own section.

```
(:method (illustrateWithIncreasedDiff ?c)
        (
        (learnerProperty hasCompetencyLevel ?c ?competencyLevel)
        (call < ?competencyLevel 2)
        )
        (
        (insertResourcesOfType ?c Example very_easy 5)
        (insertResourcesOfType ?c Example easy 5)
        (insertResourcesOfType ?c Example medium 3)
        (insertResourcesOfType ?c Example difficult 1)
        (insertResourcesOfType ?c Example very_difficult 1)
        )


        (
        (learnerProperty hasCompetencyLevel ?c ?competencyLevel)
        (call >= ?competencyLevel 2)
        (call < ?competencyLevel 4)
        )
        (
        (insertResourcesOfType ?c Example very_easy 3)
        (insertResourcesOfType ?c Example easy 4)
        (insertResourcesOfType ?c Example medium 4)
        (insertResourcesOfType ?c Example difficult 2)
        (insertResourcesOfType ?c Example very_difficult 2)
        )

        (
        (learnerProperty hasCompetencyLevel ?c ?competencyLevel)
        (call >= ?competencyLevel 4)
        )
        (
        (insertResourcesOfType ?c Example very_easy 1)
        (insertResourcesOfType ?c Example easy 2)
        (insertResourcesOfType ?c Example medium 2)
        (insertResourcesOfType ?c Example difficult 4)
        (insertResourcesOfType ?c Example very_difficult 4)
        )
        )
```

Fig. 5.71.

6

Implementation and Integration

In this chapter, I describe technical aspects of PAIGOS. The implementation, i. e., the Java classes and interfaces, is described in the first section. The interfaces work on the level of tasks: they take a pedagogical task as input and return a course that achieves the task as a result. The second section describes how the interfaces are used in the integration of PAIGOS in a Web-based learning environment, in this case ACTIVEMATH. The section illustrates the advantages that arise in a tightly coupled integration, where different components of the learning environment have direct access to the course generator: whenever a component needs to make informed decisions about content to present to the learner, it can use the functionalities offered by the course generator. Thus, knowledge is not duplicated and a coherent pedagogical approach regarding content selection is ensured in the overall system, since a single component, the course generator, is responsible for this functionality. The step from a tight, system confined integration to a service architecture is described in the final section of the chapter. In this setting, an external learning environment registers its repository at the course generation Web-service and subsequently can access PAIGOS's functionalities. The interfaces partly remain the same: pedagogical tasks are sent to the course generating service, which returns a course as a result. However, some additional interfaces are required for the repository registration, such as exchanging information about the metadata of the educational resources. As a result, if a system needs to offer course generation to its learners, it can use the functionalities offered by PAIGOS and is not required to implement the pedagogical knowledge itself.

6.1 Implementation

Since the most relevant parts of PAIGOS are formalized in the course generation planning domain, the actual Java implementation of PAIGOS consists only of a small number of classes.

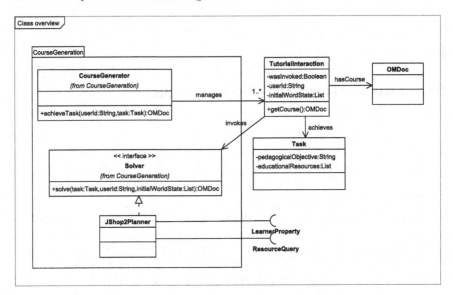

Fig. 6.1. An overview on the classes relevant for course generation

Figure 6.1 presents an UML overview on the classes that implement the course generator. The class **Task** (middle bottom right in the figure) represents a pedagogical task as described in Section 4.3. It consists of a pedagogical objective and a list of identifiers of educational resources.

The class **TutorialInteraction** serves to associate the users, pedagogical tasks and the courses that were generated for the task and for the individual users. It is initialized with a task and, if needed, an initial world state. The initial world state is mostly used when processing dynamic tasks (see Section 4.8). There, some resources have to be considered as inserted in the course in order to prevent their selection during the instantiation of the task.

In a **TutorialInteraction** object, the first invocation of the method **getCourse** starts the course generation. Once the course is generated, it is stored in the tutorial interaction, the boolean property **wasInvoked** is set to true, and the course is passed to the object that requested it. If the course is requested again at a later time, the stored course is returned.

The interface **Solver** serves to abstract from the classes that implement the course generation process. This eases a potential change of the engine that realizes the course generation (e. g., as done in ACTIVEMATH whose first course generator was implemented using an expert system). Classes that implement the **Solver** interface need to provide the method **solve** that takes a task, a user identifier and an initial world state as input and returns an OMDoc document. In PAIGOS, the class **JShop2Planner** implements this interface and encapsulates JSHOP2.

During course generation, the class **JShop2Planner** accesses the Mediator using the interface **ResourceQuery** and the learner model using the interface **LearnerProperty**. Similar to the mediator, classes that implement the interface **LearnerProperty** should cache queries, too. However, this cache becomes invalid much faster than the mediator cache since the learner's properties usually change more often than the content. In ACTIVEMATH, the cache is cleared after each planning process.

The class **CourseGenerator** manages the tutorial interactions and is used by those components that need to generate courses. It is implemented as a singleton pattern, thus a single object implements this class. The first invocation of the constructor of the class creates the **CourseGenerator** object. Later invocation of the constructor returns this single object (the singleton). Its principal method is **achieveTask** that takes as input the user identifier of the learner the course will be generated for (**userId**), a task (**task**), and optionally a list that represents the initial world state (**initialWorldState**), actually a list of atoms that are added into the world state in addition to the atoms that make up the original world state, see Section 4.4.3). Using this information, the **CourseGenerator** singleton creates tutorial interactions and then starts the course generation using the method **getCourse**. The result of the planning process is an OMDOC document. The interface of the class **CourseGenerator** is the following:

```
public OMDoc achieveTask(String userID, Task task)
public OMDoc achieveTask(String userID, Task task,
                         List initialWorldState)
```

6.2 Integration of PAIGOS in ActiveMath

In this section, I describe the integration of PAIGOS in the Web-based learning environment ACTIVEMATH. I first describe ACTIVEMATH, and then explain the integration in detail, starting with the graphical user interface, followed by the basic technique used for including references to learning-support services (Section 6.2.2), and then provide details on the specific services that were integrated: a concept map (Section 6.2.3.1), an open learner model (Section 6.2.3.2), and an exercise sequencer (Section 6.2.3.3). Section 6.2.4 describes how the symbolic representations of narrative bridges generated during planning are transformed into "real" text. The final section explains how PAIGOS is used as a service by other ACTIVEMATH components.

6.2.1 Course Generation in ActiveMath

Access to content using the course generator is an important part of ACTIVE-MATH. The manually authored courses contain only parts of the available educational resources. The remaining resources are only accessible using the search tool or the course generator. In addition, special care was taken to ensure that the user interface that handles the user's access to PAIGOS is easy to use. In the LEACTIVEMATH project, the interface was evaluated and revised twice, first by a review performed by the Fraunhofer Institute for Industrial Engineering IAO and then in a formative evaluation by usability experts of the School of Informatics at the University of Edinburgh (see Section 7.2). In the following, I describe the course generation user interface using the Figures 6.2 to 6.7.

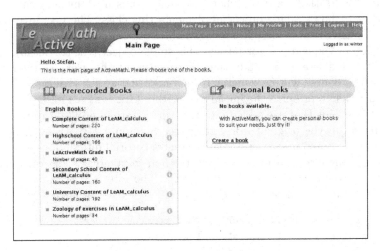

Fig. 6.2. The main menu of ACTIVEMATH

Figure 6.2 contains a screenshot of the main menu of ACTIVEMATH. The entries on the left hand side correspond to manually authored books. The menu on the right hand side allows a learner to start the course generation. In ACTIVEMATH, this process is called "personal book creation". Since the concept of course generation is unknown to almost all learners, an extensive help section explains the general approach and the scenarios in detail. The text on the link that start the course generation is phrased such that it motivates to experiment with it ("Just try it!"). If the learner follows the link, a step-by-step guide (wizard) leads him through the selection of the course generation parameters, i. e., the scenario and the target fundamentals.

Figure 6.3 illustrates the first step of the course generation wizard. There, the learner selects the mathematical domain the target fundamentals will be chosen from. In ACTIVEMATH, each of the possible choices is represented by a *grouping*. Just like a table of contents a grouping is an OMDoc `omgroup` element that consists of other `omgroup` elements and references to educational resources (for additional details about the representation of table of contents, see the following section). However, a grouping is not used to present a course, but to collect the fundamentals the learner can select from for course gen-

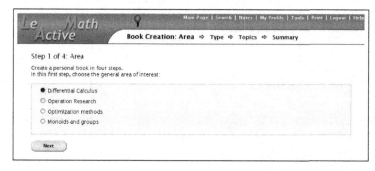

Fig. 6.3. Selecting the general area of interest

eration. Making OMDoc resources available for course generation simply requires authoring a new grouping and registering it in the ACTIVEMATH configuration. Being a regular OMDoc element, a grouping is authored using the standard OMDoc authoring tools.

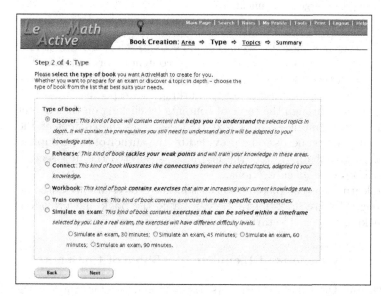

Fig. 6.4. Selecting the scenario

In the next step, illustrated in Figure 6.4, the learner selects the scenario. Each scenario is briefly described, the most relevant words being highlighted. A click on the terms in bold font opens the help menu with a more detailed description of the scenario. The evaluations showed that providing detailed help is a necessary requirement if students are to used course generation: most learners are not used to the possibility of creating books, let alone different types of books.

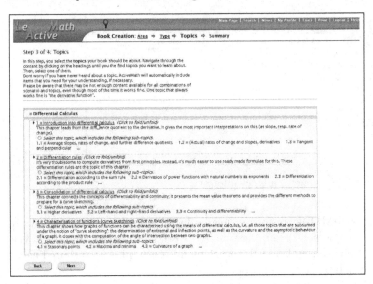

Fig. 6.5. Selecting the target fundamentals

Once the learner has chosen a scenario, he needs to select the target fundamentals (Figure 6.5). In this step, the table of contents represented by the grouping selected in the first step is presented to the learner. The learner can select one of the sections or subsections by marking the respective radio button. He can navigate through the table of contents by clicking on the chapter names. Each section contains a brief text that describes the content of the section. This information needs to be provided by the author of the grouping.

In the screenshot of Figure 6.6, the learner has selected the first section and the wizard presents its subsections.

When the learner has completed his selection, his choices are presented on a summary page (Figure 6.7). There, he can name the book and provide a summary. Clicking on "Next" starts the course generation process.

6.2.2 Dynamically Generated Elements in a Table of Contents

ACTIVEMATH uses the OMDOC elements omgroup and ref for representing tables of contents.

- the omgroup element represents and structures a table of contents in the following way: either an omgroup consists only of omgroup elements, in which case it represents a section; or it consists of ref elements and then represents a page in a course.
- the ref element references an educational resource. The value of its xref attribute contains the identifier of the resource that will be included into the page.

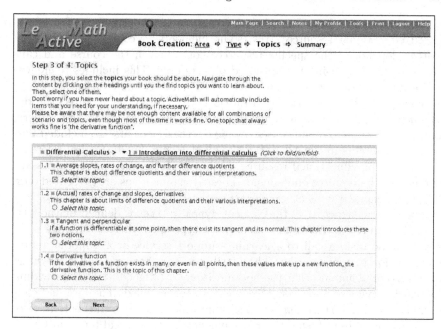

Fig. 6.6. Expanding a section

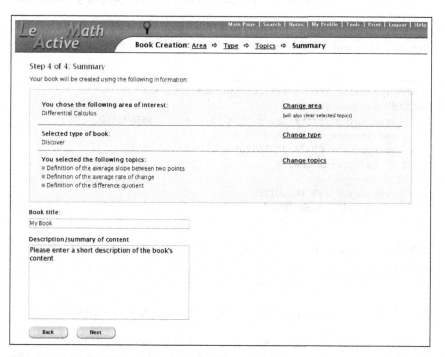

Fig. 6.7. The summary page

This approach works fine when a course consists only of previously authored educational resources. Yet, some elements of courses generated by PAIGOS depend on the specific resources contained in the course and cannot be realized by using pre-authored objects only. This includes references to learning-support services, narrative bridges and dynamic tasks.

Therefore, the integration of PAIGOS in ACTIVEMATH required the development of a new element, called `dynamic-item`, that serves as a generic container for these dynamic cases. `Dynamic-item` elements are included into a table of contents in the same way as `ref` elements, but instead of referencing an existing educational resource they contain the information necessary to generate the resource on-demand. These dynamic items are presented on a page in the same way as other educational resources.

The general structure of the element `dynamic-item` is defined by the DTD shown in Figure 6.8. A dynamic item has a type specifying whether the item is a dynamic task, a call to a learning-support service or a symbolic representation for text generation. The attributes `servicename` and `queryname` allow further differentiating the specific item to be generated by providing the exact service and method of the service to be called. The optional children of a `dynamic-item` element specify information about the context: relevant learning objects (using the `ref` element), mathematical terms in Open-Math format (`OMOBJ`), and additional parameters given as property-value pairs (`queryparam`).

The following sections describe how dynamic elements are used for the integration of learning-support services.

```
<!ELEMENT dynamic-item (ref*|queryparam*|OMOBJ*)>
<!ATTLIST dynamic-item
        type (dynamicTask|learningService|text) #REQUIRED
        servicename CDATA #REQUIRED
        queryname   CDATA #IMPLIED>
<!ELEMENT queryparam EMPTY>
<!ATTLIST queryparam
        property CDATA #REQUIRED
        value CDATA #REQUIRED>
```

Fig. 6.8. The document type description (DTD) of the dynamic item element

6.2.3 Usage of Learning-Support Services in ActiveMath

The ACTIVEMATH system offers a variety of learning-support services. This section focuses on how these services are integrated into courses generated by PAIGOS.

During course generation, references to learning-support services are inserted using specific methods and operators. In ACTIVEMATH, these references are rendered as links. Thus, for the learner, are not different from other interactive elements such as exercises and seamlessly blend into the course. Technically, the integration happens in the following way:

1. During planning, the course generator applies the operator
   (!insertLearningService *serviceName* *queryName*
                    (r_1 ... r_n) (p_1 v_1 ... p_m v_m))
   where r_x are resource identifiers and p_y and v_y denote property-value pairs.

2. After a plan was found, the above operator triggers the creation of a dynamic item that represents the above service call:
   ```
   <dynamic-item type="learningService" servicename="serviceName"
               queryname="queryName">
     <ref xref="r1" />
     ...
     <ref xref="rn" />
     <queryparam property="p1" value="v1" />
     ...
     <queryparam property="pm" value="vm" />
   </dynamic-item>
   ```

3. When the learner visits a page that contains a dynamic item, the presentation system converts the dynamic item into the requested output format (e.g., HTML) and displays it. The rendered element is presented like any other interactive element: it uses the same layout and is started by a click on a link.

I will now describe three services that were integrated using this approach.

6.2.3.1 Interactive Concept Mapping Tool

The interactive Concept Mapping Tool (iCMAP, [108]) helps the learner to reflect on his mathematical knowledge by providing a framework for the visualization and construction of structures in a mathematical domain. It supports the learning process by verifying the concept map constructed by the learner and by suggesting reasonable changes to the created map.

PAIGOS employs the concept mapping tool in two different ways: the mode display presents a complete concept map to the learner. This is used by, e. g., the scenario "connect" to offer the learner with an opportunity to inspect a visual representation of the relationships between the fundamentals covered in the course. In the mode solve, the learner's task is to construct a concept map on her own, using a given set of fundamentals.

In order to create dynamic exercises, iCMAP takes the following parameters from the course generator as input: a set of OMDOC references pointing to the initial fundamentals to be displayed (the *central fundamentals*), a set of pairs (`relationType depth`), and the mode-string (with the values `solve` and `display`). Roughly speaking, the concept map contains the initial fundamentals C and all other fundamentals that are connected to elements of C by the given set of relations up to the given depth. More precisely:

Central Fundamentals. For each central fundamental all related resources are added to the concept map exercise. The relations taken into account are specified in the parameter `relationType`:

Relation Type and Depth. The parameter `relationType` represents the relation types (as defined in the OIO) which are used to compute the additional resources to be presented to the learner. A depth parameter is attached to each specified relation representing the maximum distance ICMAP will follow to compute neighboring learning items. Each node N that is added to the concept map meets one of the following conditions:

1. N is a node representing a central fundamental, or
2. a relation type r with depth r_n defined such that N is connected by the relation r over at most r_n nodes.

Mode. The mode specified with the parameter `queryname` determines how the concept map exercise will be presented to the learner. If the mode is `display`, all computed nodes and all edges of the given types are added to the workspace; the learner is told to verify the map and, if applicable, to complete it. Launching an exercise with mode `solve` starts ICMAP with an empty concept map. All the nodes determined as central fundamentals and all those computed by ICMAP are added to the learner's palette. Therefore, in mode `solve`, the learner has to create the concept map by herself.

Example 6.1. The following operator triggers the creation of an ICMAP exercise for the resource "definition of the average slope":

```
(!insertLearningService CMap display (def_average_slope)
                    (requires 1.0 isRequiredBy 1.0
                     isA 1.0 inverseIsA 1.0))
```

Example 6.2. The application of the above operator creates the following dynamic item:

```
<dynamic-item type="learningService" servicename="CMap"
            queryname="display">
  <ref xref="def_average_slope" />
  <queryparam property="requires" value="1.0" />
  <queryparam property="isRequiredBy" value="1.0" />
  <queryparam property="isA" value="1.0" />
  <queryparam property="inverseIsA" value="1.0" />
</dynamic-item>
```

Figure 6.9 shows the presentation of the dynamic element in ACTIVE-MATH. Figure 6.10 contains of screenshot of the resulting workbench of the ICMAP exercise.

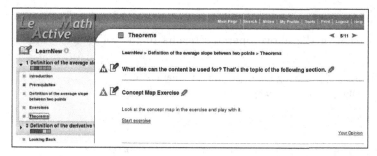

Fig. 6.9. Presentation of a dynamically generated concept mapping tool exercise in ACTIVEMATH

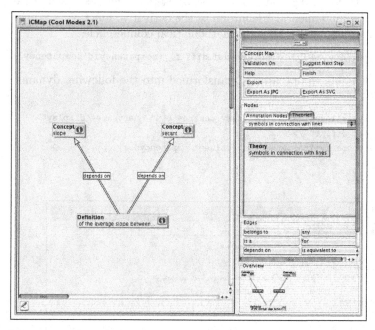

Fig. 6.10. The workbench of a dynamically generated concept mapping tool exercise

6.2.3.2 Open Learner Model

An Open Learner Model [OLM, 35] provides learners with a possibility to inspect and modify the beliefs that the learner model holds about the mastery or competencies of the learner. An OLM for ACTIVEMATH was developed in the LEACTIVEMATH project.

The course generator uses the OLM for the reflection phase to encourage the learner to reflect about her learning progress regarding the learned fundamentals. It is started with a list of fundamentals and a competency, which define the initial items presented on the OLM workbench. References to the OLM are created using the following operator:

```
(!insertLearningService OLM display (r_1 ... r_n) (competencyID competency))
```

The application of the above operator results in the following dynamic item:

```
<dynamic-item type="learningService" servicename="OLM"
              queryname="display">
  <ref xref="r_1" />
  ...
  <ref xref="r_n" />
  <queryparam property="comptencyID" value="competency" />
</dynamic-item>
```

Example 6.3. The following operator serves to insert a reference to the OLM that displays the fundamental "definition of the derivative function" and the competency that aggregates all eight mathematical competencies.

```
(!insertLearningService OLM display (def_diff_f) (competencyId competency))
```

Example 6.4. The above operator is transformed into the following dynamic item:

```
<dynamic-item type="learningService" servicename="OLM" queryname="display">
  <ref xref="def_diff_f" />
  <queryparam property="competencyId" value="competency" />
</dynamic-item>
```

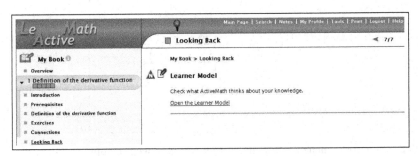

Fig. 6.11. The presentation of a dynamically generated link to the Open Learner Model

Figure 6.11 shows the link generated for the above example and Figure 6.12 an example of the workbench of the OLM after the learner has performed a few exploration steps.

6.2.3.3 Exercise Sequencer

The exercise sequencer presents to the learner a dynamically selected sequence of exercises that leads her towards a higher competency level. This functionality differs from the exercise selection of the course generator: PAIGOS generates

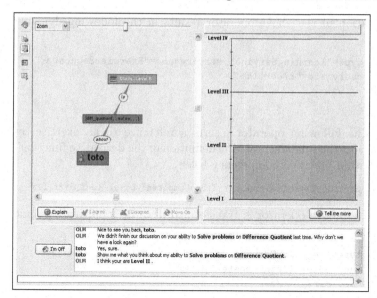

Fig. 6.12. The workbench of the Open Learner Model

a sequence of educational resources which is adapted to the learner at generation time, but once it is generated, it remains static. This behavior was a design decision to avoid confusion of the learner arising from pages changing over and over again as reported by De Bra [30].

In contrast, the exercise sequencer is completely dynamic. It selects an exercise, presents it to the learner in a window separate from the current course, and depending on the learner's problem-solving success provides feedback and terminates or selects a new exercise, thus starting the cycle again. The selection algorithm is based on competency levels.

For the selection of the exercises, the sequencer uses the course generator. It requests the course generator to select an exercise adequate to the current competency level of the learner using the pedagogical task `trainWithSingleExercise!`. The task reuses the pedagogical knowledge of PAIGOS, thus following the same principles and avoiding different ways of exercise selection.

References to the exercise sequencer created by the course generator include the fundamental that will be trained. Additionally, it is possible to specify the algorithm used by the sequencer. However, currently only the competency based algorithm is implemented. A link to a sequencer is created using the following operator, where r stands for the fundamental that will be trains and *algorithm* is the identifier of the algorithm used for the exercise selection.

```
(!insertLearningService ExerciseSequencer algorithm (r))
```

The application of the above operator results in the following dynamic item:

```
<dynamic-item type="learningService" servicename="ExerciseSequencer"
              queryname="algorithm">
  <ref xref="r" />
</dynamic-item>
```

Example 6.5. The following operator inserts a reference to an exercise sequencer that trains the fundamental "the definition of the derivative function" using the algorithm based on competency-levels.

```
(!insertLearningService ExerciseSequencer TrainCompetencyLevel (def_diff_f))
```

Example 6.6. The above operator is transformed into the following dynamic item:

```
<dynamic-item type="learningService" servicename="ExerciseSequencer"
              queryname="TrainCompetencyLevel">
    <ref xref="def_diff_f" />
</dynamic-item>
```

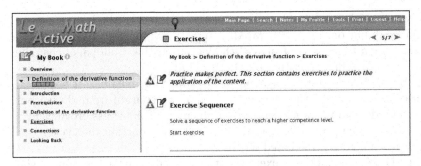

Fig. 6.13. The presentation of a dynamically generated link to the exercise sequencer

Figures 6.13 and 6.14 contain screenshots of the rendering of the link to the exercise sequencer and of an exemplary interaction.

6.2.4 Template-Based Generation of Narrative Bridges

In this section I demonstrate how the symbolic representations of bridging texts generated during course generation can be transformed into texts.

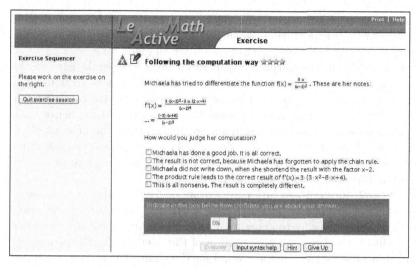

Fig. 6.14. An exemplary interaction with the exercise sequencer

6.2.4.1 NLG vs. Templates

Reiter [152] distinguishes between two principally different techniques for text generation. While natural language generation (NLG) is based on linguistic and knowledge-based techniques, the template-based approach is based on the manipulation of character strings, done at character level, without a deeper, semantic representation of text. According to [152], the advantages of NLG include the following:

Maintainability. NLG is easier to adapt than template-based techniques, especially if large amounts of texts are generated. Since NLG works on a higher level of abstraction, it uses a limited set of rules to create a potentially vast amount of individual texts. In a template-based approach, each of these text needs to specified beforehand. Therefore, whereas performing a change in NLG requires updating a limited amount of rules, in a template-based approach all involved templates need to be updated.

Improved text quality. NLG uses various techniques to improve text quality. For instance, aggregation is used to sum up several individual propositions in a single sentence.

A principal disadvantage of NLG is its need of an explicit representation of the content that is to be communicated, i.e., for learning the content that is being learned. Without this representation, no texts can be generated. In addition, the generation requires a macro-planner and micro-planner, which necessitates specialized expertise for their development, since only prototypical toolkits are available. They also make the generated language hard to internationalize.

In contrast, template-based approaches are widely-used because of their straightforward implementation. Their development and application is supported by several frameworks, for instance using phrases.

In ACTIVEMATH, the purpose of generated texts is to make explicit the structure of a course by displaying the pedagogical purpose of sections. It is possible to formulate the templates in a way independent of the fundamentals actually taught. Each purpose is expressed by a specific phrase, hence techniques such as aggregation are not required. In addition, the amount of required texts is limited. All in all, the pedagogical strategies encompass about twenty sections that need to be augmented by texts. Therefore, manually maintaining the texts is feasible.

Reiter [152] summarizes his comparison of NLG and template-based text generation as follows: "[i]f a certain portion of the output text never varies ... it would be silly to generate it with NLG, and much more sensible to simply use canned text for this portion of the document". This statement and the above discussion provide ground for the claim that a template-based approach can be adequate for the generation of bridging texts. I now describe the technical aspects of the generation.

6.2.4.2 Generation of Narrative Bridges in LeActiveMath

In ACTIVEMATH, a 2-stage presentation pipeline handles the rendering/presentation of the learning materials contained in a course [190]. In the first step, the educational resources referenced in the table of contents of a course are fetched from the database, transformed into the requested output format and cached. In the second step, these educational resources are composed into a complete page, and the resulting page is rendered for the learner. If an educational resource was already transformed, it is directly retrieved from the cache, in order to avoid repeated transformation of the same educational resource.

In contrast, dynamic items (such as symbolic representations of bridging texts) are not fetched from a database but instantiated on demand. More specifically, the controller responsible for the presentation calls the service specified in the dynamic item by the attribute `servicename` and passes the remaining attributes and sub-elements as parameters. In the case of dynamic items of type `text`, the corresponding service uses the parameters to determine the adequate template t and returns an OMDOC element whose text body consists of t. If a template is available in several languages, a specific text body is generated for each language (catering for the case that the user changes the language any later time). Because the texts are stored in OMDOC elements, they can be cached and reused using the mechanisms of the presentation pipeline.

This approach allows for a flexible on-demand generation of texts. The texts are generated at view time, i. e., when the learner actually visits the page for the first time. Therefore, the templates can integrate up-to-date learner information, such as user name, competency-level, etc.[1] If texts were generated directly after planning, some information might not be available or quickly become outdated (such as competency-level).

For the instantiation of the templates, ACTIVEMATH uses a common internationalization framework that pairs a set of keywords with texts. Such a pair is called a *phrase*. These phrases are stored in text files, one for each language. This makes editing and extending phrases easily possible for non-technical experts, e. g., translators.

Figure 6.15 contains a selection of phrases used for English bridging texts. The carpet character "#" denotes comments. The keywords at the left hand side of the equals sign are the phrases determined during the course generation. For the presentation, they are replaced by the texts following the equals sign. The last two phrases provide an example of a method-induced change of scenario. As described in Section 4.9.2, in the scenario `rehearse` two different sections present a sequence of examples. The first section serves to remind the learner how to apply the fundamental. The second section, placed after an exercise section, is used to provide additional examples. Because the same methods are used for the selection, the context is changed prior to the second examples selection.

Figure 6.16 shows a HTML rendering of the task of Example 4.21 (Section 4.9.2). The text is emphasized in order to convey to the learner that the text is on a different level of abstraction than the remaining content displayed on the page.

6.2.5 PAIGOS as a Service in ActiveMath

The most frequent usage of PAIGOS in ACTIVEMATH is to generate a course on request of the learner. Equally important and a good illustration of the features made possible by a course generator service is its usage by other components in ACTIVEMATH whenever they require pedagogically based retrieval of content. By using the course generator, these components do not have to implement themselves the knowledge required to make the selection. This reduces development time and ensures a coherent pedagogical look-and-feel, since the same pedagogical principles are used for content selection, regardless of the component.

Previously, I described how the exercise sequencer uses PAIGOS to select the exercises the learner should work on. In the following, I describe two additional components, a suggestion component and an assembly tool, that use PAIGOS's functionalities. The third subsection explains how PAIGOS is used to enhance the learner's interaction possibilities with courses presented in ACTIVEMATH. All components use the interface described in Section 6.1.

---

[1] This feature is not yet used in the current version of ACTIVEMATH.

```
# phrases for scenario "Discover"

text.NLGGenerator.Item.Discover.Introduction=Why is the mathematical
content presented in this chapter important? The following section
tries to answer that question.

text.NLGGenerator.Item.Discover.Prerequisites=This paragraph contains
the prerequisite knowledge necessary to understand the content of this
section.

text.NLGGenerator.Item.Discover.Develop=Careful now! This section
contains the principal content and some examples.

text.NLGGenerator.Item.Discover.Practice=Practice makes perfect. This
section contains exercises to practice the application of the
content.

text.NLGGenerator.Item.Discover.Connect=In this section, you will
discover the connections to other content.

text.NLGGenerator.Item.Discover.Reflect=Please think about your
learning process: How did you proceed? Did you understand everything?
If not, try to look up the necessary content using the system.

text.NLGGenerator.Item.Discover.Examples=Have a close look! In this
section you will see example applications of the content.


# phrases for scenario "Rehearse"

text.NLGGenerator.Item.Rehearse.Develop=Do you still remember what the
goal content is about? Here you can have a second look at it.

text.NLGGenerator.Item.Rehearse.Connect=What else can the content be
used for? That's the topic of the following section.

text.NLGGenerator.Item.Rehearse.Examples=If you do not recall how to
apply the goal content, have a look at these examples.

text.NLGGenerator.Item.RehearseDeeper.Examples=Here you find
additional examples of the goal content.
```

Fig. 6.15. A selection of bridging texts

Why is the mathematical content presented in this chapter important? The following section tries to answer that question.

Fig. 6.16. A rendered bridging text

6.2.5.1 Suggestion Component

ACTIVEMATH's *suggestion component* [103] analyzes the user's interactions with ACTIVEMATH to detect potential learning problems. Based on the interactions, diagnoses are formed. The diagnoses are addressed by actions that provide remediating feedback, i.e., suggestions, in case problems are diagnosed. Suggestions consists of navigational hints (e.g., pointing at a specific page in the table of contents) or of educational resources (e.g., an example that illustrates the fundamental that learner seems to not have understood). For the latter case, the suggestion component uses PAIGOS: the action only specifies the pedagogical task that can be used to address the diagnosed problem; the actual educational resources to be presented are determined by the course generator.

6.2.5.2 Assembly Tool

ACTIVEMATH's *assembly tool* allows a learner to create a book on her own by dragging educational resources from ACTIVEMATH (but also any other resource addressable by an URI). The tool was designed to support the learner's meta-cognitive reasoning, self-regulated learning and active engagement with the content.

The principal actions supported by the assembly tool are the creation of structured courses by adding chapters and drag-and-drop of resources into a table of contents. In addition, a learner has access to PAIGOS's functionality using a context menu. She can select the direct insertion of resources that fulfill a pedagogical task specified by the learner or insert a dynamic task that is achieved at a later time. Figure 6.17 contains a screenshot that illustrates the integration. In the example, the learner uses the course generator to select an example for "the definition of the difference quotient".

The interface allows an intuitive creation of a pedagogical task. First, the user selects a fundamental by clicking on it. This fundamental is the target fundamental of the pedagogical task. Then, the learner selects the pedagogical objective from the context menu. If the learner selected the direct insertion of elements, then the complete task is sent to the course generator and the resulting resources are added in the table of contents. Otherwise, in case the learner selected a dynamic item, the dynamic item is inserted in the table of contents and instantiated at the time the learner views the page in ACTIVEMATH.

The assembly tool runs on the client and thus illustrates that the course generator interfaces allow server-client communication.

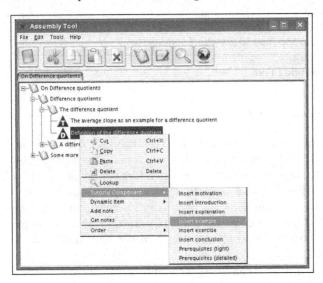

Fig. 6.17. Screenshot of the assembly tool

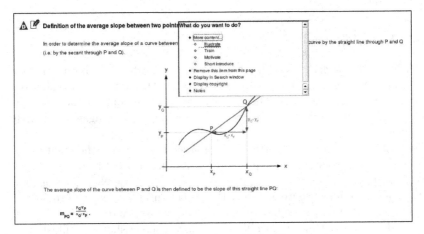

Fig. 6.18. The item menu for requesting additional content

6.2.5.3 Supporting the User's Initiative

In addition to the generation of complete courses on request of the learner, the integration of PAIGOS in ACTIVEMATH offers user-triggered course extension as an additional feature that supports the learner's active engagement in accessing the content.

In case the learner wishes to see additional educational resources about a fundamental displayed in a course, she can trigger the execution of a pedagogical task (e.g., `train`) by selecting them from a drop-down list. Then, the task is processed by PAIGOS and the resulting educational resources are presented to her. Upon the learner's request, the resources are added to the current page. Figure 6.18 contains a screenshot of the interface. The interface uses the condition element provided in the description of the task processable by PAIGOS ("public" tasks, see Section 4.3) to evaluate efficiently whether a task can be fulfilled. If it cannot be fulfilled, then the corresponding menu entry is hidden.

Compared to the search tool available in ACTIVEMATH, the item menu has the advantage that content is retrieved in "one click" using pedagogical knowledge. Using the search tool to retrieve, say, an easy exercise, requires knowledge about the ACTIVEMATH's metadata. The item menu only requires following a link.

6.3 Course Generation as a Web-Service

In this section, I describe how PAIGOS can be made available as a Web-service.[2] I start by describing a survey we conducted in order to determine the specific functionalities required by potential clients. From the collected requirements, we inferred a set of interfaces (Section 6.3.1); in contrast to a course generator integrated within a Web-based e-learning system as described in the previous section, a course generator Web-service (CGWS) needs to provide additional information, e. g., about the metadata it uses and the functionalities it offers. The final section describes the interactions between the clients and the CGWS.

In order to assess the potential interest and the requirements of third-parties regarding a CGWS, we designed a survey of 13 questions inquiring about general and specific interests of clients (e. g., interest in generating complete courses and retrieval of single resources), but also technical questions, e. g., the used metadata schema, whether a learner model is available, and the expected format of the results.

The survey was sent to three main mailing lists whose subscribers are mostly developers and researchers in the field of technology supported learning: *Adaptive Hypertext and Hypermedia*,[3] *International Forum of Educational Technology & Society*[4] and the *Internal Mailinglist of the European Network of Excellence Kaleidoscope*.[5]

25 questionnaires were completed. About 65% of the participants showed an interest in a CGWS, including 33% being strongly interested. The majority of the participants were using LOM, IMS CP and SCORM. Interestingly, even parties whose Web-based e-learning systems did not include a learner model

---

[2] The work described in this section was developed as the master thesis by Lu [89] under my supervision.

[3] http://pegasus.tue.nl/mailman/listinfo/ah [31]

[4] http://ifets.ieee.org/ [120]

[5] http://www.noe-kaleidoscope.org/ [70]

were interested in personalized course generation. Half of the Web-based e-learning systems that use learner models offer a Web-service access to their system. The results from the survey served to determine the interfaces of the CGWS.

6.3.1 Interfaces

6.3.1.1 Interfaces of the Course Generator Web-Service

The CGWS provides two main kinds of interfaces: the core interface that provides the methods for the course generation, and the repository integration interface that allows a client to register a repository at the CGWS. The core interface consists of the following methods:

- The method `getTaskDefinitions` is used to retrieve the pedagogical tasks which the course generator can process. The tasks are represented in the format described in Section 4.3.
- The method `generateCourse` starts the course generation on a given task. The client can make information about the learner available in two ways: if the learner model contains information about the specific learner, then the client passes the respective learner identifier as a parameter. In case no learner model exists, a client gives a list of property-value pairs that is used by the CGWS to construct a temporary "learner model". The course generator performs the planning in the same way as with a real learner model, however its access of learner properties is diverted by the CGWS and answered using the map. Properties not contained in the map are answered with a default value.

The result of the course generation is a structured sequence of educational resources represented in an IMS Manifest. Since the returned result does not contain the resources but only references, the return result is not an IMS CP.

The interface for repository registration consists of the following methods:

- The method `getMetadataOntology` informs the client about the metadata structure used in CGWS. It returns the ontology of instructional objects described in Section 4.1.
- The method `registerRepository` registers the repository that the client wants the course generator to use. The client has to provide the name and the location (URL) of the repository. Additional parameters include the ontology that describes the metadata structure used in the repository and the mapping of the OIO onto the repository ontology.
- The method `unregisterRepository` unregisters the given repository.

6.3.1.2 Client Interfaces

A client that wants to use the CGWS needs to provide information about the educational resources as well as about the learner (if available).

The interface `ResourceQuery` is used by the mediator to query the repository about properties of educational resources. The interface consists of the following methods (the same as described in Section 4.2.5):

- `queryClass` returns the classes a given resource belongs to.
- `queryRelation` returns the set of identifiers of those educational resources the given resource is related to via the given relation.
- `queryProperty` returns the set of property-value pairs the given resource has.

The *LearnerPropertyAPI* makes the learners' properties accessible to the CGWS in case the client contains a learner model and wants the course generator to use it. In the current version of the CGWS, this interface is not yet implemented. It would require a mediator architecture similar to the one used for repository integration.

6.3.1.3 Interaction between Client and Server

In this section we describe the communication between client and server performed when registering a repository and for course generation.

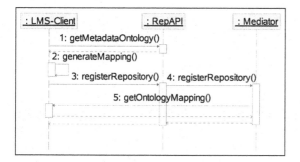

Fig. 6.19. A sequence diagram illustrating the repository registration

A repository is registered in the following way (for a sequence diagram illustrating the registration, see Figure 6.19): in a first step, the client (LMS-Client in the figure) retrieves the metadata ontology used in the CGWS (i. e., the OIO). The ontology is then used to generate a mapping between the OIO and the ontology representing the client metadata (Step 2) (the currently existing mappings were manually authored). Then, the repository is registered using the method `registerRepository` (Step 3). The repository is added to the list of available repositories and made known to the mediator (Step 4). Subsequently, the mediator fetches the ontology mapping from the client and automatically generates a wrapper for querying the `contentAPI` of the client.

A client starts the course generation using the service method **generate-Course**. In a first step, the CGWS checks whether the task is valid. If so, the course is generated by the course generator. During the generation process, PAIGOS sends queries to the mediator, which passes the queries to the repository. Like in ACTIVEMATH, the results are cached. After the course is generated, the `omgroup` generated by PAIGOS is transformed into an IMS manifest and sent to the client.

The CGWS is still in an early stage of development and further work is necessary to realize a mediator-like architecture for the generic integration of learner models. Yet, despite being a prototype, the CGWS was successfully used by the two third-party systems MATHCOACH (a learning tool for statistics, [52]) and TEAL (workflow embedded e-learning at the workplace, [156]). The following chapter will provide additional details on these use-cases.

7

Evaluation

This section describes the evaluation and use cases that assessed different aspects of PAIGOS. The first section covers technical evaluations and investigates the claims made in the previous chapters, i.e., whether the OIO can be mapped to third-party metadata (Section 7.1.1); whether the mediator can access third-party repositories (Section 7.1.2); and whether the Web-service interface of PAIGOS is usable by third-parties (Section 7.1.3). Furthermore, I describe the results of a detailed analysis of the performance of PAIGOS (Section 7.1.4). The analysis shows that PAIGOS generates courses that take a student approximately 11 hours to study in less than half a second, as long as other components such as the learner model and the repositories are able to answer requests in a timely manner. For real life usage results involving the target audience, i.e., learners are equally important as technical results. Therefore, PAIGOS was subject to formative and summative evaluations (Section 7.2). The evaluation involved about fifty students from Germany, UK, and Spain. The final summative evaluation illustrates that students like to use PAIGOS and appreciate the interactive possibilities offered by PAIGOS.

7.1 Technical Evaluations and Use Cases

The use cases and evaluations reported in this chapter have been performed in order to prepare the work and assess and improve the implemented results. The use cases are summarized in Table 7.1. I will discuss them in the following sections.

7.1.1 Evaluation of the Ontology

A major design goal of the OIO was compatibility with existing knowledge representations and metadata schemas. For that purpose, I analyzed to what extent the ontology could be mapped to the following widely-used knowledge representations and metadata used in existing e-learning systems.

Table 7.1. Realized uses cases

Type of uses case	Systems
Ontology mapping	ACTIVEMATH, DAMIT, DocBook, LEACTIVEMATH exercise repository, MATHCOACH, MATHSTHESAURUS, <ML>^{3}, OMDOC, TEAL, WINDS
Repository connection	ACTIVEMATH MBASE, DAMIT, LEACTIVEMATH exercise repository, MATHCOACH, MATHSTHESAURUS, TEAL
Usage of course generation service	LMS: MATHCOACH, TEAL, Educational services: Assembly Tool, Exercise Sequencer, Suggestion Component

- DAMIT is an adaptive learning environment for the data mining domain [66]. It adapts to the individual learning style of a user by providing different views (e.g. formal vs. informal) on the same learning content.
- DocBook [204] serves a standard for writing structured documents using SGML or XML and was selected for the evaluation because of its wide-spread use. Its elements describe the complete structure of a document down to basic entities, e.g., the parameters of functions. Here, the most relevant elements are those that describe content at paragraph level (called "block" elements). DocBook is a general-purpose standard and not specifically designed for the representation of educational resources.
- The LEACTIVEMATH exercise repository was designed in the LEACTIVE-MATH project and is a repository of interactive exercises that can be accessed by humans and machines. Its metadata is a slightly modified variant of ACTIVEMATH's metadata.
- The MATHCOACH system was developed at the University of Applied Sciences Saarland. It is a Web-based learning tool especially designed for exercises and experiments in statistics [52].
- MATHSTHESAURUS is an online multilingual mathematics thesaurus in nine languages [182] and was selected because it covers a wide range of mathematics.
- The "Multidimensional Learning Objects and Modular Lectures Markup Language" <ML>^{3} [90] was designed for use in e-learning. Several German universities used it to encode about 150 content modules in various domains.
- The TEAL project investigates task-oriented proactive delivery of educational resources in order to support learning at the workplace [156]. The TEAL project was particularly interesting since its domain was not mathematics but project management and the associated work tasks.
- WINDS [172], the "Web-based Intelligent Design and Tutoring System" provides several adaptive hypermedia features, e.g., adaptive link annotation. Its knowledge representation is based on Cisco's categorization of

learning objects [25] and was selected because its design was based on pedagogical considerations. WINDS is discussed in detail in Section 8.4.

By and large, we were able to design mappings between the OIO and the knowledge representations. Most problems were caused by the fact that often elements had no instructional semantics (e. g., para in DocBook, quotation and description in <ML>^{3}). In these cases, it is impossible to define a general mapping rule.

In contrast, it was relatively straightforward to devise mappings between the OIO and knowledge representations devised for pedagogical usage as in WINDS and <ML>^{3}. For instance, <ML>^{3} represents learning materials in "content blocks". These blocks can have one of the following types: "definition", "example", "remark", "quotation", "algorithm", "theorem", "proof", "description", "task", or "tip". Most elements directly correspond to an instructional object, however some elements, such as "quotation" and "description" cannot be mapped directly, since again the instructional purpose is unclear.

Additional evaluations of the OIO investigated its pedagogical appropriateness. School teachers (for mathematics and physics), instructional designers, and members of Klett's e-learning lab (the largest publisher of educational content in Germany), were interviewed about domain independence, pedagogical flexibility, completeness, and applicability. The feedback was largely positive and suggestions (e. g., an additional class lawOfNature) were taken into account for a revision of the ontology.

Applications of the ontology in domains other than course generation were investigated in the European Network of Excellence Kaleidoscope and published in [113]. Additionally, it was used for a revised version of the ALOCoM ontology, a recent effort in the European Network of Excellence ProLearn [82], in the e-learning platform e-aula [159], and in the CampusContent project of the Distant University Hagen [87].

7.1.2 Mediator Use Cases and Evaluations

Several repositories were successfully connected to the mediator (second row in Table 7.1, page 194): the mathematical knowledge-base of ACTIVEMATH (a Lucene database), the LEACTIVEMATH exercise repository (an EXIST-database), the database of the math tutor MATHCOACH (DerbyDB/JDBC), the MYSQL-database of the online multilingual Mathematics Thesaurus, and the DB2 database of the TEAL project. As a result, all these repositories can be accessed during course generation.

7.1.3 Course Generation Use Cases and Evaluations

The remote access to the course generation was successfully applied in MATH-COACH and the TEAL project (third row of Table 7.1, page 194). While the two

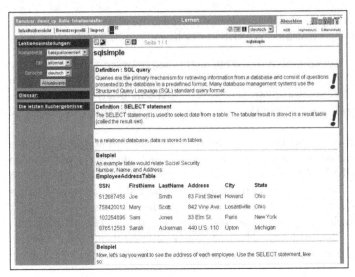

Fig. 7.1. A course generated by PAIGOS for the TEAL learning system

former use cases focus on teaching mathematics, the latter targets e-learning in office environments. This illustrates that PAIGOS is applicable in other areas than mathematics. In both cases, PAIGOS was accessed as a Web-service using the approach described in Section 6.3: MATHCOACH and TEAL registered their repositories and then started the course generation by providing a task. Information about the learner was passed as a map of property-value pairs. Figure 7.1 contains a screenshot of a course generated by PAIGOS and presented in TEAL.

7.1.4 Performance of PAIGOS

If PAIGOS is to be used in real-life learning situations, it has to generate courses quickly. In this section, I describe the results of a number of test of PAIGOS that allow making claims about its performance, i. e., the time it takes to generate courses under varying conditions.

In order to minimize influences of latency caused by the network, all components, i. e., the testing framework, ACTIVEMATH and its repository and learner model ran on the same computer, a standard PC with 2.8GH Intel Pentium 4 CPU with 2GB RAM (thus not a server).

Since the tests were designed to assess the performance of PAIGOS, influences of other components were minimized as much as possible. The learner model was replaced by a dummy learner model that returned a standard value for each query. In addition, most of the tests were performed with a pre-filled mediator cache: the course was generated once, thereby causing the mediator to store the results of the queries. Then, the actual test runs were performed, on the same set of target fundamentals and thus resulting in the same queries.

The tests were performed using the scenario "discover". This scenario involves a large variety of different educational resources and is not as specialized as, say, "exam preparation". The data was collected by generating six courses on 1, 4, 8, 12, 16, and 20 target fundamentals. Each course generation was repeated 10 times and the data was averaged. Prior to the test, the mediator cache was filled as described above.

Table 7.2. The amount of fundamentals, pages and resources of the courses generated in the technical evaluations

Number of Fundamentals	1	4	8	12	16	20
Pages	6	19	36	52	79	83
Resources	37	105	202	254	319	365

Table 7.2 provides details on the length of the created courses. The course generated for a single fundamental consists of six pages and a total of 37 educational resources if all dynamic tasks are expanded. A course generated for 20 fundamentals consists of 83 pages and 365 resources. If each resource has a typical learning time of about two minutes, completing this course would take between 11 and 12 hours. These figures illustrate that course generation requires a large amount of educational resources: a course for 4 fundamentals consists of more than 100 educational resources.

Table 7.3. Required time of course generation vs. increasing amount of fundamentals

Number of Fundamentals	1	4	8	12	16	20
Expanded	429	1 204	1 875	2 562	3 360	4 834
Dynamic Tasks	205	288	415	446	617	617

Table 7.3 and Figure 7.2 plot the number of fundamentals (called concepts in the Figure) against the time required for course generation (in milliseconds). In the table, the condition **Expanded** provides the time required for a completely expanded course, i. e., all dynamic tasks are directly instantiated. The generation of the smallest course (a single fundamental, six pages and 37 educational resources in total) takes less than half a second. The generation of a course for 20 fundamentals takes less than five seconds, an acceptable delay in a Web-based environment.

The condition **Dynamic Tasks** contains the values obtained for course generation with dynamic tasks. The figures illustrate that not planning the complete plan can result in a significant performance improvement: a course for 20 fundamentals is generated in slightly more than half a second.

Table 7.4 compares the times it takes to generates courses using a filled cache (the same data as in the previous tables) versus an empty cache. The

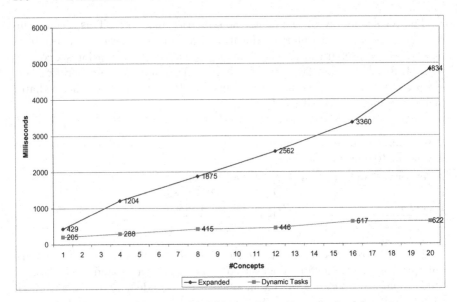

Fig. 7.2. A plot of the number of fundamentals vs. time required for course generation in milliseconds

Table 7.4. Times for generating a course with filled and empty mediator caches.

Number of Fundamentals	1	4	8	12	16	20
Filled Cache	205	288	415	446	617	617
Empty Cache	1 218	2 176	4 258	6 502	8 975	11 405

Table 7.5. Numbers of queries to the mediator and of expanded queries

Number of Fundamentals	1	4	8	12	16	20
Mediator Queries (Exp.)	1 519	5 297	9 826	13 123	16 901	21 499
Expanded Queries (Exp.)	11 400	29 697	49 565	62 992	83 923	100 421
Mediator Queries (DT)	148	496	1 043	1 503	2 002	2 707
Expanded Queries (DT)	1 204	3 349	7 810	9 702	11 510	14 155

increase is significant: the generation of a course for a single fundamental with an empty cache takes more than a second, compared to 200 milliseconds with filled cached. A course for 20 fundamentals takes about 11 seconds compared to half a second. This data was obtained with the repository running on the same location as the course generator. Hence, accessing a repository over the Web would increase the required time even more. The reasons for the increase can be found by taking a closer look at the mediator.

Table 7.5 provides details about the number of queries that are sent to the mediator during course generation and about the number of queries that the mediator sends to the repository. The figures differ since the mediator expands a query for a class c to include its subclasses. The data is provided for expanded

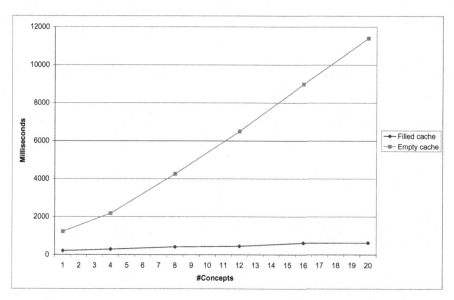

Fig. 7.3. Plot of the number of fundamental vs. times required for course generation with empty and filled cache

Table 7.6. Time required for course generation with different learner models (in milliseconds)

no LM	288
SLM	463
LM-x	161 085

courses (condition **Exp.**) as well as for courses with dynamic tasks (condition **DT**). The high amount of queries came as a surprise. Generating an expanded course for a single fundamental results in about 1 500 mediator queries that are expanded to more than 11 000 queries to the repository. The figures are significantly less in condition **DT**. Approximately 150 queries are sent to the mediator, which expands them to about 1 200 queries. On the other end of the spectrum, generating an expanded course for 20 fundamentals results in 21 500 mediator queries and more than 100 000 expanded queries. Condition **DT** requires approximately 2 700 and 14 100 mediator and repository queries.

The above results show that PAIGOS generates courses very efficiently, however it strongly depends on the performance of the repository. An additional test examined effects on the learner model on course generation. In the previous tests, learner property queries were handled by a dummy learner model. Table 7.6 and Figure 7.4 compare the time required by course generation with the dummy leaner model, the standard learner model of ACTIVEMATH (SLM) and an external learner model that was integrated in ACTIVEMATH on a provisional basis in the LEACTIVEMATH project (I will refer to it as LM-x).

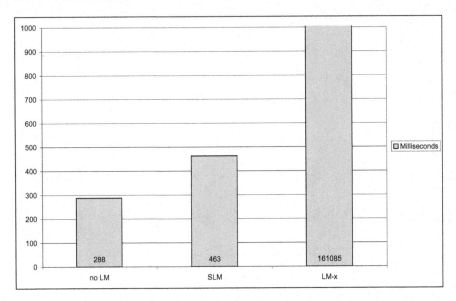

Fig. 7.4. Plot of the time required for course generation with different learner models (in milliseconds)

During course generation, PAIGOS caches learner property queries. The cache is cleared after each planning run. The course was generated for four fundamentals. Not surprisingly, the required time depends on the learner model: if it provides fast response times, then course generation is not substantially affected (see the increase from 288 to 463 milliseconds when using the SLM). In contrast, a low-performing learner model like the LM-x deteriorates the course generator's performance: generating a course takes about 2:30 minutes instead of half a second.

Table 7.7. Required average time of 50 concurrent course generation processes (in milliseconds)

Dynamic Tasks	7 713
Expanded	31 029

A final test investigated the performance of concurrent access to the course generator. In the test, fifty concurrent course generation processes were started, for a course with four target fundamentals. Table 7.7 illustrates the results: on average, a completely expanded course takes 30 second to generate. Using dynamic tasks, it takes about 8 seconds.

7.1.5 Discussion

The results show that PAIGOS on its own generates courses fast, especially if dynamic tasks interrupt the expansion of subtasks. Thus, dynamic tasks improve the performance and enable adaptivity in generated and authored courses.

The tests were designed to assess the performance of PAIGOS. As a consequence, external factors needed to be minimized. In particular, PAIGOS retrieved all resource queries from the mediator's cache. However, this test design is not completely artificial: in classroom usage, each lesson covers a limited set of fundamentals. After a few course generations, the majority of queries will be cached. In addition, since the topics are known beforehand, the teacher or the e-learning environment can fill the cache before the lesson.

Yet, PAIGOS's real-life performance considerably depends on the repositories and the learner model. In case the components reside on different servers, the network latency alone reduces the overall performance: the LeActive-Math exercise repository is located in Eindhoven, the Netherlands. When accessed from Saarbrücken, Germany, it answers a single query in about 80 milliseconds. As a consequence, the generation of a 4 concepts course that requires 3 300 queries requires 4:30 minutes instead of 290 milliseconds.

On the Web, four minutes are an eternity. Few learners will wait patiently for the course to appear: the experiments conducted by Bhatti et al. [14] showed that subjects rate a response time of over 11 seconds as unacceptable. This suggests adapting the user-interface metaphor of the course generator. Instead of making the users expect an immediate course assembly, a course should be "downloadable", like a PDF document or PowerPoint slides. A download often takes several minutes. After the "download" the user is notified and can access her course from the main menu.

7.2 Formative and Summative Evaluation

This section presents the results of several evaluations of PAIGOS performed in the LeActiveMath project. The reported work was done in collaboration with Marianne Moormann (Mathematical Institute of Ludwig-Maximilians-University, Munich), Tim Smith (School of Informatics at the University of Edinburgh) and Eva Millán (University of Malaga). PAIGOS was subject to two formative evaluations and a summative evaluation.

Formative Evaluation

Formative evaluations are performed during the development of a product (a software, a lesson, etc.). The evaluators monitor how users interact with the product and identify potential problems and improvements. According to Scriven [165], p. 20, "[f]ormative evaluation is evaluation designed, done, and intended to support the process of improvement, and normally commissioned or done by, and delivered to, someone who can make improvements."

Summative Evaluation

A summative evaluation is performed at the end of the development of the product. It describes the outcome of the product, by summarizing whether the product is able to do what it was supposed to do. Scriven [165], p. 20 characterizes summative evaluation as "the rest of evaluation: in terms of intentions, it is evaluation done for, or by, any observers or decision makers (by contrast with developers) who need evaluative conclusions for any reasons besides development".

The difference between formative and summative evaluation is illustrated by Robert Stake's analogy: "when the cook tastes the soup, that's formative evaluation; when the guest tastes it, that's summative evaluation [165, p. 19]."

The evaluations focused on the scenario "discover". It is the first scenario learners will work with and does not require prior contact with the content in contrast to, say, rehearse and connect. The final summative evaluation included the remaining scenarios.

We conducted the first formative evaluation in December 2005 in Saarbrücken and Munich, Germany (Section 7.2.1). At that time we had completed a first prototypical implementation of the scenario "discover". The results of the evaluation were taken into account in the further implementation of PAIGOS. In June 2006, the second formative evaluation took place in Munich and repeated the methodology employed in the first evaluation (Section 7.2.1.2). The result showed that we successfully addressed the problems identified in the first evaluation. The summative evaluation was performed in January 2007 in Edinburgh, UK, and Malaga, Spain (Section 7.2.2). It investigated the complete set of scenarios developed in LEACTIVEMATH. The results were positive: the subjects judged the generated courses being useful and well-structured. The following sections describe the evaluations in detail.

7.2.1 Formative Evaluations

7.2.1.1 First Formative Evaluation (Germany)

A first formative evaluation assessed the scenario "discover". It took place at the universities in Munich and in Saarbrücken. The subjects were five students for pre-service mathematics teachers in their final year of study (Munich) and six computer science students attending a seminar on "e-learning and mathematics" (Saarbrücken).

In both places the procedure was as follows: an introduction (15 minutes) introduced the subjects to ACTIVEMATH (the book metaphor, navigation, online help and search, and exercises). Then, we randomly split the students in two groups. One group worked with a generated course, the other with an authored book that contained the complete content. The aim of the evaluation was to assess whether an automatic selection of the educational resources would show an advantage over accessing the complete content within a single book. Usage of the search facility was not restricted.

The subjects worked on the task to learn about derivatives, from the basic concept up to the differentiation rules. The duration of the evaluation was 45 minutes. Afterwards, each subject completed a questionnaire that assessed attitudes (e.g., like and dislike of the book they worked with) and how they judge the effectiveness of the book. The questionnaire asked for both structured (Likert scale questions) and open feedback.

For the quantitative analysis, the answers were encoded numerically ranging from 1 for complete agreement or positive judgment to 4 for complete disagreement or a negative judgment. We merged all questions inquiring about similar topics into one category, thus resulting in the following categories: overall positive views on the system, quality of navigation, content quality, and value for learners new to the content.

The subjects rated the overall ACTIVEMATH system as average (2.54), which is not surprising given the early state of the system. The subjects from Saarbrücken gave better, i. e., lower, ratings (2.31) than the Munich subjects (2.82). This was a general tendency throughout all the answers. We believe it is caused by the Saarbrücken students being more familiar with software in general. The subjects rated the content averagely, too (mean 2.37, Saarbrücken and Munich 2.07).

Several question assessed whether the subjects judged the content as being useful for learners without prior knowledge. The overall mean was 2.85, hence neutral. Contrary to our expectations the group that worked with authored books gave a more positive statement (2.66) than the group working with generated books (3.01). However, the difference between the two locations was more significant: the subjects of Saarbrücken rated the usefulness higher than the Munich subjects (2.48 vs. 3.01).

The evaluation was severely hampered by the fact the mathematical skills of the subjects were much lower than we expected. Both groups exhibited problems while working with content we considered being prerequisites. Hence, in the limited time of the study some subjects did not reach the principal content of the books, which was the content that was adapted.

The qualitative feedback given in the open feedback questions provided valuable suggestions that were taken into account for the development of the course generation scenarios, e. g., about the order of the exercises and examples, the insertion of prerequisites (axiom `readyAux`) and duplication of resources). Although the evaluation focused on the scenario "discover", these modifications are relevant to all scenarios.

7.2.1.2 Second Formative Evaluation (Germany)

We conducted a second formative evaluation in June 2006 in Munich. Although the number of participants was limited (4 pre-service teachers), the feedback of the subjects showed that the modifications implemented as a reaction to the first evaluation were beneficial.

The used methodology was almost equivalent to the one of the first study. Due to the small number of participants, the subjects all worked with generated courses. In addition, the task was formulated slightly differently. In order to avoid that the subjects try to work through all pages of the book and run in danger to get stuck in the very first pages, they were told to assess the book with respect to its adequateness for learners new to the concept of derivation.

In this evaluation, the subjects were very positive regarding the structure of the generated courses. They rated the structure of the book as being beneficial for "new learner" (mean 1.67). Similarly, the structure of the sections are rated as being very coherent (mean 1.25).

7.2.1.3 Formative Evaluation (UK)

During February and March 2007 a lab-based University-level formative evaluation of PAIGOS was performed. At that time, the system was in an early stage of development. The learner model and course generator was not yet completely functional. Nevertheless, the evaluation was able to identify potential problems and to identify the potential contributions of the course generator to the student's learning and experience of ACTIVEMATH.

A cooperative evaluation design was used for this study. This design actively engages the student in the evaluation process and enables them to step back and critique the system's performance and comment on their experience. Students were set tasks to complete and asked to "think aloud" describing how they are carrying out the task and any problems they are having. During their interaction audio and video was recorded and later analyzed to identify metrics of performance. This data was then combined with the student's answers to pre- and post-use questionnaires.

Eleven students (6 male; mean age 19.45 years) from University of Edinburgh first year Mathematics courses took part in the evaluation. The participants had been studying calculus for 2.6 years on average and rated their own confidence with calculus as "good". All participants were frequent computer users who were very familiar with web interfaces. All had previously used some form of math software although the tasks they had performed were mostly limited to generating graphs and inputting mathematical formulae. These participants were considered representative of the University-level target users of ACTIVEMATH.

The content in the primitive version of ACTIVEMATH evaluated was divided into either authored courses which had been constructed by a teacher or personal courses which the student could construct themselves using the course generator. Due to the preliminary state of the learner model the content presented in these courses was not adapted to the competency levels of the students. Essentially the student's experience of the content was as an electronic text book with hyperlinked concepts.

The evaluation showed that students found the structure and navigation of the content "quite" easy to use and "quite" useful. Responses were made on a 5-point Likert scale ranging from 1 ("not at all") to 5 ("very much"). The two above values ("quite") correspond to 4. 91% of students said that the book metaphor used to structure the content was useful and intuitive and the web interface worked as expected. However, 63% of the students commented that the content structure became confusing when there were more than two sublevels of content. When a course was subdivided into only one top level and bottom level (chapters and pages), students navigated the content without any problem. If a course contained further subdivision they were unable to use the book metaphor to refer to the content and their efficiency of navigation suffered.

Learners used a course generation wizard for selecting content topics to appear in the course. On average students rated the course generator as "quite" easy to use but of only "moderate" usefulness. When asked for more details 63% of students commented that they found it difficult to relate the list of content items presented in the course creation tool to the resulting form of that content in the generated course. The relationship between content item and page was not one-to-one as expected.

When asked to identify ACTIVEMATH's weaknesses students commented that the system was not as good as a human tutor as it could not direct them towards content and exercises based on their knowledge or give them tailored guidance. However, no requests for these functions were made when given the opportunity to suggest improvements. This mismatch possibly indicates students' assumptions about what a computer system is capable of. This suggests that the functionality offered by the course generator in combination with the learner should be unexpected but beneficial to the student's experience of ACTIVEMATH and their learning. This was confirmed in the summative evaluation.

7.2.2 Summative Evaluation

The summative evaluation took place in January 2007 in Edinburgh, UK, and Malaga, Spain. It involved 39 students of mathematics, engineering, science, and computer science, with an age range of 17–21 (average age of 18). 28 students were male, 11 female.

The evaluation used a cooperative evaluation methodology. A cooperative evaluation usually involves a user working together with a physically present experimenter to use and critique a system [118]. The physical presence of the experimenter allows them to modify the evaluation to the user, ensures that they communicate any problems they are experiencing, any issues, incompatibilities they identify and also to ensure that they explore the important features of the system. The upside of this approach is that a detailed insight into the system's usability and acceptance can be gained. The downside is that only one user can be run at a time, the scenario in which the system is used is highly artificial, and the experiences of multiple users cannot be directly compared as the experimenter tailors each session.

These problems were addressed in the in-depth summative evaluation by taking the cooperative evaluation design and automating it. As ACTIVEMATH is an on-line system tailored to a specific student a realistic evaluation of the system should be performed by solitary students, on-line whilst in their usual work environment, whether that is at home or in an open-access computer lab. To achieve this, the experimenter in the cooperative evaluation has to be replaced by a system that both guides the student and probes them for feedback. On-line surveys were used to set the student tasks, provide hints on how to solve the tasks, and ask for both structured (Yes/No or Likert scale questions) and open feedback.

At the time of the study, course generation was new to the students and not part of their learning routine. This certainly affects the judgment of some of the scenarios, especially those that correspond to unfamiliar ways of structuring content, e. g., the scenario "connect". In addition, the subjects had no experience how and when to use generated courses, e. g., to start with "discover", followed by "rehearse", etc. Nevertheless, the evaluation allowed to collect data regarding the subject's attitude towards generated courses, e. g., to assess whether the students accept and appreciate the generated books.

The evaluations were impaired by severe problems with the learner model component. Access to the learner model was often very slow, which caused some courses not to be generated. In addition, sometimes the competency values were not updated and existing values forgotten. Nevertheless, since we were able to take these problems into account, the evaluation provided us with valuable data how learners value the courses generated by PAIGOS.

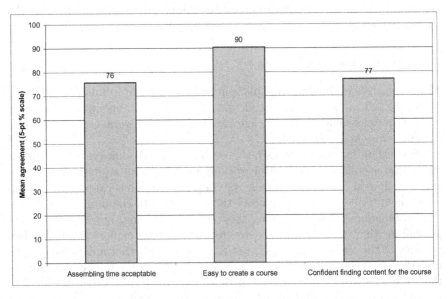

Fig. 7.5. General usability regarding the scenario "discover"

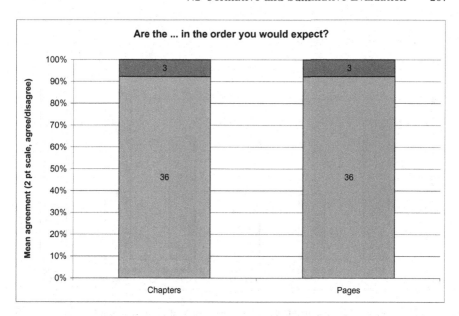

Fig. 7.6. Agreement with the order of elements

Figure 7.5 shows that the subjects appreciate PAIGOS's general usability. The subjects stated their agreement (100) or disagreement (0) using a 5-point Likert scale. The assembling time is judged being acceptable (first column). The subjects highly value the course generation wizard: they agree that it is easy to create a course and that they are confident that they will find the content they want (second and third column). Given that course generation was previously unknown to the subjects, these results show that the revised wizard is able to convey the concept of course generation to the learners.

The following figures present results concerning the scenario "discover". Figure 7.6 illustrates that PAIGOS orders chapters (first column) and pages (second column) in a way the subjects expect. They could either agree or disagree with the given statement. About 92% agreed that the chapters were in the expected order.[1] The subject's agreement with the order of the pages is similarly high (92%). These results show that automatic course generation as implemented in PAIGOS structures courses in a way that students understand.

As shown in Figure 7.7, the subjects agree with the way PAIGOS adapts courses to their knowledge if they agree with the learner model. Students were asked to rate how well they think the content of the book has been tailored to their current knowledge using a 5-point Likert scale (0 not tailored at all, 100 perfectly tailored). The course was generated for content the subjects had worked with previously. The mean value of about 60 (first column) shows that

---

[1] Due to a programming bug, the raw data results in a lower percentage (70%). If the bug is taken into account and the data cleaned up, we reach 92% agreement.

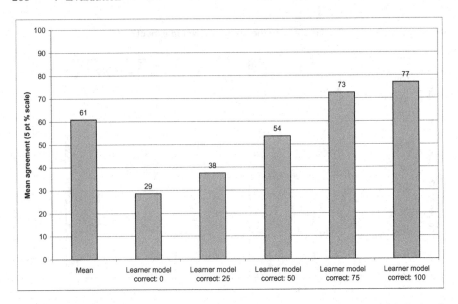

Fig. 7.7. Results for the question "rate how well you think the content of the book has been tailored to your current knowledge", in relation to the perceived correctness of the learner model

the subjects agree with PAIGOS's adaptivity. However, a closer look on these figures shows that the rating of the quality of the tailoring increases with the perceived correctness of the learner model. One question in the evaluation asked the subjects to rate how well they think the learner model reflects their competency. Columns 2 to 6 in Figure 7.7 show that the rating of the tailoring increases with the perceived quality of the learner model. With a very low rating of the correctness of the learner model, the quality of the tailoring is low, but not zero. This may be due to the tailoring with respect to the selected fundamentals. A high perceived learner model quality (10 students for column 5, and 13 for column 6) increases the rating of the tailoring to almost 80. We think that this data allows drawing two conclusions: firstly, the learners are able to see that the courses generated by PAIGOS are adapted to the learner. Otherwise, the ratings would not differ depending on the rating of the learner model. Secondly, the realized adaptivity is appreciated by the learners.

Figure 7.8 presents the subjects' agreement/disagreement with the level of difficulty of the selected exercises (the numbers give the numbers of subjects as well as the percentage). As described in the previous chapter, the scenario "discover" presents exercises directly on a page, but also includes a link to the exercise sequencer. Since the evaluation surveys instructed the subjects to use the sequencer, the figures comprises the data for both selection processes (which both use the same pedagogical task). The data contains the answers of those students who stated that the estimations by the learner model were

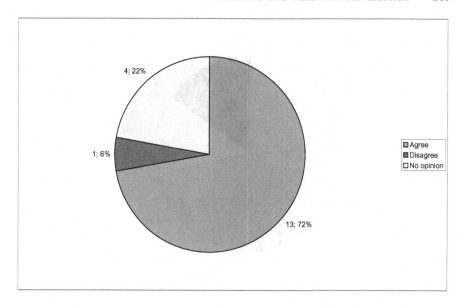

Fig. 7.8. Results for the question "do you think the level of difficulty of the exercises was correct" for learners who state that the learner model values are correct

correct. Almost three quarter of the learners state that the selected exercises have the appropriate difficulty level, and only a single subject disagrees. Again, this result indicates that PAIGOS's pedagogical knowledge is adequate.

Data that investigates the preferred way of exercise selection is presented in Figure 7.9. The subjects were asked whether they preferred exercises being presented using the sequencer or on a page. The results are not clear cut. Even if more than half of the subjects prefer the sequencer, about a quarter prefer the "traditional" way. Thus, the current formalization that caters for both groups is reasonable.

Subjects like working with generated courses of the type "discover". Figure 7.10 shows that only a single subject stated that he would never use a generated course. One third would use it mostly or as often as authored books; forty percent would use it occasionally.

An additional set of questions investigated the subjects' attitudes towards the remaining scenarios. For each scenario, the subjects first read its description and then answered the question how much they think they could learn from a generated course of this type. Subsequently, they generated the corresponding course. After examining the course, the subjects answered the following questions.[2]

- "I understand how the personal book is structured."

---

[2] The subjects use the terminology of ACTIVEMATH: generated courses are called personal books; authored courses are called prerecorded books.

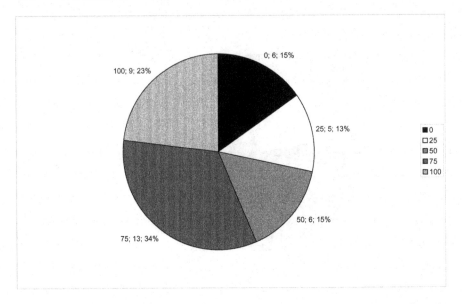

Fig. 7.9. Results for the question "do you prefer exercises to be sequenced in this way or presented in a book that you can work through on your own?" Answers were given on a 5-point scale, with 0 corresponding to "on a book page" and 100 to "in the exercise sequencer"

- "The book is very tailored to my knowledge."
- "I would learn a lot from using this type of personal book."
- "How much do you think you would use a book this type when learning a topic?"

The Figures 7.11 and 7.12 contain the results for scenario "connect". The first column in Figure 7.11 shows how much the learners think they could learn a lot from a "connect" book (with 0 corresponding to "disagree" and 100 to "agree"). Even though the aim of the book, i. e., to make explicit the connections between fundamentals, is usually not a focus in teaching and thus unfamiliar to the learners, they still think they can learn from books of this type after reading the scenario's description. Albeit the structure of "connect" books is more complicated than of the other scenarios, students seem to understand it (second column). They have a neutral opinion regarding the adaptivity. Interestingly, the subjects appreciate the scenario less after having seen a generated course (column 4) than after having read the description (column 1). We think this indicates that the students value learning about connections between fundamentals, but that the formalization of the course needs to be refined. This conclusion is supported by the data in Figure 7.12. More than half of the subjects state that they would use a book of type "connect" occasionally and more often, and an additional 20% would use it at least once. In this and the following figures, the total number of subjects

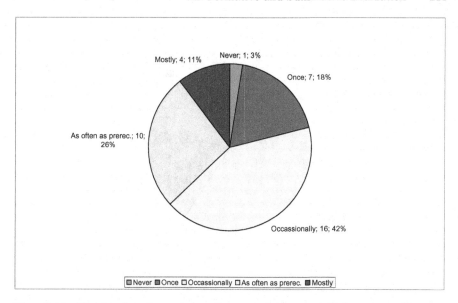

Fig. 7.10. Results for the question "how much do you think you would use a Discover book when learning a new topic?"

differ since due to the problems with the learner model some subjects were

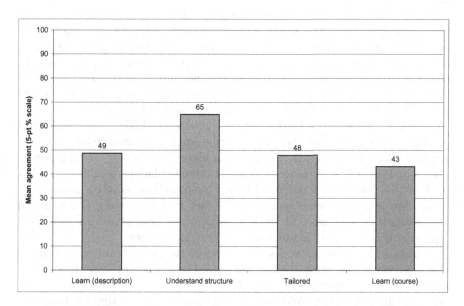

Fig. 7.11. Results for the scenario "connect", on a 5-point scale, with 0 corresponding to complete disagreement and 100 corresponding to complete agreement

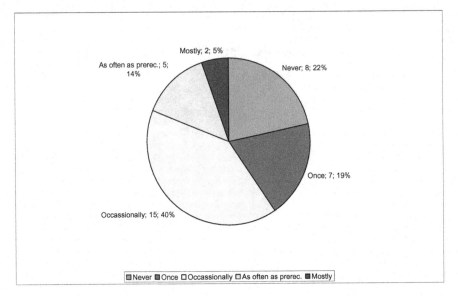

Fig. 7.12. Results for the question "How much do you think you would use a book of type 'connect' when learning a topic?"

unable to generate courses for all scenarios. These subjects were not included in the respective data.

Figure 7.13 and 7.14 contains the results for the scenario "exam simulation". In Figure 7.13, the discrepancy between the agreement after reading the description (85) and after inspecting the course (54) is striking. We attribute this fact to the long time it takes to generate this particular type of book. In this scenario, all exercises have to be determined during the course generation in order to fill the selected time-span and hence, dynamic tasks cannot be used. But still, 90% of the subjects would use books of this type.

The data in Figure 7.15 shows that the subjects highly value generated courses of the type "rehearse": the average agreement after reading the description and after generating a course is about 75. The high rating is confirmed by Figure 7.16. None of the subjects claimed he/she would never use a book of this type, about two third would use mostly or as often as authored books. We attribute these results to the fact that rehearsing is a common task when learning and that students appreciate support during rehearsal, especially if the support is tailored to their competencies.

Figure 7.17 contains the data for books of the type "train competency". The appreciation is lowest of all scenarios (56) but increases after the subjects have inspected a generated course (61). We think these results are due to the unfamiliarity of the concept of "competencies". This would explain the increase: by only reading the description, the learners do not have a sufficiently concrete idea of the scenario. After inspecting a generated course, the subjects

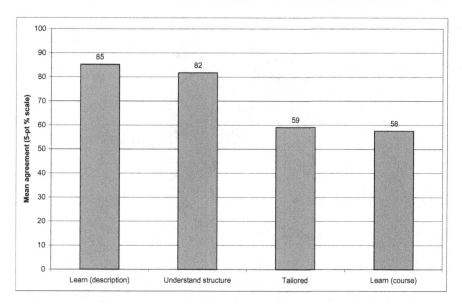

Fig. 7.13. Results for the scenario "exam simulation", on a 5-point scale, with 0 corresponding to complete disagreement and 100 corresponding to complete agreement

become aware that it mainly consists of exercises that train a specific aspect of a fundamental. Two third of the students would use such a course at least occasionally (Figure 7.18).

The most appreciated type of book is "train intensively" (called "workbook" in ACTIVEMATH). The mean agreement both before and after a course of this type was generated is about 80 (see Figure 7.19). About 85% of the subjects would use it at least occasionally (see Figure 7.20), and half of the subject as least as often as an authored book.

7.2.3 Discussion

The results of the formative and summative evaluations show that the subjects understand the structure of the generated courses and appreciate the tailoring to their competencies. Those scenarios that support the students in working with exercises are valued highest. The in-depth evaluations performed in the LEACTIVEMATH project confirm that students primarily appreciate ACTIVE-MATH as a tool for rehearsing and training. Scenarios such as connect that are new to students are rated lower.

The open feedback questions provide other valuable insights. Two subjects commented that they were afraid to miss important content when using generated courses. One of the subject said "the personal book was at a good level, but if I was revising for maths I would be worried that it would miss

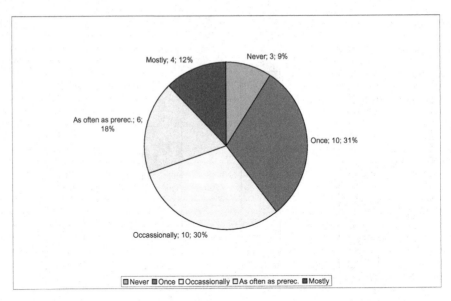

Fig. 7.14. Results for the question "How much do you think you would use a book of type 'exam simulation' when learning a topic?"

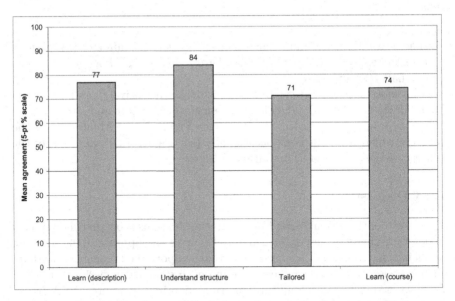

Fig. 7.15. Results for the scenario "rehearse", on a 5-point scale, with 0 corresponding to complete disagreement and 100 corresponding to complete agreement

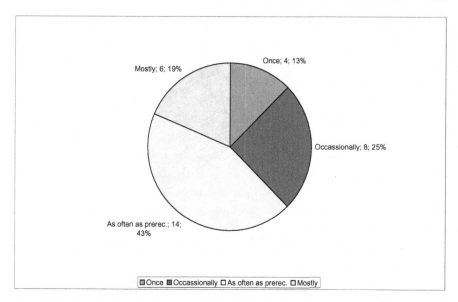

Fig. 7.16. Results for the question "How much do you think you would use a book of type 'rehearse' when learning a topic?"

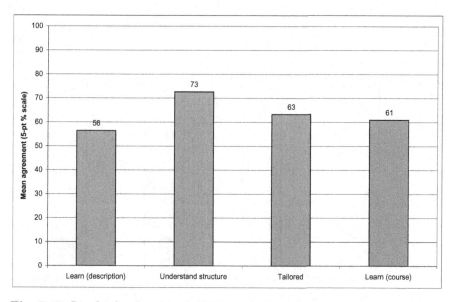

Fig. 7.17. Results for the scenario "train competency", on a 5-point scale, with 0 corresponding to complete disagreement and 100 corresponding to complete agreement

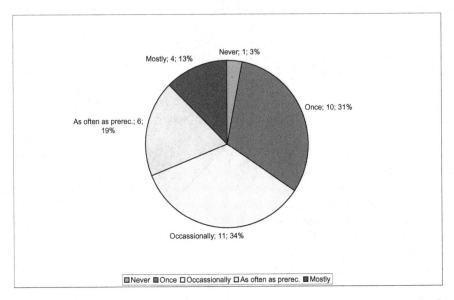

Fig. 7.18. Results for the question "How much do you think you would use a book of type 'train competency' when learning a topic?"

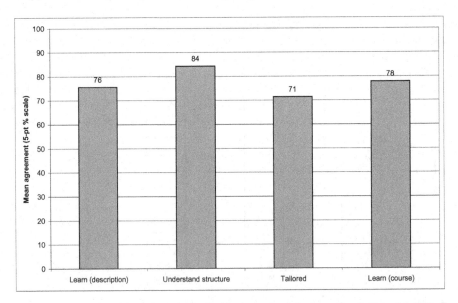

Fig. 7.19. Results for the scenario "train intensively", on a 5-point scale, with 0 corresponding to complete disagreement and 100 corresponding to complete agreement

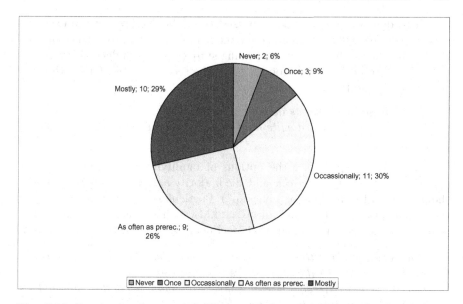

Fig. 7.20. Results for the question "How much do you think you would use a book of type 'train intensively' when learning a topic?"

out something important, and just read the prerecorded books anyway". This underlines the importance of making the concept of generated courses familiar to the students if they are to be used in daily learning.

Another point emphasized by the subjects in the open feedback was that they understand and appreciate the notion that a generated course is indeed personal, that is, it is tailored to and modifiable by the individual learner. In fact, all subjects agreed that they should be able to modify generated courses using the item menu.

I conclude this chapter by discussing some of the subjects' remarks (spelling errors were not corrected). These comments are of general interest since they show that students will criticize pedagogically questionable course generation knowledge, but at the same time appreciate the flexibility that course generation makes possible. Appendix A contains the complete list of the students' comments.

The two following quotes illustrate that the subjects detected incorrect order of chapters, but were also aware of the intended structure in case of correct order.

> difference quotient is first but i think it should come later. pages are in a logical order.
> They get progressively more difficult and the later ones require the knowledge of the first ones

Three quarter of the subjects judged the difficulty level of the exercises as appropriate considering their competency level; several provided comments like the first quote below. The remaining subjects either judged the exercises either being too difficulty or too easy (see the second quote). Often, this was caused by the problems with the learner model.

> *the exercises are good as they grow in difficulty"*
> *These problems seemed quite hard considering how weakly I have met the prerequisites.*

The subjects appreciate the options of modifying generated courses by adding and removing resources. and the majority agrees that authored books should remain fixed ("kind of a backup"). Particularly interesting are the last two comments: the "freedom" of ACTIVEMATH helps learners to find they own way of learning and makes them feel being respected, treated as adults.

> *One is responsible utterly for a personal book, but should always have a kind of backup in the form of pre-recorded book.*
> *I think the more freedom a user is given, the more likely they will find the best way to learn the material for them.*
> *As I understand, LAM is designed for students; as students are adults, they should be able to easily decide about contents of their books, to suit their particular needs.*

The final four comments are a representative set of quotes of the subjects describing whether they prefer working with authored books or generated courses. Most subjects value the clear structure of personal books and that they are focused on the selected target fundamentals. These quotes show that subjects perceive the adapted courses that PAIGOS generates as an added value compared to traditional access to content.

> *In Personal Book topics are more friendly segregated.*
> *personal book offers a better means of understanding the product rule as it gives information bit by bit ie in sequence*
> *The prerecorded books were set out ideally and in an acceptable order, I'd use that.*
> *I prefer personal book because it is only about the product rule and no other topics would interrupt me. The pre-recorded book is quite big and is therefore not as clear as the personal book.*

Part III

Conclusions

8

Related Work

Course generation has long been a research topic and appears in the literature under a number of names, for instance curriculum sequencing [175] and trail generation [79]. The subsequent sections provide an overview of existing course generation approaches. The focus lies on well-known approaches that use (or claim to use) educational knowledge to inform the sequencing and selection of learning objects.

8.1 Early Work

The early work (e. g., [143]) introduced techniques upon which some of today's course generation is still based, in particular those approaches that model pedagogical knowledge. In the beginning, the distinction between course generation and ITS was fuzzy. The goal was to model the complete process of one-to-one tutoring as a dialogue between a system and a learner, including interactions while solving exercises. Some of these systems (e. g., [121]) used learning materials retrieved from repositories to support the tutoring process — a technique that later became the basic technique for course generation.

The early approaches applied a number of AI-techniques to guide the tutorial interaction, e. g., skeletal plans retrieved from a plan library [213], expert systems [26], STRIPS-based planning [143], blackboard-based architectures [121], and task-based approaches [196]. For a recent discussion on modeling tutorial interactions, see [37].

The early work was done at a time when the Internet was in its very infancy: there was no notion of standardized learning objects, and Web-based learning environments did not exist. With the advent of the Web, the research focus in course generation moved from modeling tutorial interactions to exploring Web-based techniques such Adaptive Hypermedia, generic descriptions of learning objects (metadata), and re-use as well as interoperability of resources and tools. While pedagogical knowledge was present in each developed system to some extent, often it was marginalized and seldom extensively and explicitly modeled.

Since the modeling of pedagogical knowledge plays a significant role in this volume, I restrict the following discussion of related work to approaches which have a similar objective.

8.2 Generic Tutoring Environment

The "Generic Tutoring Environment" (GTE) [195, 197] is a learning environment that is based on the explicit modeling of knowledge. It was developed in the Third EU Framework Programme, in the scope of several Delta projects. To my knowledge, despite the time that has passed since the development of GTE, no other course generation system possesses a comparable large instructional knowledge base up to now, aside from PAIGOS.

GTE was the first system that followed the line of thought of Steels' *Components of Expertise* [174]. Based on this paradigm, the instructional knowledge represented in GTE was divided into instructional tasks, instructional methods, and instructional objects. Tasks represent activities to be accomplished during the teaching process. They are performed by methods that decompose tasks into subtasks down to a level of primitives. The tree that results from the repeated decomposition of tasks into subtasks by methods is called a task structure. PAIGOS is also based on the task-based paradigm.

The early descriptions of GTE [196] show that the original system was not designed as a course generator. The complete instructional process was supposed to be modeled as a dialogue, which includes interactions while solving exercises. This aim is reflected in the process model of GTE, which handles the interaction with the learner. The process model includes the selection/presentation of the educational resources and interpretation of learner input during problem solving.

GTE does not use any standard (AI) technique but implements its own algorithm, based on *proceed signals*. A proceed signal tells the system to advance the interaction step by step. It is sent to the top-level task of the interaction and pushed through the tasks and methods of the task structure down to the currently active bottom task. In case the bottom task can be decomposed, a method that is applicable on the task is selected using a complex set of rating conditions. If the interactions associated with task were completed successfully (e. g., the learner solved the associated exercise(s)), then the task is marked as "finished". Otherwise a failure signal was sent to the method that created the task. A method that receives a process signal passes it to its first unfinished task. A failure signal causes the method to select a different subtask or to fail.

Van Marcke [197] argues that process signals provide a great deal of flexibility, as it enables tasks to interrupt the execution of its children. The downside is that no analysis of this algorithm exists (at least not published) and thus its complexity is unknown. In contrast, the formal underpinnings of HTN planning were developed in the mid-90s by [40] and complexity results are available.

Despite the amount of pedagogical knowledge modeled in GTE, it has no notion of scenarios as developed in PAIGOS. While the methods for teaching a concept do represent different ways of doing so (e. g., following a tutorial or discovery approach), the selection of the method is done using ratings encoded within the methods. A learner can not tell the system to apply, say, a discovery approach for the complete tutorial session.

In addition, the selection of exercises is limited. GTE takes difficulty and prior performance into account but does not use properties such as competencies, although it is in principle possible within the GTE framework.

8.3 Dynamic Courseware Generator

Just like GTE, the "Dynamic Courseware Generator" (DCG) [198, 199, 200] is one of the early systems. It uses rules for pedagogically-based decision making, e. g., for deciding how to present a concept. DCG is based on the ideas of [143] who first proposed to use AI planning for technology-supported learning.

DCG distinguishes between the domain concepts and the educational resources used to explain/teach the concepts. The domain structure is represented in a graph. Nodes correspond to domain concepts, and edges to relations that hold between the concepts, e. g., domain prerequisites. The educational resources are stored as HTML pages and they are linked to the domain concepts. Each resource has a role (e. g., teach, explain, exercise, and test).

Course generation in DCG is separated in two consecutive steps: the selection of the concepts the course will cover and the way how these concepts are explained. Based on [205], Vassileva named these steps *content planning* and *presentation planning*.

Given a learner and a goal concept, content planning generates paths through the concept graph that connect the concepts known by the learner with her learning goal. DCG uses an AI-planner to search for the paths. A plan is then selected as a course skeleton for presentation planning.

Presentation planning selects which of those educational resources that are linked to a concept are to be presented to the learner and in what order. DCG uses four different methods for teaching a concept: "hierarchical", "advanced organizer", "basic concept", and "discovery". The hierarchical method uses the sequence "introduce", "explain", "give example", "give exercises", and "give a test". The "advance organizer" method uses the same sequence, but starts by informing the learner of the structure of the course to come and of the learning objectives. The "basic concepts" method starts with an exercise. The "discovery" method presents a motivating problem and an analysis of the problem and then lets the learner solve the problem on her own.

DCG is a course sequencer, that is, the next page is selected dynamically at the time the learner requests it. While this allows better reactivity, the learner is not able to see the structure of the complete course, which inhibits, for instance, free navigation.

The distinction between content and presentation planning raises the problem that for each concept it is decided separately what educational resources will be selected for it. The selection only takes the current concept into account. Using the published rules, it is not possible to construct a page that contains, say, the definition of a concept and all the definitions of its prerequisite concepts. Aside from the case of re-planning, it is also not possible that the same concept occurs in the course several times, which is necessary, for instance, when a theorem is used in several proofs and should be presented each time.

8.4 ACE/WINDS

The "Adaptive Courseware Environment" (ACE)[171] offers similar features as DCG. ACE was an extension of one of the first Web-based e-learning systems ELM-ART [20, 207], and combined ELM-ART's adaptive hypermedia techniques with DCG's presentation planning.

In ACE's concept graph, each node represents a concept or a set of concepts. Each concept is linked to different types of learning materials that explain different aspects of the concept. The edges of the domain structure represent prerequisite relations. In addition, authors can specify a sequence relation that is used as the default path through the domain.

Whereas in DCG the rules that govern presentation planning are independent of the concepts and hence re-used, in ACE an author has to provide them explicitly by specifying the sequence of educational resource to present for each concept (otherwise a default strategy is used). The sequence can change depending on values of the learner model, for instance easy examples might be skipped. Unfortunately, Specht and Oppermann do not describe the expressiveness of these rules, which makes them hard to assess. An adaptive sequencing component tries to keep the student on an optimal path but allows skipping sections if the learner proves to master them in a test.

Specht continued research in course generation and developed the "Web-based Intelligent Design and Tutoring System" (WINDS) [172]. Based on WINDS' description, ACE and WINDS seem closely related, which, however, is hard to assess precisely as the available descriptions of WINDS are very abstract. WINDS may possess more complex adaption methods, such as one deciding whether to present a concrete example before or after an abstract statement.

Both ACE and WINDS are conceptually very similar to DCG. In particular, they follow the distinction between content and presentation planning and hence suffer from the same drawbacks.

Another drawback is that the rules informing the presentation planning are attached to the individual concepts, which is a step backwards from the goal of *generic* instructional knowledge. The same applies to the requirement that the path through the domain structure needs to be specified by the author and is not generated automatically taking into account the learning goals.

8.5 Former Course Generator of ActiveMath

The former course generator of the learning environment ACTIVEMATH (see Section 2.4.2) generates a personalized course in a three-stage process, where stage one and two correspond to content and presentation planning [88]:

Retrieval of content. Starting from the goal concepts chosen by the user, all concepts they depend upon and corresponding additional educational resources (e.g., elaborations, examples for a concept) are collected recursively from the knowledge base. This process uses the dependency metadata information specified in metadata. The result of this retrieval is a collection of all educational resources that are available for the goal concepts and their prerequisites.

Applying pedagogical knowledge. In step second step, the collection of educational resources is processed according to the information in the user model and in the pedagogical module. This results in a personalized instructional graph of the learning material. This process is detailed below.

Linearization. In the final step, the instructional graph is linearized.

The result of the presentation planning is a linearized instructional graph of references to educational resources.

The goal of the application of pedagogical knowledge is to select resources from the collection of educational resources that was gathered in the first stage of course generation and to assemble them into a course. ACTIVEMATH employs pedagogical information represented in pedagogical rules. It evaluates the rules with the expert system shell JESS [43]. The rules consist of a *condition* and an *action* part. The condition part of a rule specifies the conditions that have to be fulfilled for the rule to be applied, the action part specifies the actions to be taken when the rule is applied.

The course generator employs the pedagogical rules to decide: (1) which information should be presented on a page; (2) in what order this information should appear on a single page; (3) how many exercises and examples should be presented and how difficult they should be; (4) whether or not to include exercises and examples that make use of a particular learning-supporting service, such as Computer Algebra Systems.

The former course generator of ACTIVEMATH offered the following scenarios: overview, guided tour, workbook, exam preparation. A prototypical Polya-style proof presentation targets the presentation of proofs in a manner based on guidelines by [146]. For more details on the scenarios, see [188, 105].

The former course generation of ACTIVEMATH had the following limitations. First, the content on a page was limited. Only a single concept could be contained in a page, and all other educational resources on that page had to be for the concept — a recurrent limitation of course generators that follow the paradigm of distinguishing between content and presentation planning.

A severe technical problem arouse due to the usage of the expert system approach. There, it is required that first the fact base that is used as a basis for the reasoning process is filled with the facts that are relevant for the reasoning. Only then, the reasoning process starts. This required to collect all potentially useful educational resources beforehand and then perform the selection. Naturally, this created performance problem, in particular high memory usage.

Additional limitations included the following. The rules that decided which auxiliaries to select for a concept were limited; they consisted of fixed schemas. In addition, the reasoning process happened on OMDOC level, using the metadata it provided, therefore, other repositories could not be integrated. Finally, the resulting course only contained educational resources; no learning goals, text templates, or services.

8.6 APeLS/iClass

In the "Adaptive Personalised e-Learning Service" (APeLS) [27, 28] an author can represent his courses using what the authors call "narratives" and "candidate groups". A narrative is a sequence through the content where each step consists of sets of educational resources that share the same learning goal (candidate groups). The specific resource presented to the learner is selected at run-time. This approach seems very similar to Vassileva's paths through the domain structure but instead of having concepts linked with educational resources, the nodes of the domain structure consist of the sets of educational resources. Unfortunately, the authors do not provide any details on this topic (nor citations). Different from DCG, where the paths were generated during content planning, in APeLS they are authored.

In APeLS, presentation planning is restricted to selecting the specific candidate group. The candidate groups are pre-defined and differ in the structure/layout in which the educational resources are placed and their output format.

Conlan and Wade continued their research on course generation in the European FP6 Integrated Project "iClass" (Intelligent Distributed Cognitive-based Open Learning System for Schools)[1] that "adapts to learners' needs, both intelligently and cognitively" [78]. In iClass, two components are responsible for course generation (or, to follow the terms of Keeffe et al. 78, "the

---

[1] http://www.iclass.info [60].

delivery of customized learning experiences"). A "Selector Service" does content planning and part of the presentation planning and a "LO Generator" performs additional functionalities similar to presentation planning.

The authors stress that the fact that unlike in APeLS, the iClass system separates pedagogical information and the domain structure into two distinct entities. However, they do not provide information to what extent this is different from the approach as advocated by [143] and implemented by, e. g., Vassileva in DCG. A potential difference might be that the selector's domain structure contains "skills" as well as concepts, and the selector service uses "skills" as a basis for determining the content. However, as there exists a one-to-one relationship between skills and concept, the approach is not fundamentally different. Once the selector has determined a set of concepts, it decides how each concept is presented, i. e., it selects the suited instructional method. The LO Generator then determines the exact educational resources to be used, based in learner preferences and context.

8.7 SeLeNe

The "SeLeNe" (self e-learning networks) project investigated technology-supported learning in networks of Web-based learning objects.[2] SeLeNe was an Accompanying Measure in the Fifth Framework Programme of the EU; part of its research was continued in the TRAILS-project of the European Network of Excellence Kaleidoscope.[3] A techniques investigated in SeLeNe is adaptive sequencing. Keenoy et al. [79, 80] call a linear sequence of educational resources a *trail*.

In SeLeNe, a learner searches for educational resources using simple keyword-based queries that are matched against author and subject information. A "Trails and Adaptation service" personalizes the queries by reformulating and adding conditions to the query (e. g., the learner's language), and by ranking the results in order of relevance to the learner. The learner can request a personalized sequence of interactions through the resources (a trail). Trails are calculated based on relationship types that hold between resources.

Most of the pedagogical knowledge used in SeLeNe is embedded in the algorithm that ranks the search results. The sequencing of the educational resources is done using the relationships given in the metadata of the resources. In the current version, it is rather limited, since essentially it consists of presenting all prerequisite concepts. When searching for resources, the learner can only specify a learning goal from the content. She can not specify more sophisticated learning goals as they are available in PAIGOS.

---

[2] http://www.dcs.bbk.ac.uk/selene/ [191].
[3] http://www.noe-kaleidoscope.org/ [70].

8.8 Statistical Methods for Course Generation

In contrast to the above approaches to course generation that rely on a more or less detailed explicit representation of instructional knowledge, Karampiperis and Sampson [71, 72] suggest to use statistical methods for determining the best path through the educational resources.

The approach works as follows. Instead of first selecting the concepts and then for each concept selecting the educational resources, they first calculate all possible courses that reach a set of concepts and then select the best suited one, according to a utility function.

Generating all possible sequences requires merging the concepts contained in the domain structure with the educational resources. This is achieved by replacing every concept in the domain structure by the related set of resources. The resulting structure ("Learning Paths Graph") inherits the relations represented in both the domain structure and among the resources.

The utility function encodes how good a particular educational resource is suited for a given learner. The utility function maps learning object characteristics to learner characteristics and vice versa. The function is determined through statistical methods: for a set of reference learners, an instructional designer rates a training and generalization set of educational resources with respect to their usefulness for the learner. Subsequently this data is used to train and evaluate the resulting utility function.

In a final step, the edges in the learning paths graph are inversely weighted with to the utility function: the more appropriate an educational resource is, the lower the weight. Determining the best sequence through the learning paths graph is done by using a shortest path algorithm

The authors evaluated their approach by comparing automatically calculated sequences with sequences authored by an instructional designer, as well as through simulations that measure how close the generated sequences are to ideal paths. They claim that their approach can produce sequences that are almost similar to the ideal ones (generated and authored) if the educational resources are well described by metadata and consist of collections of small-size resources.

This statistical method is a novel approach to course generation and hence it is hard to assess it suitability in real-life applications. A major drawback is that the educational resources are rated by an instructional designer with respect to a specific learner. The rating does not take into account that the same learner can have different learning goals regarding the same concepts. Another drawback is that educational resources will only appear in a course if there exists a direct relation between them. However, it will often be the case that two educational resources for the same concept have no relationship to each other, e. g., two exercises of different difficulty level. They will never be presented in the same course, unless a different educational resource exists that aggregates both resources. This criticism is supported by the evaluation, where best results were obtained for small-size resources.

8.9 Approaches Using Hierarchical Task Network Planning

Course generation approaches based on HTN planning are rare – in the literature, only a single system is described, apart from PAIGOS. Méndez et al. [111] propose to use HTN planning for course generation in the e-learning environment FORHUM. Their approach automatically generates HTN methods and operators from the domain model. So called "educational objectives", which practically correspond to concepts are "achieved" by educational resources, called "educational units". Each educational unit has an associated learning style.

The generation of the methods and operators happens according to a set of five rules: for each concept c, a method m is generated. The preconditions of m are the prerequisites of c. The subtasks of m are the concepts that are linked to c by a `part-of` relation (called "component"). For each educational resource e, a method and an operator are generated. The method has as a precondition the learning style associated with e (hence, the resource will only be "applied" if the learning style is the one of the learner); the single subtask consists of the resource itself. The operator has as precondition the prerequisites of e, the delete list is empty, and the add list consists of the concept associated with e. Therefore, a resource is presented after its prerequisites were presented. The remaining three generation rules are similar.

In contrast to PAIGOS, the generation of the pedagogical knowledge happens automatically, once the domain structure is defined. The system can then generate courses for given concepts adapted to a given learning style. The drawback is that the pedagogical knowledge is encoded in the generation process and it is rather limited. Basically, it says: teach the prerequisites first and select educational resources according to the learner's learning style. PAIGOS, in contrast, has an explicit representation of pedagogical knowledge, which was derived by interviewing from pedagogical experts and from pedagogical theory. In addition, PAIGOS allows generating courses for the same concepts but with different learning goals, which is not possible in the planner of FORHUM.

Sicilia et al. [167] present the idea to use HTN planning to generate IMS LD instances. Their description is on a very abstract level and sketches some basic operators and methods. By using two HTN methods as an example, they hint at how different pedagogical approaches ("content-oriented" vs. "sociocultural") might be implemented. Their work provides evidence that course generation techniques can be used for the generation of learning designs, however they do not provide any detailed formalization as done within the context of this volume.

8.10 Ontologies for Instructional Design

Closely related are applications of ontological modeling in instructional design. Seminal work in this direction by Mizoguchi and Bourdeau [117] describes general directions of research regarding how ontologies might help to overcome some problems of the area of artificial intelligence techniques in education. Building on that work, Aroyo and Mizoguchi [8] describe how an assistant layer uses an ontology to support the complete authoring, for instance by providing hints on the course structure.

Recent work by [56, 55] develops "an ontology of learning, instruction and instructional design". Conceptually similar to PAIGOS's pedagogical tasks and methods, this ontology formalizes the learning process by describing how high-level events (called "educational events") can be decomposed into smaller events. The approach makes assumptions about the changes in the state of minds of learners: An educational event combines an instructional action with a presupposed mental change. For instance, the instructional action "preparing the learner for learning" is associated with the state change "being ready to learn". There is no notion of preconditions, i. e., one cannot specify the context under which a specific decomposition is applicable. The ontology is used for author support and provides guidelines what learning materials to author in a given learning theory. Currently supported learning theories encompass cognitive as well as constructivist theories.

The authors do not list the automatic generation of courses as a potential application for the ontology, and accordingly, the ontology misses some requirements necessary for this task. First, the event decomposition does not contain preconditions and the selection of an event depends only on the instructional theory used in the current authoring process. Additionally, the connection to the resource layer is missing: basic events are not coupled with partial descriptions of educational resources that can be used to locate resources that support the achievement of the educational event. Furthermore, different scenarios are not represented. Nevertheless, it would be an interesting research direction to combine their complex ontology with the approach provided by PAIGOS.

9

Future Work and Acknowledgments

9.1 Future Work

The declarative representation of the course generation knowledge and the modular architecture of PAIGOS ensures that extensions can be realized easily. The following work could be worth investigating.

Increased Generality. The course generation knowledge and the ontology of instructional objects were designed for applicability in domains other than mathematics. However, the majority of the test cases and evaluations of PAIGOS used mathematics as a domain. Due to its formal nature, mathematical knowledge is well structured into educational resources and thus an ideal candidate for course generation. Other domains such as language learning exhibit different characteristics [58]. Exploring these but also domains that are more closely related to mathematics such as computer science and physics will allow insights into the generality of course generation knowledge. In addition, PAIGOS's handling of competencies could be made more abstract. The current formalization of the competency-based scenarios uses the PISA competency model. Yet, there exist other similar models, the best known being Bloom's taxonomy of educational objectives [15]. Currently, the competencies used by PAIGOS are encoded within the methods. For increased generality the competencies should be externalized and the methods should adapt themselves dynamically to the specific competency framework used by the course generation client.

Mediator. The mediator translates queries about the metadata of educational resources. However, in its current state it requires that identical resources have the same identifier throughout the repositories. Extending the mapping algorithm of the mediator to include mappings between instances, that is to translate between different names of the same fundamentals, would allow a more flexible integration of repositories. Similarly, PAIGOS's current access of learner information is not sufficiently flexible: adding a learner model requires changes to PAIGOS's source code in contrast to the plug-and-play registration and access to repositories. As a consequence, further research might investigate how to increase applicability of course generation by applying the mediator framework to learner models.

Rapid Prototyping/Evaluation Tool. Due to the declarative representation of the course generation knowledge, the knowledge can be changed and extended easily. Therefore, PAIGOS is an ideal candidate for rapid prototyping of adaptive systems. By using the basic axioms, operators and methods and by modifying the existing scenarios, hypotheses about the effects of adaptive features can be tested faster than if the adaptive system was to be implemented from scratch. The rapid-prototyping process could be supported by tools that allow a drag-and-drop construction/modification of scenarios.

Deeper Integration into the Learning Process. During the evaluation of PAIGOS in the LEACTIVEMATH project it became obvious that students and teachers need detailed information about how to integrate advanced tools such as PAIGOS into their learning process. In a first step, we designed a user manual for course generation that describes how to use the scenarios, for instance, by suggesting a sequence of the different scenarios. It would be worth investigating the general problem, namely how to integrate course generation into a learning management system. For instance, a suggestion component could recommend which scenario a learner should use at a specific point during learning. This would require formalizing the complete learning process, which might be possible with IMS LD.

Authoring Support. PAIGOS could support the authoring process in various ways. For instance, authors could use PAIGOS to assess whether they produced a sufficient amount of educational resources. In case PAIGOS is not able to find a specific resource, it could make this information available to an authoring tool.

A

Complete List of User Comments

This appendix contains the complete list of the comments[1] made by the English speaking students during the summative evaluation. In the evaluation, the subjects were asked to state their agreement to a variety of statements about the course generator using yes/no questions and Likert scales. After each set of statements, the students had the opportunity to briefly explain their answers in their own words.

The first comments are the students' explanations of their answers the following questions:

- Are the chapters in the order you would expect?
- Are the pages in the order you would expect?

The comments are as follows:

> These are in order of the topic I wanted. So that's ok.
>
> expected chapters in the order Average Slopes, rates of change, and further difference quotients. The pages not also ordered in the same way
>
> differnce quotient is first but i think it should come later. pages are in a logical order.
>
> The order of the chapters seems fine. I cannot suggest a more suitable order.
>
> I would expect chapters regaarding the same subject (ie. derivatives, or slope) to be one after the other. I would also put chapters containg concepts (ie. slope) useful to others (derivatives) to be presented before.
>
> The chapters follow on from each other and each chapter follows a logical order of pages - introduction, explanation, exercises
>
> yes, with the connections and look back at correct place, exercises at end of chapter. chapters lead on well from each other.
>
> They get progressively more difficult and the later ones require the knowledge of the first ones
>
> in correct order, ie intro, explanation, exercises
>
> The order is fine. First introduction − > Theory − > Exercises.
>
> The chapters are in a good order- starting from basics, moving on into concepts based on the previous ones. The pages are similarily well - ordered.

---

[1] I did not correct spelling and grammar mistakes.

equation of a tangent was after equation of normal

the pages go throgh the order of having inroduction then the concept then the exercises. which seems to be a locigal order

All looks like I would expect really, it is fairly standard to have a looking back excercise at the end etc.

Because the chapters are in the order that they were in step 4 of making the book and the pages link on from each other

I would expect the order to be 'Definition of the Average Slope', 'Definition of the Average Rate of Changes' and then 'Definition of the Difference Quotient'. To me this is a more natural progression of knowledge. However, inside the chapters, the pages seem to be in a logical order.

The topics are in logical order and the pages build from concepts towards exercises.

Each chapter is layed out starting with an Intro, Prerequisites and then into the information for the topic and then exercises which is a sensible order.

The chapters and pages were in a good order, but too similar to the prerecorded books.

I expected the slope chapter to come before the rate chapter. The pages are arranged in introduction, definition, then excercises which is how I would work through them.

Each page/chapter seems to be in a logical order....

Opposite order to that listed when creating book. Prerequisites, Information, Exercises is logical order.

The chapters seem to be in a logical order with the definitions first then moving onto exercises. The pages started with the simple content before moving onto what appears to be the more advanced parts.

each chapter and page follows on logically from what you've learned before in the previous chapter/page

Chapters and pages are ordered from the easiest to most difficult.

the order seems logical

Well i didn't really think about chapter order but the page orders seem logical. Definition should come first etc..

a- follow order selection when creating the book b- sequenced

The next comments are the students' explanations of their answers the following questions:

- Should exercises be added to the same page as the definition or to the designated exercise page?
- Should users be permitted to remove items from personal books?
- Should users be permitted to add items from personal books?
- Should users be permitted to remove items from pre-recorded books?
- Should users be permitted to add items from pre-recorded books?

One is responsible utterly for a personal book, but should always have a kind of backup in the form of pre-recorded book.

users should be free do do as they wish, if removing or adding items makes a more personalized environment that sustains learning then it should be allowed personal books should be allowed to be customised and these should be used to add more knowledge to not the pre-recorded books.

Custom-made books should the modifiable, after all, that is the key reason for making them in the first place. Pre-recorded books shouldn't be modifiable as they were made as they were for a good reason.

I think it's up to the user how they structure the pages they want but removal of set books is pintless as they have the badics for the course.

if a user makes a personal book he wants it for certain purposes. It is natural for him to decide the contents of the book in order to suit the purposes in the way he finds most useful. He should be able to do this by adding or removing Items from the book. The user should be able to expand the contents of a book if he chooses to, ie. by adding excercises. He should also be able to take these exercises he has added off, by removing them.

I think the more freedom a user is given, the more likely they will find the best way to learn the material for them.

personal books, being tailored for the individual should have the control over them. for the per-recorded books i think theres a reason for all the pages being in it so shouldnt be able to remove at will.

b) They are customized for them c) They are customized for them d) No they are designed the way they are for a reason e) No they are designed the way they are for a reason

this tidys up the book and makes it more relevant

personal books should be completely editable whereas pre-recorded books should be left as they are but users should be able to add things to them and from them.

As I understand, LAM is designed for students; as students are adults, they should be able to easily decide about contents of their books, to suit their particular needs.

whenever you need to change a personal book you wouldnt want to create a new one, however editing pre-recorded books may result in an incomplete knowledge of topics

you should be able to do anything with your own personal book. and assuming the pre recorded books dont work like a wiki for everyone signing in. then its reasonable to change whatever you want

Users should be able to modify their books to their needs but the pre-recorded books should be there just for reference

Allowing the removal of things from books could lead to content being missed. adding content will help the user to learn in their own style.

Personal books should be just that, personal. The computer should suggest what goes in a book but ultimately if the user doesn't want somehting in the book tey should be able to remove it. On the other hand, a pre-recorded book should be 'locked' just in case a user deleted a piece of content (these books contain the content of the course so should also be standard).

The more customisation the better as users can tailor the books/pages to their own needs.

Its a very useful feature.

I think the personal books should have the ability to be edited, but not the prerecorded books, this keeps things tidy in the personal book (i.e. has only *the things that you want in it) , but also means that you can refer to the prerecorded books if there is something missing.*

Adding and removing pages from both types of book will allow the user to further personalise their learning experience and make it more useful to them.

a user can customize a personal book to his or her needs & it would be easier for them to add or remove things that were relevant or irrelevent accordingly........ pre-recorded books should be Read Only because accidental deleting could occur

Personal books by definition should contain whatever the user wants Customised books are what the personal feature is for, and it could be dangerous to make pages inaccessible, or even to put an item in an inappropriate book.

Users should be able to customise how they learn

all things should be able to be altered, so that the user can get the most out of the information, like having their own notes

Users should have influence on their personal book.

editing custom books is acceptable, however editing premade ones isnt, the user would end up deleting the book eventually. however it would be helpful to hide certain items

4d would be yes if these changes were reversable. altho im not sure they should be allowed to mess around with the pre recorded books at all

b - If comfortable that they kno the info already c - Yes, update the book and keep themselves aware of things they kno/don't d - No, they were not made for them e - Yes, helps update them

The following statements were made with respect to the exercise sequencer. The students also commented the content. I included the statements since they show how the subjects judge the appropriateness of the selected exercises.

- How matched to your level of knowledge are the exercises?
- How suitable are the types of exercises to your position as a beginner in this area?

According to results of early completed exercises I would be in a position to finish successfully those too.

to me the level of the maths is not challenging. a beginner would find it some what difficult to follow through

the exercises are good as they grow in difficulty

These problems seemed quite hard considering how weakly I have met the prerequisites.

The examples weren't particularly challenging and suite a 1st year easily.

all the excercise required the knowledge of derivatives and in particulare of the Product Rule, which is probably something I don't know if I create a book to "Discover Product Rule"

It is quite frustrating to be presented with this format of exercise [open exercises] as a beginner.

open ended are a bit iffy but besides that questions seemed suited

All the exercises i have attempted before have not shown a direct way to calculate dy/dx of a function making this task impossible for someone who has never done it before

For me personally they could be harder but for beginners they are very good.

1b) the difficulty seems perfect- some of the excercises were easy and would just remind me about the principles, some required some effort and one would actually require me to search for more knowledge. 1c) too many open questions I think.

Some of the questions were a bit easy but others made me think a bit harder. Some people who are just beginning might find a few of the questions challenging

I think the exercises are fairly testing but within the reach of someone starting this topic. However, there were a few questions that needed knowledge of other differentiation methods which someone who was just learning the product rule would not know.

The sort of language used in the notes seem convulated and not very clear, so it wouldn't be very good for a beginner. But the questions seem to be more or less on the right lines, although i'd never use the words "difference quoteient" The loading time for the excersise sequencer and pretty much everything is ureasonably long. takeing 2 about mins to load one question. I'd never use it if it took that long.

Exercises seemed to be at around the correct level for someone new to the topic

The exercises were at a really good level for my knowledge, there was a good spread of exercises for the subject.

The questions were mainly open questions that could not give feedback on how you were doing.

the questions seemed a bit challenging for a beginner but they were not TOO hard either.........

Perhaps excessive use of variables rather than numbers would be hard on a beginner as a first example?

questions seem to scale to how you cope with previous questions. It starts slightly difficult for beginners in this area.

the exercises are fairly simple and straight forward, not requiring advanced knowledge

Some exercises may be too difficult for beginners.

The questions are well suited if the user has the right prerequisite knowledge

The level seems ok...

b- questions match level of maths I know c- quite suitable

The next comments address the following questions:

- How tailored to you as a learner is the content in your personal book, Discover Quotient Rule?
- Which would you rather use to learn about the Product Rule?

In Personal Book topics are more friendly segregated.

personal book offers a better means of understanding the product rule as it gives information bit by bit ie in sequence

i think the personal books as it's tailored to your knowledge and level on comprehension

The personal book is much leaner but I would still prefer the complete pre-recorded book just so that I don't miss anything that may be important.

The prerecorded books were set out ideally and in an acceptable order, I'd use that.

in the personal book the rule is presented in a way which is more friendly to learning. rule, application of rule, examples and then animated proof, proof, in a separate page. In the prerecorded everything is in a less inutitive order and all on the same page.

The personal book explained concepts such as polynomials which I didnt know about.

pre-recorded book has more links to help with wider grasp but personal book is more explicitly designed for the user.

I think i would use either

It is more advanced than anything i have used active math for. The pre-recorded book is good as it proves the quotient rule

they are specifically designed and more appropriate

I prefer personal book because it is only about the product rule and no other topics would interrupt me. The pre-recorded book is quite big and is therefore not as clear as the personal book.

I dont think the differences between the books are particularly significant-maybe because I didnt use LAM long enough yet. However, my personal book is better structured and therefore easier to use.

i got the message - Sorry, there are no more exercises available! We have to abort this exercise session. Close the window to get back to the course. when loading the Exercise Sequencer

Personal books seem a lot better as they give content that is specific and that is good as most people learning maths i presume will be using this to touch up on little things they have not understood.

In the personal book they do an example of the product rule, it might be useful to have more than one though

Whilst the personal book seems to be good for my level of knowledge, I like to have all of the information at one time so form my point of view I would prefer to be able to access all of the information in the pre-recorded book.

The personal book is a bit more direct and less in-depth.

Its hard to tell what has been tailored to me as all the mastery squares are grey even though i'm on SLM. It seems not too bad. I'd prefer the Pre recorded book to learn about the Product rule mainly as it seems the only one acutally mentioning the product rule. The personal book doensn't seem to mention the product rule

The page introduces it well and then uses several examples to show the rule which is ideal.

The book did not seem well tailored to the standards of a beginner in the topic but the pre-recorded book provided a wide base for the subject.

pre-recorded books would tend to maybe go into too much detail while personal books would register the concepts that you have already grasped etc.....

Quotient Rule is not in my personal book Either is fine for (f)

A mixture of both is best.

both books are useful, i would start with the personal book and move on to the pre-recorded one

In personal book I can chose the content on my own.

pretty well tailored, but i would be scared i missed something important

I would rather have the information pre-recorded as making a personal book is quite alot of effort.

e-more detail given f-easily understanable due to detail given

References

[1] ActiveMath Group: Activemath home (2007), http://www.activemath.org/. This is an electronic document. Date retrieved: January 29, 2007

[2] American: The American Heritage Dictionary of the English Language, 4th edn. Houghton Mifflin Company (2004)

[3] Anderson, J.R.: The Architecture of Cognition. Harvard University Press, Cambridge (1983)

[4] Anderson, J.R., Boyle, C.F., Farrell, R.G., Reiser, B.J.: Cognitive principles in the design of computer tutors. In: Morris, P. (ed.) Modeling Cognition, John Wiley, New York (1987)

[5] Anderson, J.R., Corbett, A.T., Koedinger, K.R., Pelletier, R.: Cognitive tutors: Lessons learned. The Journal of the Learning Sciences 4(2), 167–207 (1995)

[6] Andre, T.: Selected microinstructional methods to facilitate knowledge construction: implications for instructional design. In: Tennyson, R.D., Schott, F., Seel, N., Dijkstra, S. (eds.) Instructional Design: International Perspective: Theory, Research, and Models, vol. 1, pp. 243–267. Lawrence Erlbaum Associates, Mahwah (1997)

[7] ARIADNE: ARIADNE – foundation for the european knowledge pool (2004), http://www.ariadne-eu.org. This is an electronic document. Date retrieved: January 31, 2007

[8] Aroyo, L., Mizoguchi, R.: Authoring support framework for intelligent educational systems. In: Hoppe, U., Verdejo, F., Kay, J. (eds.) Proccedings of AI in Education, AIED-2003, pp. 362–364. IOS Press, Amsterdam (2003)

[9] Ausubel, D.: The Psychology of Meaningful Verbal Learning. Grune & Stratton, New York (1963)

[10] Bartle, R.G., Sherbert, D.R.: Introduction to Real Analysis. John Wiley& Sons, New York (1982)

[11] Beck, R.J.: Learning objects collections (2001), http://www.uwm.edu/Dept/CIE/AOP/LO_collections.html. This is an electronic document. Date of publication: May 17, 2001. Date retrieved: January 19, 2007. Date last modified: January 10, 2007

[12] Berners-Lee, T., Fielding, R., Masinter, L.: Uniform resource identifiers (uri): Generic syntax. Technical report, RFC Editor, United States (1998)

[13] Berners-Lee, T., Hendler, J., Lassila, O.: The semantic web. Scientific American 284(5), 34–43 (2001)

[14] Bhatti, N., Bouch, A., Kuchinsky, A.: Integrating user-perceived quality into web server design. In: Proceedings of the 9th international World Wide Web conference on Computer networks: the international journal of computer and telecommunications netowrking, Amsterdam, The Netherlands, pp. 1–16. North-Holland, Amsterdam (2000), doi: http://dx.doi.org/10.1016/S1389-1286(00)00087-6

[15] Bloom, B.S.: Taxonomy of educational objectives: The classification of educational goals: Handbook I, cognitive domain. Longmans, Green, New York, Toronto (1956)

[16] Brown, J.S., Collins, A., Duguid, P.: Situated cognition and the culture of learning. Educational Researcher 18(1), 32–41 (1989)

[17] Bruner, J.S.: On knowing: Essays for the left hand. Harvard University Press, Cambridge (1967)

[18] Brusilovsky, P.: Methods and techniques of adaptive hypermedia. User Modeling and User Adapted Interaction 6(2–3), 87–129 (1996)

[19] Brusilovsky, P., Vassileva, J.: Course sequencing techniques for large-scale web-based education. International Journal of Continuing Engineering Education and Lifelong Learning 13(1/2), 75–94 (2003)

[20] Brusilovsky, P., Schwarz, E., Weber, G.: ELM-ART: An Intelligent Tutoring System on the World Wide Web. In: Lesgold, A., Frasson, C., Gauthier, G. (eds.) ITS 1996. LNCS, vol. 1086, Springer, Heidelberg (1996)

[21] Brusilovsky, P., Eklund, J., Schwarz, E.: Web-based education for all: A tool for developing adaptive courseware. Computer Networks and ISDN Systems 30(1-7), 291–300 (1998)

[22] Burnard, L., Sperberg-McQueen, C.M.: TEI Lite: An introduction to text encoding for interchange (2002)

[23] Caprotti: The Open Math Standard, Open Math Consortium (1998), http://www.nag.co.uk/projects/OpenMath/omstd/

[24] Carr, B., Goldstein, I.P.: Overlays: A theory of modeling for computer aided instruction. AI Memo 406, MIT (Feb. 1977)

[25] Cisco Systems, Inc.: Reusable learning object strategy: Designing and developing learning objects for multiple learning approaches (2003)

[26] Clancey, W.: Tutoring rules for guiding a case method dialogue. International Journal of Man-Machine Studies 11, 25–49 (1979)

[27] Conlan, O., Wade, V., Bruen, C., Gargan, M.: Multi-model, metadata driven approach to adaptive hypermedia services for personalized elearning. In: De Bra, P., Brusilovsky, P., Conejo, R. (eds.) AH 2002. LNCS, vol. 2347, pp. 100–111. Springer, Heidelberg (2002)

[28] Conlan, O., Lewis, D., Higel, S., O'Sullivan, D., Wade, V.: Applying adaptive hypermedia techniques to semantic web service composition. In: de Bra, P. (ed.) Proceedings of AH2003: Workshop on Adaptive Hypermedia and Adaptive Web-Based Systems, Budapest, Hungary, May 20-24, pp. 53–62 (2003)

[29] Currie, K., Tate, A.: O-plan: The open planning architecture. Artificial Intelligence 52(1), 49–86 (1991)

[30] De Bra, P.: Pros and cons of adaptive hypermedia in web-based education. Journal on CyberPsychology and Behavior 3(1), 71–77 (2000)

[31] De Bra, P.: ah — adaptivehypertext and hypermedia (2007), `http://pegasus.`
     `tue.nl/mailman/listinfo/ah` This is an electronic document. Date retrieved:
     March 19, 2007

[32] De Bra, P., Houben, G.-J., Wu, H.: AHAM: a Dexter-based reference model for
     adaptive hypermedia. In: HYPERTEXT '99: Proceedings of the tenth ACM
     Conference on Hypertext and hypermedia: returning to our diverse roots,
     Darmstadt, Germany, pp. 147–156. ACM Press, New York (1999)

[33] de Bruijn, J., Foxvog, D., Zimmermann, K.: Ontology Mediation Patterns
     Library V1. D4.3.1, SEKT-project (February 2005)

[34] Dijkstra, S., Seel, N.M., Scott, F., Tennyson, R.D.: Instructional Design: Inter-
     national Perspectives. Solving Instructional Design Problems, vol. 2. Lawrence
     Erlbaum Associates, Mahwah (1997)

[35] Dimitrova, V.: STyLE-OLM: Interactive open learner modelling. International
     Journal of Artificial Intelligence in Education 13, 35–78 (2002)

[36] Dodds, P., Thropp, S.E.: Sharable content object reference model 2004 3rd
     edition overview version 1.0. Technical report, Advanced Distributed Learning
     (2004)

[37] du Boulay, B., Luckin, R.: Modelling human teaching tactics and strategies
     for tutoring systems. International Journal of Artificial Intelligence in Educa-
     tion 12(3), 235–256 (2001)

[38] Duval, E.: Metadata standards: What, who & why. Journal of Universal Com-
     puter Science 7(7), 591–601 (2001)

[39] Duval, E.: Metadata, but not as you know it: electronic forms are dead. In:
     Proceedings of Interactive Computer aided Learning, ICL2005, Villach, Aus-
     tria, published on CD-ROM (2005)

[40] Erol, K., Hendler, J., Nau, D.S.: Complexity results for hierarchical task-
     network planning. Annals of Mathematics and Artificial Intelligence 18(1),
     69–93 (1996)

[41] Fikes, R.E., Nilsson, N.J.: STRIPS: A new approach to the application of
     theorem proving to problem solving. Artificial Intelligence 2, 189–208 (1971)

[42] Fox, M., Long, D.: PDDL2.1: An extension to PDDL for expressing temporal
     planning domains. Journal of Artificial Intelligence Research, Special Issue on
     the 3rd International Planning Competition 20, 61–124 (2003)

[43] Friedman-Hill, E.: Jess, the java expert system shell. Technical Report
     SAND98-8206, Sandia National Laboratories (1997)

[44] Gagné, R.M.: The Conditions of Learning and Theory of Instruction. Holt,
     Rinehart & Winston, New York (1965)

[45] Gardner, H.: Multiple approaches to understanding. In: Reigeluth, C.M. (ed.)
     Instructional Design Theories and Models: A New Paradigm of Instructional
     Theory, vol. 2, pp. 69–89. Lawrence Erlbaum, Mahwah (1999)

[46] GEM Consortium: GEM 2.0: Element descriptions. Technical report, Gateway
     to Educational Materials Project (November 2004)

[47] IMS Global Learning Consortium. IMS content packaging information model,
     June (2003a)

[48] IMS Global Learning Consortium. IMS learning design specification, February
     (2003b)

[49] IMS Global Learning Consortium. IMS simple sequencing specification, March
     (2003c)

244   References

[50] IMS Global Learning Consortium. IMS question and test interoperability: ASI information model specification, final specification version 1.2 (2002)

[51] Goguadze, G., Palomo, A.G., Melis, E.: Interactivity of Exercises in Active-Math. In: In Proceedings of the 13th International Conference on Computers in Education (ICCE 2005), Singapore, pp. 107–113 (2005)

[52] Grabowski, B.L., Gäng, S., Herter, J., Köppen, T.: MathCoach und Laplace-Skript: Ein programmierbarer interaktiver Mathematiktutor mit XML-basierter Skriptsprache. In: Jantke, K.P., Fähnrich, K.-P., Wittig, W.S. (eds.) Leipziger Informatik-Tage. LNI, vol. 72, pp. 211–218. GI (2005)

[53] Gruber, T.R.: A translation approach to portable ontology specifications. Knowl. Acquis. 5(2), 199–220 (1993), doi: http://dx.doi.org/10.1006/knac.1993.1008

[54] Halasz, F., Schwartz, M.: The dexter hypertext reference model. Communications of the ACM 37(2), 30–39 (1994)

[55] Hayashi, Y., Bourdeau, J., Mizoguchi, R.: Ontological support for a theory-eclectic approach to instructional and learning design. In: Nejdl, W., Tochtermann, K. (eds.) EC-TEL 2006. LNCS, vol. 4227, pp. 155–169. Springer, Heidelberg (2006a)

[56] Hayashi, Y., Bourdeau, J., Mizoguchi, R.: Ontological modeling approach to blending theories for instructional and learning design. In: Mizoguchi, R., Dillenbour, P., Zhu, Z. (eds.) Proceedings of the 14th International Conference on Computers in Education, Beijing, China, pp. 37–44. IOS Press, Amsterdam (2006b)

[57] Heflin, J.: OWL web ontology language use cases and requirements. W3C recommendation, W3C (Feb. 2004), http://www.w3.org/TR/2004/REC-webont-req-20040210/

[58] Heilman, M., Eskenazi, M.: Language learning: Challenges for intelligent tutoring systems. In: Aleven, V., Pinkwart, N., Ashley, K., Lynch, C. (eds.) Proceedings of the Workshop of Intelligent Tutoring Systems for Ill-Defined Domains at the 8th International Conference on Intelligent Tutoring Systems (2006)

[59] Henze, N., Nejdl, W.: A logical characterization of adaptive educational hypermedia. Hypermedia 10(1), 77–113 (2004)

[60] IClass Consortium: iclass (2004), http://www.iclass.info. This is an electronic document. Date retrieved: January 20, 2007

[61] IEEE Learning Technology Standards Committee: IEEE learning technology standards committee (2005), http://ieeeltsc.org/. This is an electronic document. Date of publication: March 19, 2005. Date retrieved: January 29, 2007. Date last modified: November 16, 2006

[62] Ilghami, O.: Documentation for JSHOP2. Technical Report CS-TR-4694, Department of Computer Science, University of Maryland (February 2005)

[63] Ilghami, O., Nau, D.S.: A general approach to synthesize problem-specific planners. Technical Report CS-TR-4597, Department of Computer Science, University of Maryland (October 2003)

[64] IMS Global Learning Consortium: Welcome to IMS global learning consortium, inc. (2007), http://www.imsglobal.org/. This is an electronic document. Date retrieved: January 31, 2007. Date last modified: January 28, 2007

[65] International Organization for Standardization: Electronic manuscript preparation and markup, document number: ANSI/NISO/ISO 12083 (April 1995)

[66] Jantke, K.P., Grieser, G., Lange, S., Memmel, M.: DaMiT: Data Mining lernen und lehren. In: Abecker, A., Bickel, S., Brefeld, U., Drost, I., Henze, N., Herden, O., Minor, M., Scheffer, T., Stojanovic, L., Weibelzahl, S. (eds.) LWA 2004, Lernen — Wissensentdeckung —Adaptivität, Oct. 2004, pp. 171–179. Humboldt-Universität Berlin (2004)

[67] Jeffery, A., Currier, S.: What is... IMS learning design? Standards briefings series, cetis (2003)

[68] Jonassen, D.: Designing constructivist learning environments. In: Reigeluth, C.M. (ed.) Instructional Design Theories and Models: A New Paradigm of Instructional Theory, vol. 2, pp. 215–239. Lawrence Erlbaum, Mahwah (1999)

[69] Jones, M., Li, Z., Merrill, M.D.: Domain knowledge representation for instructional analysis. Educational Technology 10(30) (1990)

[70] Kaleidoscope: Kaleidoscope (2007), http://www.noe-kaleidoscope.org. This is an electronic document. Date retrieved: January 20, 2007

[71] Karampiperis, P., Sampson, D.: Adaptive learning resources sequencing in educational hypermedia systems. Educational Technology & Society 8(4), 128–147 (2005a)

[72] Karampiperis, P., Sampson, D.: Automatic learning object selection and sequencing in web-based intelligent learning systems. In: Ma, Z. (ed.) Web-Based Intelligent e-Learning Systems: Technologies and Applications, pp. 56–71. Information Science Publishing (2005b)

[73] Kärger, P.: Ontologie-basierter Mediator zum Zugriff auf heterogene und verteilte Lerninhalte. Master's thesis, Universität des Saarlandes (March 2006)

[74] Kärger, P., Ullrich, C., Melis, E.: Integrating learning object repositories using a mediator architecture. In: Nejdl, W., Tochtermann, K. (eds.) EC-TEL 2006. LNCS, vol. 4227, pp. 185–197. Springer, Heidelberg (2006a), http://www.carstenullrich.net/pubs/kaergeretal-mediator-ectel06.pdf

[75] Kärger, P., Ullrich, C., Melis, E.: Querying learning object repositories via ontology-based mediation. In: Kinshuk, Kopers, R., Kommers, P., Kirschner, P., Sampson, D.G., Didderen, W. (eds.) Proceedings of the 6th IEEE International Conference on Advanced Learning Technologies, July 2006, pp. 845–846. IEEE Computer Society Press, Los Alamitos (2006b), http://www.carstenullrich.net/pubs/icalt06_mediator.pdf

[76] Kay, J., Kummerfeld, B., Lauder, P.: Personis: A server for user models. In: De Bra, P., Brusilovsky, P., Conejo, R. (eds.) AH 2002. LNCS, vol. 2347, pp. 203–212. Springer, Heidelberg (2002)

[77] Kearlsey, G.: Authoring considerations for hypertext. Educational Technology 28(11), 21–24 (1988)

[78] Keeffe, I.O., Brady, A., Conlan, O., Wade, V.: Just-in-time generation of pedagogically sound, context sensitive personalized learning experiences. International Journal on E-Learning 5(1), 113–127 (2006)

[79] Keenoy, K., Levene, M., Peterson, D.: Personalisation and trails in self e-learning networks. WP4 Deliverable 4.2, IST Self E-Learning Networks (2003)

[80] Keenoy, K., Poulovassilis, A., Papamarkos, G., Wood, P.T., Christophides, V., Maganaraki, A., Stratakis, M., Rigaux, P., Spyratos, N.: Adaptive personalisation in self e-learning networks. In: Proceedings of First International Kaleidoscope Learning Grid SIG Workshop on Distributed e-Learning Environments, Napoly, Italy (2005)

[81] Klieme, E., Avenarius, H., Blum, W., Döbrich, P., Gruber, H., Prenzel, M., Reiss, K., Riquarts, K., Rost, J., Tenorth, H., Vollmer, H.J.: The development of national educational standards - an expertise. Technical report, Bundesministerium für Bildung und Forschung / German Federal Ministry of Education and Research (2004)

[82] Knight, C., Gašević, D., Richards, G.: An ontology-based framework for bridging learning design and learning content. Educational Technology and Society 9(1), 23–37 (2006)

[83] Koch, N., Wirsing, M.: The Munich reference model for adaptive hypermedia applications. In: De Bra, P., Brusilovsky, P., Conejo, R. (eds.) AH 2002. LNCS, vol. 2347, pp. 213–222. Springer, Heidelberg (2002)

[84] Kohlhase, M.: OMDOC: Towards an internet standard for the administration, distribution, and teaching of mathematical knowledge. In: Campbell, J.A., Roanes-Lozano, E. (eds.) AISC 2000. LNCS (LNAI), vol. 1930, p. 32. Springer, Heidelberg (2001)

[85] Kohlhase, M.: OMDoc – An Open Markup Format for Mathematical Documents. Springer, Heidelberg (2006)

[86] Koper, R.: From change to renewal: Educational technology foundations of electronic learning environments. published online (2000), http://eml.ou.nl/introduction/docs/koper-inaugural-address.pdf

[87] Krämer, B.J.: Reusable learning objects: Let's give it another trial. Forschungsberichte des Fachbereichs Elektrotechnik, ISSN 0945-0130, Fernuniversität Hagen (2005)

[88] Libbrecht, P., Melis, E., Ullrich, C.: Generating Personalized Documents Using a Presentation Planner. In: Montgomerie, C., Viteli, J. (eds.) Proceedings of World Conference on Educational Multimedia, Hypermedia and Telecommunications 2001, Norfolk, VA, pp. 1124–1125. AACE (2001), http://www.carstenullrich.net/pubs/edmedia01.pdf

[89] Lu, T.: Kursgenerator für e-learning syteme als web-service. Master's thesis, Hochschule für Technik und Wirtschaft des Saarlandes (2006)

[90] Lucke, U., Tavangarian, D., Voigt, D.: Multidimensional Educational Multimedia with ML3. In: Richards, G. (ed.) Proceedings of World Conference on E-Learning in Corporate, Government, Healthcare, and Higher Education 2003, Phoenix, Arizona, USA, pp. 101–104. AACE (2003)

[91] Lumsden, L.S.: Student motivation to learn. ERIC Digest 92 (1994)

[92] Mann, W.C., Thompson, S.A.: Rhetorical structure theory: Toward a functional theory of text organization. Text 8(3), 243–281 (1988)

[93] Manola, F., Miller, E.: RDF primer. W3C recommendation, W3C (Feb. 2004), http://www.w3.org/TR/2004/REC-rdf-primer-20040210/

[94] Mantyka, S.: The Math Plague: How to Survive School Mathematics. MayT Consulting Cooperation (2007)

[95] Mayer, R.E.: Multimedia Learning. Cambridge University Press, New York (2001)

[96] Mayes, J.T.: Cognitive tools: A suitable case for learning. In: Kommers, P.A.M., Jonassen, D.H., Mayes, J.T. (eds.) Cognitive Tools for Learning. NATO ASI Series, Series F: Computer and Systems Science, vol. 81, pp. 7–18. Springer, Berlin (1992)

[97] McCarthy, B.: About Learning. Excell Inc., Barrington (1996)

[98] McCarthy, J., Minsky, M.L., Rochester, N., Shannon, C.: A proposal for the Dartmouth summer research project on Artificial Intelligence (1955), http://www-formal.stanford.edu/jmc/history/dartmouth/dartmouth.html

[99] McCollum, B.: Advanced distributed learning - home (2005), http://www.adlnet.gov/. This is an electronic document. Date of publication: April 13, 2005. Date retrieved: January 31, 2007. Date last modified: January 12, 2007

[100] McDermott, D.: The 1998 AI planning systems competition. AI Magazine 21(2), 35–55 (2000)

[101] McDermott, D.: PDDL, the planning domain definition language. Technical Report 1165, Yale Center for Computational Vision and Control, New Haven, CT (1998), ftp://ftp.cs.yale.edu/pub/mcdermott/software/pddl.tar.gz

[102] Meder, N.: Didaktische Ontologien. Accessed online (2003)

[103] Melis, E., Andres, E.: Global Feedback in ACTIVEMATH. Journal of Computers in Mathematics and Science Teaching 24, 197–220 (2005)

[104] Melis, E., Siekmann, J.: Knowledge-based proof planning. Artificial Intelligence 115(1), 65–105 (1999)

[105] Melis, E., Ullrich, C.: How to teach it – Polya-scenarios in activemath. In: Hoppe, U., Verdejo, F., Kay, J. (eds.) Artificial Intelligence in Education, pp. 141–147. IOS Press, Amsterdam (2003), http://www.carstenullrich.net/pubs/HowToTeachItPolyaScenariosActiveMath.pdf

[106] Melis, E., Andrès, E., Büdenbender, J., Frischauf, A., Goguadze, G., Libbrecht, P., Pollet, M., Ullrich, C.: Activemath: A generic and adaptive web-based learning environment. International Journal of Artificial Intelligence in Education 12(4), 385–407 (2001), http://www.carstenullrich.net/pubs/Melisetal-ActiveMath-AIEDJ-2001.pdf

[107] Melis, E., Büdenbender, J., Goguadze, G., Libbrecht, P., Pollet, M., Ullrich, C.: Knowledge representation and management in activemath. Annals of Mathematics and Artificial Intelligence, Special Issue on Management of Mathematical Knowledge 38(1–3), 47–64 (2003), http://www.carstenullrich.net/pubs/Knowledge_Representation_in_ActiveMath.pdf

[108] Melis, E., Kärger, P., Homik, M.: Interactive Concept Mapping in ActiveMath (iCMap). In: Haake, J.M., Lucke, U., Tavangarian, D. (eds.) Delfi 2005: 3. Deutsche eLearning Fachtagung Informatik, Rostock, Germany, Sept. 2005. LNI, vol. 66, pp. 247–258. Gesellschaft für Informatik e.V., GI (2005)

[109] Melis, E., Goguadze, G., Homik, M., Libbrecht, P., Ullrich, C., Winterstein, S.: Semantic-aware components and services of ActiveMath. British Journal of Educational Technology 37(3), 405–423 (2006), http://www.carstenullrich.net/pubs/Melisetal-SemanticAware-BJET-2005.pdf

[110] Melis, E., Shen, R., Siekmann, J., Ullrich, C., Yang, F., Han, P.: Challenges in search and usage of multi-media learning objects. In: Lu, R., Siekmann, J.H., Ullrich, C. (eds.) Joint Chinese German Workshops. LNCS (LNAI), vol. 4429, pp. 36–44. Springer, Heidelberg (2007), http://www.carstenullrich.net/pubs/Melisetal-MultimediaLOs-WSCS-2007.pdf

[111] Méndez, N.D.D., Ramírez, C.J., Luna, J.A.G.: IA planning for automatic generation of customized virtual courses. In: Frontiers In Artificial Intelligence And Applications, Proceedings of ECAI 2004, Valencia (Spain), vol. 117, pp. 138–147. IOS Press, Amsterdam (2004)

[112] Merceron, A., Yacef, K.: A web-based tutoring tool with mining facilities to improve learning and teaching. In: Proceedings of the 11th International Conference on Artificial Intelligence in Education, Sydney, Australia (2003)

[113] Merceron, A., Oliveira, C., Scholl, M., Ullrich, C.: Mining for content reuse and exchange – solutions and problems. In: Poster Proceedings of the 3rd International Semantic Web Conference, ISWC2004, Hiroshima, Japan, Nov. 2004, pp. 39–40 (2004), http://www.carstenullrich.net/pubs/Merceronetal-Mining-ISWC-2004.pdf

[114] Van Merriënboer, J.J.G.: Training Complex Cognitive Skills. Educational Technology Publications, Inc., Englewood Cliffs (1997)

[115] Merrill, M.D.: First principles of instruction. Educational Technology Research & Development 50(3), 43–59 (2002)

[116] Miklos, Z., Neumann, G., Zdun, U., Sintek, M.: Querying Semantic Web Resources Using TRIPLE Views. In: Kalfoglou, Y., Schorlemmer, M., Sheth, A., Staab, S., Uschold, M. (eds.) Semantic Interoperability and Integration, Dagstuhl, Germany. Dagstuhl Seminar Proceedings, Internationales Begegnungs- und Forschungszentrum (IBFI), Schloss Dagstuhl, Germany (2005)

[117] Mizoguchi, R., Bourdeau, J.: Using ontological engineering to overcome AI-ED problems. International Journal of Artificial Intelligence in Education 11(2), 107–121 (2000)

[118] Monk, A., Wright, P., Haber, J., Davenport, L.: Improving your human-computer interface: A practical technique. Prentice-Hall, Englewood Cliffs (1993)

[119] Moodle: Moodle (2007), http://moodle.org/. This is an electronic document. Date retrieved: May 16, 2007

[120] Mularczyk, D.: International forum ofeducational technology & society (2004), http://ifets.ieee.org/. This is an electronic document. Date retrieved: March 19, 2007. Date last modified: October 9, 2004

[121] Murray, W.R.: Control for intelligent tutoring systems: A blackboard-based dynamic instructional planner. In: Bierman, D., Breuker, J., Sandberg, J. (eds.) Proc. 4th International Conference of AI and Education, Springfield VA, Tokyo, pp. 150–168. IOS Press, Amsterdam (1989)

[122] Nau, D.S., Smith, S.J.J., Erol, K.: Control strategies in HTN planning: theory versus practice. In: AAAI '98/IAAI '98: Proceedings of the fifteenth national/tenth conference on Artificial intelligence/Innovative applications of artificial intelligence, Madison, Wisconsin, United States, pp. 1127–1133. AAAI Press, Menlo Park (1998)

[123] Nau, D.S., Cao, Y., Lotem, A., Muñoz-Avila, H.: SHOP: Simple hierarchical ordered planner. In: IJCAI '99: Proceedings of the Sixteenth International Joint Conference on Artificial Intelligence, San Francisco, CA, USA, pp. 968–975. Morgan Kaufmann, San Francisco (1999)

[124] Nau, D.S., Muñoz-Avila, H., Cao, Y., Lotem, A., Mitchell, S.: Total-order planning with partially ordered subtasks. In: Nebel, B. (ed.) Proceedings of the Seventeenth International Joint Conference on Artificial Intelligence, IJ-CAI 2001, Seattle, Washington, USA, pp. 425–430. Morgan Kaufmann, San Francisco (2001)

[125] Nau, D.S., Au, T.-C., Ilghami, O., Kuter, U., Murdock, J.W., Wu, D., Yaman, F.: SHOP2: An HTN Planning System. Journal of Artificial Intelligence Research 20, 379–404 (2003)

[126] Nau, D.S., Au, T.-C., Ilghami, O., Kuter, U., Muñoz-Avila, H., Murdock, J.W., Wu, D., Yaman, F.: Applications of SHOP and SHOP2. Technical Report CS-TR-4604, Department of Computer Science, University of Maryland (2004)

[127] Nejdl, W., Wolf, B., Qu, C., Decker, S., Sintek, M., Naeve, A., Nilsson, M., Palmér, M., Risch, T.: Edutella: a P2P networking infrastructure based on RDF. In: WWW '02: Proceedings of the 11th international conference on World Wide Web, Honolulu, Hawaii, USA, pp. 604–615. ACM Press, New York (2002)

[128] Nelson, L.M.: Collaborative problem solving. In: Reigeluth, C.M. (ed.) Instructional Design Theories and Models: A New Paradigm of Instructional Theory, vol. 2, pp. 241–267. Lawrence Erlbaum, Mahwah (1999)

[129] Nielsen, J.: Heuristic evaluation. In: Nielsen, J., Mack, R.L. (eds.) Usability inspection methods, pp. 25–62. John Wiley & Sons, Inc, New York (1994)

[130] Nilsson, M., Palmér, M., Brasse, J.: The LOM RDF binding – principles and implementation. In: Proceedings of the 3rd Annual Ariadne Conference, Leuven, Belgium (2003), Published online: http://www.kbs.uni-hannover.de/Arbeiten/Publikationen/2003/LOM_binding_nilsson_brase.pdf

[131] Niss, M.: Mathematical competencies and the learning of mathematics: the danish KOM project. Technical report, IMFUFA, Roskilde University (2002)

[132] Noble, D.D.: The Classroom Arsenal: Military Research, Information Technology and Public Education. The Falmer Press, New York (1991)

[133] Novak, J.D., Gowin, D.B.: Learning How to Learn. Cambridge University Press, New York (1984)

[134] Noy, N.F., McGuinness, D.L.: Ontology development 101: A guide to creating your first ontology. Stanford Medical Informatics Technical Report SMI-2001-0880, Stanford University (2001)

[135] OASIS: OASIS SOA reference model (2006), http://www.oasis-open.org/committees/soa-rm/faq.php. This is an electronic document. Date retrieved: January 22, 2007

[136] Object Management Group: Object Management Group — UML (2007), http://www.uml.org/. This is an electronic document. Date retrieved: January 22, 2007. Date last modified: January 2, 2007

[137] OECD (ed.): Learning for Tomorrows World — First Results from PISA 2003. Organisation for Economic Co-operation and Development (OECD) Publishing (2004)

[138] OECD (ed.): Measuring Student Knowledge and Skills – A New Framework for Assessment. OECD Publishing, Paris, France (1999)

[139] OECD (ed.): PISA – the OECD programme for international student assessment. Brochure (2007)

[140] Papert, S.: Mindstorms: Children, Computers, and Powerful Ideas. Basic Books, New York (1980)

[141] Pawlowski, J.M.: Das Essener-Lern-Modell (ELM): Ein Vorgehensmodell zur Entwicklung computerunterstützter Lernumgebungen. PhD thesis, Universität Gesamthochschule Essen, Essen (2001)

[142] Pazienza, M.T., Stellato, A., Vindigni, M., Zanzotto, F.M.: XeOML: An XML-based extensible Ontology Mapping Language. In: Workshop on Meaning Coordination and Negotiation, held in conjunction with 3rd International Semantic Web Conference (ISWC-2004) Hiroshima, Japan (November 2004)

[143] Peachy, D.R., McCalla, G.I.: Using planning techniques in intelligent tutoring systems. International Journal of Man-Machine Studies 24(1), 77–98 (1986)

[144] Pintrich, P.R.: The role of motivation in promoting and sustaining self-regulated learning. International Journal of Educational Research 31, 459–470 (1999)

[145] PLATO Learning, Inc.: Plato learning (2007), http://www.plato.com/. This is an electronic document. Date retrieved: January 16, 2007

[146] Polya, G.: How to Solve it. Princeton University Press, Princeton (1973)

[147] Prenzel, M., Drechsel, B., Carstensen, C.H., Ramm, G.: PISA 2003 - Eine Einführung. In: Deutschland, P.-K. (ed.) PISA 2003 - Der Bildungsstand der Jugendlichen in Deutschland - Ergebnisse des zweiten internationalen Vergleichs, pp. 13–46. Waxmann Verlag, Münster (2004)

[148] Random: Random House Unabridged Dictionary. Random House, Inc. (2006)

[149] Reigeluth, C.M.: Instructional Design Theories and Models: An Overview on their Current Status, vol. 1. Lawrence Erlbaum Associates, Hillsdale (1983)

[150] Reigeluth, C.M.: Instructional Design Theories and Models: A New Paradigm of Instructional Theory, vol. 2. Lawrence Erlbaum Associates, Mahwah (1999)

[151] Reinmann-Rothmeier, G., Mandl, H.: Unterrichten und Lernumgebungen gestalten. In: Krapp, A., Weidmann, W. (eds.) Pädagogische Psychologie. Ein Lehrbuch, 4th edn., pp. 601–646. Beltz PVU, Weinheim (2001)

[152] Reiter, E.: NLG vs. Templates. In: Proceedings of the Fifth European Workshop on Natural Language Generation, Leiden, The Netherlands, May 1995, pp. 95–105 (1995)

[153] Reiter, E., Dale, R.: Building Natural Language Generation Systems. Cambridge University Press, Cambridge (2000)

[154] Reusable Learning. Reusable learning (2007), http://www.reusablelearning.org/glossary.asp. This is an electronic document. Date retrieved: January 29, 2007

[155] Rich, E.: User modeling via stereotypes. Cognitive Science 3, 329–354 (1979)

[156] Rostanin, O., Ullrich, C., Holz, H., Song, S.: Project TEAL: Add adaptive e-learning to your workflows. In: Tochtermann, K., Maurer, H. (eds.) Proceedings: I-KNOW'06, 6th International Conference on Knowledge Management, Graz, Austria, Sept. 2006, pp. 395–402 (2006), http://www.carstenullrich.net/pubs/Rostaninetal-TEAL-IKNOW-2006.pdf

[157] Russell, S.J., Norvig, P.: Artificial Intelligence: A Modern Approach. Pearson, London (2003)

[158] Sacerdoti, E.: The nonlinear nature of plans. In: The Proceedings of the 4th International Joint Conference on Artificial Intelligence, Tiblisi, USSR, September 1975, pp. 206–214. Morgan Kaufmann, San Francisco (1975)

[159] Sancho, P., Martínez, I., Fernández-Manjón, B.: Semantic web technologies applied to e-learning personalization in e-aula. Journal of Universal Computer Science 11(9), 1470–1481 (2005)

[160] Schank, R.C., Berman, T.R., Macperson, K.A.: Learning by doing. In: Reigeluth, C.M. (ed.) Instructional Design Theories and Models: A New Paradigm of Instructional Theory, vol. 2, pp. 161–181. Lawrence Erlbaum, Mahwah (1999)

[161] Schöch, V., Specht, M., Weber, G.: ADI - an empirical evaluation of a tutorial agent. In: Ottmann, T., Tomek, I. (eds.) Proceedings of ED-MEDIA/ED-TELECOM'98 - 10th World Conference on Educational Multimedia and Hypermedia and World Conference on Educational Telecommunications, Freiburg, Germany, pp. 1242–1247 (1998)

[162] Schulmeister, R.: Grundlagen hypermedialer Lernsysteme. Oldenbourg, München, Germany (2002). English version available online at http://www.izhd.uni-hamburg.de/paginae/Book/Frames/start_frame.html, Last accessed 29.10.2007

[163] Schulmeister, R.: eLearning: Einsichten und Aussichten. Oldenbourg, München, Germany (2006)

[164] Schwartz, D.L., Lin, X., Brophy, S., Bransford, J.D.: Toward the development of flexibly adaptive instructional designs. In: Reigeluth, C.M. (ed.) Instructional Design Theories and Models: A New Paradigm of Instructional Theory, vol. 2, pp. 183–213. Lawrence Erlbaum, Mahwah (1999)

[165] Scriven, M.: Beyond formative and summative evaluation. In: McLaughlin, M.W., Phillips, D.C. (eds.) Evaluation and Education: A Quarter Century, pp. 18–64. University of Chicago Press, Chicago (1991)

[166] Shneiderman, B., Plaisant, C.: Designing the User Interface: Strategies for Effective Human-Computer Interaction. Addison-Wesley, Reading (2004)

[167] Sicilia, M.-A., Sánchez-Alonso, S., García-Barriocanal, E.: On supporting the process of learning design through planners. In: Virtual Campus 2006 Post-proceedings. Selected and Extended Papers, pp. 81–89 (2006)

[168] Simon, B., Massart, D., van Assche, F., Ternier, S., Duval, E., Brantner, S., Olmedilla, D., Miklos, Z.: A simple query interface for interoperable learning repositories. In: Simon, B., Olmedilla, D., Saito, N. (eds.) Proceedings of the 1st Workshop on Interoperability of Web-based Educational Systems, Chiba, Japan, May 2005, pp. 11–18. CEUR (2005)

[169] Skinner, B.F.: The Technology of Teaching. Appleton-Century-Crofts, New York (1968)

[170] Spaulding, S.: Technology in education: Past, present, and future. In: Bianchéri, A., Hilgard, E.R., Hurwitz, H.M.B., Komoski, P.K., Randell, G.A., Schaefer, H.H., Schultze, W. (eds.) International Konferenz: Programmierter Unterricht und Lehrmaschinen, July 1964, pp. 134–148. Franz Cornelsen Verlag (1964)

[171] Specht, M., Oppermann, R.: ACE - adaptive courseware environment. The New Review of Hypermedia and Multimedia 4, 141–162 (1998)

[172] Specht, M., Kravcik, M., Pesin, L., Klemke, R.: Authoring adaptive educational hypermedia in WINDS. In: Henze, N. (ed.) Proc. of the ABIS 2001 Workshop (2001)

[173] Sperberg-McQueen, C.M., Bray, T., Yergeau, F., Maler, E., Paoli, J.: Extensible markup language (XML) 1.0 (fourth edition). W3C recommendation, W3C (Aug. 2006), http://www.w3.org/TR/2006/REC-xml-20060816

[174] Steels, L.: Components of expertise. AI Magazine 11(2), 30–49 (1990)

[175] Stern, M.K., Park Woolf, B.: Curriculum sequencing in a web-based tutor. In: Goettl, B.P., Halff, H.M., Redfield, C.L., Shute, V.J. (eds.) ITS 1998. LNCS, vol. 1452, pp. 574–583. Springer, Heidelberg (1998)

[176] Studer, R., Hotho, A., Stumme, G., Volz, R.: Semantic web - state of the art and future directions. KI 17, 5–8 (2003)

[177] Tate, A.: Generating project networks. In: Proceedings of the Fifth International Joint Conference on Artificial Intelligence, pp. 888–893. Morgan Kaufmann, San Francisco (1977)

[178] Tennyson, R.D., Scott, F., Seel, N.M., Dijkstra, S.: Instructional Design: International Perspectives. Theory, Research, and Models, vol. 1. Lawrence Erlbaum Associates, Mahwah (1997)

[179] Tergan, S.O.: Hypertext und Hypermedia: Konzeption, Lernmöglichkeiten, Lernprobleme und Perspektiven. In: Klimsa, P., Issing, L.J. (eds.) Information und Lernen mit Multimedia und Internet – Lehrbuch für Studium und Praxis, pp. 99–112. MIT Press, Cambridge (2002)

[180] IEEE Learning Technology Standards Committee. 1484.12.1-2002 IEEE standard for Learning Object Metadata (2002)

[181] MERLOT: MERLOT – multimedia educational resource for learning and online teaching (2006), http://www.merlot.org/merlot/index.htm. This is an electronic document. Date retrieved: May 15, 2007

[182] Thomas, R.: Millenium mathematics project - bringing mathematics to life. MSOR Connections 4(3) (2004)

[183] Ullrich, C.: Course generation based on HTN planning. In: Jedlitschka, A., Brandherm, B. (eds.) Proceedings of 13th Annual Workshop of the SIG Adaptivity and User Modeling in Interactive Systems, pp. 74–79 (2005a), http://www.carstenullrich.net/pubs/Ullrich-CourseGenerationHTN-ABIS-2005.pdf

[184] Ullrich, C.: Description of an instructional ontology and its application in web services for education. In: Poster Proceedings of the 3rd International Semantic Web Conference, ISWC2004, Hiroshima, Japan, November 2004, pp. 93–94 (2004a), http://www.carstenullrich.net/pubs/Ullrich-InstructionalOntology-ISWC-2004.pdf

[185] Ullrich, C.: Description of an instructional ontology and its application in web services for education. In: Proceedings of Workshop on Applications of Semantic Web Technologies for E-learning, SW-EL'04, Hiroshima, Japan, November 2004, pp. 17–23 (2004b), http://www.carstenullrich.net/pubs/Ullrich-InstructionalOntology-SWEL-2004.pdf

[186] Ullrich, C.: The learning-resource-type is dead, long live the learning-resource-type! Learning Objects and Learning Designs 1(1), 7–15 (2005b), http://www.carstenullrich.net/pubs/Ullrich-LearningResource-LOLD-2005.pdf

[187] Ullrich, C.: Tutorial planning: Adapting course generation to today's needs. In: Looi, C.-K., McCalla, G., Bredeweg, B., Breuker, J. (eds.) Proceedings of 12th International Conference on Artificial Intelligence in Education, p. 978. IOS Press, Amsterdam (2005c), http://www.carstenullrich.net/pubs/Ullrich-TutorialPlanning-AIED-2005.pdf

[188] Ullrich, C.: Pedagogical rules in ActiveMath and their pedagogical foundations. Seki Report SR-03-03, Universität des Saarlandes, FB Informatik (2003), http://www.carstenullrich.net/pubs/Ullrich-PedRules-Techrep03.pdf

[189] Ullrich, C., Ilghami, O.: Challenges and solutions for hierarchical task network planning in e-learning. In: Penserini, L., Peppas, P., Perini, A. (eds.) STAIRS 2006, Proceedings of the Third Starting AI Researchers' Symposium, Riva del Garda, Italy, Aug 2006. Frontiers in Artificial Intelligence and Applications, vol. 142, pp. 271–272. IOS Press, Amsterdam (2006), http://www.carstenullrich.net/pubs/UllrichOkhtay-HTNEL-Stairs-2006.pdf

[190] Ullrich, C., Libbrecht, P., Winterstein, S., Mühlenbrock, M.: A flexible and efficient presentation-architecture for adaptive hypermedia: Description and technical evaluation. In: Kinshuk, Looi, C., Sutinen, E., Sampson, D., Aedo, I., Uden, L., Kähkönen, E. (eds.) Proceedings of the 4th IEEE International Conference on Advanced Learning Technologies (ICALT 2004), Joensuu, Finland, pp. 21–25 (2004), http://www.carstenullrich.net/pubs/Ullrichetal-Presentation-ICALT04.pdf

[191] University of London. Self e-learning networks (2005), http://www.dcs.bbk.ac.uk/selene/. This is an electronic document. Date retrieved: January 20, 2007.Date last modified: January 21, 2005

[192] van der Linden, E.: Does feedback enhance computer-assisted language learning? Computers & Education 21(1-2), 61–65 (1993)

[193] van Harmelen, F., McGuinness, D.L.: OWL web ontology language overview. W3C recommendation, W3C (Feb. 2004), http://www.w3.org/TR/2004/REC-owl-features-20040210/

[194] van Joolingen, W.R.: Cognitive tools for discovery learning. International Journal of Artificial Intelligence in Education, 385–397 (1999)

[195] Van Marcke, K.: Instructional expertise. In: Frasson, C., McCalla, G.I., Gauthier, G. (eds.) ITS 1992. LNCS, vol. 608, pp. 234–243. Springer, Heidelberg (1992)

[196] Van Marcke, K.: A generic tutoring environment. In: Aiello, L. (ed.) Proceedings of the 9th European Conference on Artificial Intelligence. Stockholm, Sweden, pp. 655–660. Pitman, London (1990)

[197] Van Marcke, K.: GTE: An epistemological approach to instructional modelling. Instructional Science 26, 147–191 (1998)

[198] Vassileva, J.: Dynamic Courseware Generation: at the Cross Point of CAL, ITS and Authoring. In: Proceedings International Conference on Computers in Education, ICCE'95, Singapore, pp. 290–297 (1995)

[199] Vassileva, J.: Dynamic courseware generation. Communication and Information Technologies 5(2), 87–102 (1997)

[200] Vassileva, J., Deters, R.: Dynamic courseware generation on the WWW. British Journal of Educational Technology 29(1), 5–14 (1998)

[201] Vygotsky, L.S.: Mind in society. Harvard University Press, Cambridge (1978)

[202] W3C. World wide web consortium (2007), http://www.w3.org/. This is an electronic document. Date retrieved: February 6, 2007. Date last modified: February 2, 2007

[203] Walmsley, P., Fallside, D.C.: XML schema part 0: Primer second edition. W3C recommendation, W3C (Oct. 2004), http://www.w3.org/TR/2004/REC-xmlschema-0-20041028/

[204] Walsh, N., Muellner, L.: DocBook: The Definitive Guide. O'Reilly, Sebastopol (1999)

[205] Wasson, B.: Determining the Focus of Instruction: Content planning for intelligent tutoring systems. PhD thesis, Department of Computational Science, University of Saskatchewan, Research Report 90-5 (1990)

[206] Watson, J.B.: Psychology as the behaviorist views it. Psychological Review 20, 158–177 (1913)

[207] Weber, G., Brusilovsky, P.: ELM-ART: An adaptive versatile system for web-based instruction. International Journal of Artificial Intelligence in Education 12(4), 351–384 (2001)

[208] Wiederhold, G.: Mediators in the architeture of future information systems. The IEEE Computer Magazine (1992)

[209] Wiley, D.A.: Connecting learning objects to instructional design theory: A definition, a metaphor, and a taxonomy. In: Wiley, D.A. (ed.) The Instructional Use of Learning Objects: Online Version (2000)

[210] Wilkins, D.E.: Can AI planners solve practical problems? Computational Intelligence 6(4), 232–246 (1990)

[211] Wilson, B., Cole, P.: A review of cognitive teaching models. Educational Technology Research and Development 39(4), 47–64 (1991)

[212] Winer, D.: XML-RPC specification (October 1999), http://www.xmlrpc.org/spec

[213] Woolf, B.P., McDonald, D.D.: Building a computer tutor: Design issues. IEEE Computer 17(9), 61–73 (1984)

[214] Yaman, F., Cao, Y., Nau, D.S., Goldmann, R.P.: Documentation for SHOP2. Department of Computer Science, University of Maryland (May 2005)

[215] Zech, F.: Grundkurs Mathematikdidaktik. Beltz Verlag, Weinheim (2002)

Index